The Magic of
Terry Pratchett

For Sir Terry, whose name will always be spoken

The Magic of
Terry Pratchett

Marc Burrows

WHITE OWL
AN IMPRINT OF PEN & SWORD BOOKS LTD.
YORKSHIRE – PHILADELPHIA

First published in Great Britain in 2020 by
White Owl
An imprint of
Pen & Sword Books Ltd
Yorkshire – Philadelphia

ISBN 978 1 52676 550 5

A CIP catalogue record for this book is
available from the British Library.

Typeset by Mac Style
Printed and bound in the UK by TJ International Ltd,
Padstow, Cornwall.

Pen & Sword Books Limited incorporates the imprints of Atlas,
Archaeology, Aviation, Discovery, Family History, Fiction, History,
Maritime, Military, Military Classics, Politics, Select, Transport,
True Crime, Air World, Frontline Publishing, Leo Cooper, Remember
When, Seaforth Publishing, The Praetorian Press, Wharncliffe
Local History, Wharncliffe Transport, Wharncliffe True Crime
and White Owl.

For a complete list of Pen & Sword titles please contact

PEN & SWORD BOOKS LIMITED
47 Church Street, Barnsley, South Yorkshire, S70 2AS, England
E-mail: enquiries@pen-and-sword.co.uk
Website: www.pen-and-sword.co.uk

Or

PEN AND SWORD BOOKS
1950 Lawrence Rd, Havertown, PA 19083, USA
E-mail: Uspen-and-sword@casematepublishers.com
Website: www.penandswordbooks.com

Contents

Acknowledgements

This book is the result of a year of hard work, but without the support, generosity and good faith of a handful of people, it could never have been completed.

First of all, I'd like to thank Terry's longstanding agent and first publisher, Colin Smythe. Though we never sat down for a formal interview, he has been patient and helpful in answering my queries, and his excellent website, colinsmythe.co.uk, is very much the key to the map of Terry's life. I couldn't have found my way through the forests and mountains of the Discworld without it. I'd also like to thank the staff of the Senate House Library, where much of Colin's archive of material is now housed, especially Maria Castrillo and her team, who were never anything but helpful.

This book would be nowhere near as interesting without the input of those that knew or worked with Terry over the years and helped me to see the man behind the hat. Huge thanks to David Langford, Roger Peyton, Rob Hansen, Charles Platt, Christopher Priest, Robert Rankin, Nigel Planer, Ed James, Julius Welby, Ivan Sparrow, Janice Raycroft (and by extension, Helen Clarke), Martin Wainwright, Gerald Walker, Tony Bush, Barbara Steinberg, the estate of Josh Kirby and the marvellous Jo Fletcher, all of whom added a pinch (or in the case of some, a handful or even a bucketload) of much-needed spice to the gumbo.

Thanks to Jason Rincewind Anthony-Rowlands and, especially, Rachel Anthony-Rowlands of the insanely comprehensive DiscworldMonthly. co.uk, who have been *absolutely invaluable* in this endeavour. I'm forever grateful for their assistance and will be standing them several drinks at DWCon.

I'd also like to acknowledge Neil Gaiman, Rhianna Pratchett, Rob Wilkins, Stephen Briggs, Paul Kidby, Bernard and Isobel Pearson and, especially, the Estate of Sir Terry Pratchett for their parts in this story.

This book could never have happened without the enthusiasm and patience of my editor (and headhunter), Kate Bohdanowicz, who had to put up with far too many nervous and impatient emails. She also deserves a bottle of something nice for letting me keep more of the jokes than I expected, especially the one about sub-editors. Thanks to everyone at Pen and Sword, especially Lori, Aileen, Jonathan, Laura and Alice.

I'd like to thank Amanda Angus for her eagle-eyed proofing and well-timed suggestions, which have been more helpful than she'll ever know. Has it been so long? I'd also like to thank Andrew, Andy and Jez for the much needed distractions.

I couldn't have done this without the everlasting patience and support of my darling wife, Nicoletta, who believes in me when I lose faith in myself. LAWD, she has had to put up with *a lot* during the writing of this book. And thanks to Princess for curling up in my lap whenever I needed it.

And finally … without my mum and dad handing a nerdy 11 year old *The Colour of Magic* and *Guards! Guards!* back in 1992, I would never have started on this journey. So for that and a million, billion other things, I will be saying thank you forever.

If you enjoyed this book, you can thank those people. If you didn't, you can blame me.

Marc Burrows,
December 2019, London

Foreword

I t's hard to sum up Terry Pratchett properly. On the surface there's a temptation to think of him as a little bit like Santa Claus. White beard, distinctive hat, delivered goodies (at least) once a year, usually towards the end. But he was more complicated than that saint, and far superior to his own equivalent, the Hogfather, however much one likes sausages. Pratchett knew that the good weren't always rewarded and the bad did not always get coal in their stockings. He knew that virtue often had to be its own reward because no-one else would thank you much for it. He knew that people are not essentially bad or good but essentially people, and that to impute too much else to their actions leads to madness. He taught me – all of us – more than Father Christmas ever did. But that's because he cannot be reduced to a cheery portrait.

Like most bookworms of my generation, I don't remember the first time I saw a Terry Pratchett book. They were always just there, around, bright colours and sinuously intricate Josh Kirby shapes calling to me even as the dense, picture-free insides suggested they were for older readers. I finally picked up *Mort* in my local library and fell instantly in love with the tone and the language and the entire damn Discworld. Over the next few years I devoured all the Pratchett I could get my hands on and then started over again (something I still do whenever I need a lift). When I decided, age 17, to sit the entrance exam for Oxford University, I noticed that there was always a question on the English paper along the lines of, 'Make a case for the inclusion of any writer not covered in this paper'. Aha! Here was a chance to read Discworld books all day and call it study instead of prepping yet another Shakespeare essay. I'll never know if that paper helped or hindered my chances of getting in, but I like to think it was the former (I did get the offer). After all, by then respectable journalists were comparing Pratchett to Charles Dickens (faint praise as far as my teenage self was concerned) so I figured I could make my case.

I never wrote Pratchett a fan letter, caught between a desire not to waste his time and a sense of doubt that I had anything worth saying beyond 'OMG why are you so great? Will you be my friend?' Arguably I still do not have much beyond that to say, despite having followed his footsteps into journalism and writing. But when Marc Burrows asked me to introduce this deeply researched and lovingly crafted book, I saw a chance to make up for my failure, because Marc's whole book is a tribute. This considers how a guy called Terry Pratchett became *the* Sir Terry Pratchett, how he honed his writing abilities from his earliest days until he could casually knock off several gloriously comic, beautifully nuanced stories each year. It paints a detailed, rounded picture of a man who was not a 'jolly elf', as Neil Gaiman puts it, but also not the old curmudgeon that Pratchett sometimes liked to pretend. The life that Marc recounts, in its ordinariness and its extraordinariness, is inspiring.

The thing is that Terry Pratchett was dependably funny, unfailingly sharp, deeply caring, but often furious as well, and it was the combination of all those elements that made his work sing. I'm a relatively well-read person, but phrases and theories from his books echo in my head more than almost anyone else's because of that simmering sense of outrage. The Vimes 'boot' theory of economics is an immensely useful tool in convincing people how expensive it is to be poor. The odd compassion and even-handed respect of his Death is an encouraging alternative to traditional religion. And Granny Weatherwax's 'headology' sums up humanity's foibles better than most philosophical textbooks. It is, I think, no accident that she featured in the last book he wrote, *The Shepherd's Crown*. There's a lot of Pratchett in Granny's capacity for quick, keen insight and her unyielding conviction of what's right. But he's also there in her well-hidden soft heart.

Many of Pratchett's most memorable characters grew in the same direction in the end. Vimes became a family man and upright citizen, sitting behind a desk and casting a gimlet eye over the world (just like the dwarf delicatessen). Granny ended up more mentor to young witch Tiffany Aching than hero in her own right. As Pratchett's final illness limited his physical boundaries, his signature characters seemed to become similarly restricted, at least in body. But those final years, and that final book, also include Tiffany. His youngest heroine stepped further into her power as a leader of the ever-changing landscape of the Chalk and the world was left in good hands. That is surely no accident. Even at the end, Pratchett looked forwards, showing hope over experience that the next generation might prove wiser and better than their elders. His fundamental optimism tempered his anger at the world's injustices and stupidities, and shone alongside his humour. It's why the Santa Claus comparison isn't *completely* absurd. The man Marc reveals here, under the cynicism and wariness, did believe in people, I think. Then he wrote books that make our lives better. For that, I'll always be grateful. GNU Terry Pratchett.

Helen O'Hara, 2020

Introduction

I missed the only chance I ever had to meet Terry Pratchett. He had been my favourite author since I was 11 years old, back in the early '90s, but I'd never been attracted to the idea of queueing for a signing, or attending a convention. I was happy for my fandom to take place in my bedroom via obsessive re-reading, with a side deal in annoying my friends with quotes.

In 2010, Terry was a guest on the Radio 4 panel show *The Museum of Curiosity*, devised and produced by my friend, Dan. Knowing I was a huge fan, Dan invited me to the recording, but for whatever reason – and a decade on, I genuinely can't remember the reason – I couldn't make it. The next day Dan told me about the marvellous time he had spent in the pub after the show with Terry and his assistant, Rob Wilkins, cracking jokes and putting the world to rights. I was horrified. I had missed the opportunity to connect properly with my favourite author of all time. I became determined that I would befriend, interview or possibly mug Terry Pratchett and meet him by any means necessary.

Sadly, there were no available means. I shirked at the 2012 Discworld convention, could never land an interview, and Terry, as he became more frail, reduced his public exposure. I never met Terry Pratchett. It's probably for the best – an oft-repeated comment about Terry was that he didn't suffer fools. Since I consider myself to be, quite definitively, a fool, even on my best days, then maybe we wouldn't have got on.

I mentioned this to Terry's friend and one-time editor, Jo Fletcher when I met her for coffee to ask if she'd be willing to be interviewed for this book, and she asked me a question I hadn't considered before. If I didn't know Terry Pratchett, if I'd never even *met* Terry Pratchett, then why on earth did I want to write a book about him? I went away from that meeting pondering the answer. This is what I arrived at.

This book is my chance to meet Terry Pratchett. It's yours as well. It's our chance to explore his long (though not long enough) and endlessly fascinating life, his wit, his spikiness and his dyed-in-the-wool geekery. The more I researched and the more I wrote, the more I felt that I *had* met Terry Pratchett, not just through my research, but through the pages of the books I'd read obsessively for twenty-five years. His compassion, his decency, his wit, his anger, and if we're honest, his tendency to really, really, not suffer fools – all of that is contained in every single one of his books, from *The Carpet People* to *The Shepherd's Crown*.

Alas, there is more Terry Pratchett than I could fit into this biography. There is an essay to be written on each of his novels, and a whole separate book on the exploits of his fans. The alt.fan.pratchett newsgroup alone could fill its own volume. I've tried to stick to the relevant stuff, the events of his life that impacted his work, and the examples of his work that impacted his life.

Here's a word of caution. Don't believe everything you read. One of Terry's favourite authors was Mark Twain, the great American satirist and teller of tall tales and adventure stories. Twain was known for putting a shine on his anecdotes; work he presented as autobiographical often had only the barest toehold on historical fact. There is a hint of this, often unintentionally, in Terry's own rememberances. Many of his well-honed anecdotes were – once you trace them back to their origin – just that tiny bit more narratively satisfying than reality would usually provide. Often, he told such stories so many times that he lost track of where the original stopped and his extra bit of shine began. As he said himself, during his inaugural lecture at Trinity College, Dublin, where he was given an honourary professorship – 'my subconscious is that of an author and former journalist, and probably believes that every quote would benefit from a bit of a polish by an expert. As I believe Douglas Adams once said, sometimes after talking about yourself so often you're not exactly sure how real some things are.'

I've done my best to mark the stories I think might be embellished, or highlight when there are conflicting accounts. In some places I'm relatively sure of my facts, in others I'm guessing, at which point I've made sure to say so, and in still more I'm taking the risky tactic of trusting the author, something of an unreliable witness. Anyway, who are we to say which version is true? In fact, in an infinite universe, on the quantum level, *every* version is true and every version is valid. It's a matter of choosing the trouser leg of time in which you'd prefer to live. And if you can't decide, then there's always some fun to be had if you hang around for long enough in the crotch.

At some point in the coming years, Terry's assistant and friend Rob Wilkins, the man described by Neil Gaiman as 'Terry's representative on Earth', will write the definitive biography of the man he knew, based on Terry's notes and his own experiences. Perhaps then some of those questions can be answered, or then again perhaps not. Terry was trained as a journalist, but he was also a storyteller, and those are not always the same thing. You got the truth he wanted to tell you.

The year I have spent working on this book has been one of the most enjoyable of my working life. I feel like I met Terry, or at least a version of Terry, *my* version of Terry, every day. It's been a pleasure spending time with him. I hope it is for you too.

Chapter 1

Once Upon A Time

Let us begin as Terry might …

See the universe, frosted with stars, streaked with the tails of comets. There are no turtles here, but it's still pretty impressive.

Focus.

Let a strange, spherical world roll awkwardly into view like a badly hit snooker ball. It has continents and oceans and ice caps you'd swear were a little smaller than they were the last time you looked.

Focus …

… on a rain-soaked island on the upper right-hand side of the ball, a smudge of green amid the steely blue, and …

… focus …

… on the south east of the island. Find the biggest city, a sprawling, smoggy tangle of grey, and let your eye drift to the left and up a little; to where there's a lot more green between the grey bits, and …

… focus …

… on a large village, or perhaps it's a small town, surrounded by woods and hills, and …

… focus …

… on a tiny library, really just two rooms of books. Not even very big rooms. But still, a library. And …

… focus …

… on a boy, small for his age, attempting to wedge more books than he can possibly carry into a school satchel. This is Terence David John Pratchett, heading home to nearby Forty Green where he will lose himself in words. It will take his feet only a few minutes to get him back, but the words are going to carry him, oh, so much further.

Forty Green, in Buckinghamshire, England, shouldn't really exist anymore. It's one of those tiny hamlets that's been around for so long it stays on the map out of sheer force of habit. A census in 1881 listed just ten houses there, and seventy years later that figure had, just about, doubled. Gradually the town of Beaconsfield has swollen and swallowed it whole, along with neighbouring hamlets such as Knotty Green and Holtspur. Forty Green is where Beaconsfield ends, tagged on to the side of the town like a limpet clinging to a toy boat. Beyond its borders, there are miles and miles of wooded countryside, full of rolling hills, ponds, streams and copses. Terry Pratchett grew up with the Chiltern Hills as his back garden, a landscape perfect for the adventures of a young boy armed with a wild imagination and a bicycle. He had The Shire on his doorstep.

Terry was born on 28 April, 1948, in the Kinellan Nursing Home, Beaconsfield. His parents, David and Eileen, had married in nearby Amersham in 1942 but waited a while before having children. Their lives, as Terry would later tell BBC Radio 4's *Desert Island Discs*, had been interrupted by the outbreak of the Second World War. David had been just 19 when war broke out and enlisted voluntarily in the Royal Air Force after turning 21. He spent the war stationed near Karachi in what was then British India and is now Pakistan. He returned to a post-war England of bombsites, rationing and young people quite desperate to make babies. However, unlike many of their generation, who wasted absolutely no time in playing their part in the coming population boom, it would be a further three years before Eileen fell pregnant. Terry was in no hurry to enter the world either, arriving days later than his due date.

The family were poor, though not alarmingly so. Both David and Eileen were in work during the whole of Terry's childhood: his father was a motor mechanic[1] and his mother a company secretary. They were perfectly suited to those jobs. David was a tinkerer. He loved to build things and rebuild them, messing about with radio equipment and

---

1. Many profiles of Pratchett have described his father with the rather grander word 'engineer', which while technically true doesn't really give an accurate impression. David Pratchett wasn't building steam engines or designing bridges; he was fixing cars, which is a skilled and important job in itself, and there's no need to dress it up as something it isn't. The world would struggle without mechanics.

a never-ending list of projects. Eileen, meanwhile, was practical and organised, and loved words and stories. The family lived in a small cottage with no electricity that shared its one (cold) water tap with the house next door. Every other day David would run a hose pipe from the shared tap and fill up a tank in the kitchen for the family's water needs. The house was lit by gas lamps and candles, and Eileen would buy the huge 90-volt Ever Ready radio batteries that powered the family wireless. Bathroom needs were taken care of by an old Elsan privy – essentially a seat over a septic tank, contained in a shed – which had to be emptied by hand once a week, to the benefit of the tomatoes at the bottom of the garden. It's a life that sounds hard by modern standards, but in late-1940s Britain such conditions were neither extreme nor unusual for a working-class family. Terry would say on many occasions that in those post-Blitz years, living close to London, you were grateful if you had a house at all.

The Pratchetts were a fairly typical British family of the times. David and Eileen were attentive parents, though not outwardly affectionate. Their granddaughter, Rhianna, would later describe them in a 2018 piece she wrote for *The Guardian* as kind, but matter-of-fact people, not given to outward displays of affection.[2] Instead, they expressed love through creativity and craft. David helped his son make carts and treehouses, and the two built their own shortwave radio sets, even joining the Chiltern Amateur Radio Club where they used the handle 'Homebrew R1155'. Much of Terry's pocket money would go on batteries, capacitors and other electrical components. One of David's proudest moments was when his son rigged the garden shed using a magneto generator to give him an electric shock when he tried the handle.

For her part, Eileen would sit down with Terry and encourage him to read and be creative. She was of Irish descent, though she had grown up in London, and would tell her son stories and snatches of folklore passed on to her by her grandfather. She was a clever and knowledgeable woman, full of tidbits of trivia, with a wicked sense of humour, exemplified by the fact she named the family tortoise Phidippides, after the Greek hero who ran from Marathon to Athens. Terry was raised with a working definition

---

2. This makes a great deal of sense when you read Pratchett's work. Honestly, how many Pratchett characters can you think of that could be comfortably described as 'a hugger'?

of irony plodding slowly around the back garden eating lettuce. Eileen was always one to 'put a shine' on a story, a habit she passed on to her son who would often tweak his own anecdotes to make them more narratively satisfying. She was the loudest cheerleader when Terry eventually expressed an interest in becoming a writer.

But writing and even reading were latecomers to Terry's world. Initially, his creativity manifested as a dreamy, curious and introspective character. He would describe people in terms of colour; saying he liked them because they seemed 'purple' or 'brown', descriptions that had nothing to do with their skin. His childhood was full of occasions where his imagination added an unusual spin and shape to the world, creating possibilities and scenarios quite different from the mundane reality in front of him. He remembered walking through an old quarry on the way home from school and imagining odd, prehistoric fish swimming in the walls and floor of the chalk pit, as if underwater. An old iron bedstead at the bottom of his garden became a pirate ship, a flying saucer or a castle as his imagination demanded. When he was 5 years old, his mother took him to Gamages department store in London to meet Father Christmas. Awestruck by the shelves full of toys, lights and glitter, he wandered off on his own. A panicked Eileen found him riding the escalator, lost in a dream world. To the young Terry, the store was an entire universe of possibility. The experience stayed with him and became the inspiration for his children's novel, *Truckers*. He later told an audience at a 2005 convention in Bloomington, Minnesota, that many of the ideas that became the Discworld had their roots in that day.

Terry was raised within the Church of England system, but only because most people were. He attended Church of England schools, went to Sunday school in a tin-roofed tabernacle (he told *The Scotsman* in 2012 that he suspected Sunday school was just an excuse for his parents to get some intimate alone time) and, like his parents, was eventually married in an Anglican church. Much later he would tell the *Telegraph* that, despite spending his career being openly critical of organised religion, he was fond of the Church of England because of how tied up it was with the English national character. Both of his parents practised a fairly typical go-through-the-motions-when-we-have-to religious indifference, and faith of any kind barely factored in family life. When the local vicar called unexpectedly and saw a model Buddha David Pratchett had brought back from his wartime travels, he declared it 'a pagan icon' and was promptly thrown out of the house.

Eileen had Catholicism somewhere in her background, but left almost all trace of it behind when a devout family member disapproved of her Anglican marriage and declared that her children would be 'bastards'.[3] The only nod to her Papist roots in the Pratchetts' home was an old crucifix, which she kept until her dying day. Terry had stumbled across it when he was about 6 and, much to his mother's amusement, assumed that the lifelike Christ hanging from the cross was some sort of trapeze artist. Religion had factored so little in his life that he simply hadn't recognised it. The image would surface later in his science fiction novel *Strata*.

Nevertheless a basic Christian message did manage to penetrate as a type of 'Jesus-lite', as he told an audience during a talk at the Sydney Opera House in 2013: 'People know what Jesus said – basically Bill and Ted said it as well, "be excellent to each other", you don't need anything else. It's a good starting point, you don't need to go to church, you just need to accept the "golden rule".' It's an ethos that would find its way into his writing, where common decency would be a constant theme.

When Pratchett talked of his early childhood, the word he used most often was 'idyllic'. The endless fields that bordered Forty Green contained the potential for limitless adventures, of a sort familiar to anyone who grew up in the English countryside. It's a landscape full of trees made for climbing, brooks ideal for damming, and abandoned quarries, woods and scrubland perfect for dens and dares. In a contribution to a 1996 book called *Playground Memories*, a collection of celebrity childhood reminiscences, he explained how he and a gang of four or five other grubby, scabby-kneed kids would assemble in Roundhead Wood, a little copse of trees surrounding a chalk pit that would become, in their imaginations, ancient forests, alien worlds or any other landscape their games required. There they could battle monsters, get into fights and indulge in that quintessential hobby of small boys everywhere: throwing themselves recklessly from the top of something high. In this case, it

3. Pratchett recounted the story during a 2013 appearance at a *Live at the House* event at the Sydney Opera House, telling interviewer and fellow author Garth Nix that, figuratively speaking, they turned out to be correct.

involved climbing a young beech tree, then leaping across to another and sliding down its smooth trunk, hopefully avoiding the spiky embrace of the holly bushes below. His childhood, as he told *The Times* in 2005, felt like a summer's day that never ended.

Unusually for one of the baby boomer generation, Terry never had brothers or sisters. Later he would say that he was an only child but not a lonely one, a theme that would recur many times in his work. As an adult author he would create many young characters, from the troubled and thoughtful Johnny Maxwell in *Only You Can Save Mankind* to Adam in *Good Omens*, Eskarina in *Equal Rites* and Tiffany Aching, one of his finest creations, in *The Wee Free Men*. All are either only children or have siblings who barely feature in their lives. They're sensible children, content in the company of their friends and themselves. In truth, the only time Pratchett regretted his lack of siblings was on the odd occasion when a bigger brother would have come in handy against a playground bully. Otherwise, he saw nothing but upsides: he got more attention from his parents, the money didn't have to stretch as far so he got better presents, and he never had to share his toys.

There are many melancholy tropes of the impoverished only child who grew up to become a famous writer. An entire genre of misery-based literature is built on this very fact. None of those is present in the life of the young Terry Pratchett. He was well-loved at home and well-liked by his friends. It would have been a perfect childhood had it not been for one crucial factor – eventually, he would have to go to school.

Terry's formal education began in the autumn of 1953, one day later than everyone else in his class. The Pratchetts had been on holiday, and their trip had overlapped with the start of the school year. A family vacation would have meant months of saving, so why would they cut it short for a single day of school? It's characteristic of David and Eileen, who would often prioritise quality family time over more mundane commitments.

Terry arrived at the school gates on day two of term and found that the other children had already formed friendship groups, established a class hierarchy, worked out who sat where and claimed all the cooler coat pegs. (Terry was left with a peg marked with a pair of cherries while other kids hung their jackets beneath soldiers or space rockets. Those boring cherries were a glossy, scarlet representation of his outsider status.) His school career began on the back foot.

He was attending Holtspur County Primary School on Cherry Tree Road; a short walk from his Forty Green home. Holtspur was a fairly typical village school, catering for around 100 pupils. It had opened its doors just two years earlier and consisted of modern, red-brick buildings and a huge playing field. The school was overseen by headmaster Henry William Tame, known professionally as H. W. Tame and informally as Bill, an experienced and energetic educator who had a hand in the design of the new school and would remain head at Holtspur for another thirty years. Tame's ethos would have a profound effect on the young Terry Pratchett, giving him a lifelong distrust of teachers and formal education.

In many ways, Tame was a pioneer. He published two books on sex education, *Time To Grow Up* in 1966 and *Peter and Pamela Grow Up* in 1969, which were at odds with the stuffy views of the time. He composed the school song and wrote – and often starred in – an annual pantomime. Many of the children under his care adored him, and there was a great outpouring of affection from the local community when he died in 2002, at the age of 85. Among the various tributes printed in the local press at the time the words 'Terry Pratchett' are conspicuous by their absence. It's no surprise. When Terry was just 6 years old, Tame had already marked him down as someone unlikely to succeed in life.

The Education Act, passed in 1944, required pupils in English and Welsh schools to sit an exam during their final year of primary school – the famous eleven plus – after which they would be sent to a grammar school (for the academically gifted), technical college (for the practical) or a secondary modern (for everyone else), their destination determined by their grades. In theory, they would enter a crucial stage of their education in an environment where they could be taught according to their academic needs by a teacher who wasn't having to cater lessons to those further up or down the intellectual scale. The practice, known as the 'tripartite system', has long been controversial, with many politicians and teachers arguing that it locks social structures in place. The kids that need the most help, invariably from poorer backgrounds, lose their chance to thrive in academia; while apparently brighter children, often from wealthier families with access to better tuition, who are more likely to be encouraged to read at home, are given every opportunity to shine. The practice fell out of favour with the Labour government of the 1960s and several studies over the years have questioned the effectiveness of segregating children by attainment. Still, versions of the tripartite system have come in and out of fashion with various post-war governments, right up to the 2010s.

Infant and primary schools were under no obligation to segregate classes, though many of them did. It was common practice to begin the process early, and children were often grouped by ability from the age of 6. Many teachers believed that an assessment of a child of 6 could accurately predict their academic progress through life. H. W. Tame was one such teacher.

Holtspur pupil, Julius Welby, who attended the school a few years after Terry, provides a neat summary of Tame:

> He was forward-thinking, especially in terms of sex education and yet strangely backwards in his emotional perception. He seemed to think there was only one way in which a child should develop, hitting the various milestones – physical and mental – on time and in the approved manner. If you fit the mould, Mr Tame was a great influence and teacher. If you didn't, one was left looking back, like Terry, with polite bafflement, pain and the most mixed of mixed feelings.

A 1963 book, *Selected at Six* by the Holtspur teacher, Joan Goldman, charts a year in a primary school suspiciously similar to Holtspur, with a headmaster suspiciously similar to Tame.[4] In it she says of her headmaster, 'Mr Collins': 'At the age of five and a half, he can tell which of [the pupils] will be invited to occupy a seat in the local Grammar School ... and which of them won't.' Goldman has 'Collins' dividing the youngest members of his school into A or B groups, also knowns as 'wills' and 'won'ts' or, more crudely, 'sheep' and 'goats'. 'Collins' would freely use these phrases in front of the children, a practice that seems jarringly

---

4. In the introduction to a piece about Holtspur School in *A Slip of the Keyboard*, a collection of his non-fiction, Terry mentions a book about Tame called *Selected at Six*. It's possible he's referring to another book entirely, but I've been unable to find any trace of it, so we can assume he means Goldman's and that she changed names and details to protect the innocent. Either that or Terry got muddled up somewhere.

cruel by modern standards. That Terry uses exactly the same language in his various remembrances suggests that so-called 'Mr Collins' may have been more than familiar to him.

Terry was an introspective little boy who arrived a day late, out of step with his classmates and possessing a wild imagination that meant he would rather be daydreaming his own stories than learning to read other people's. Tame, as fellow alumni Julius Welby notes, delivered his opinions with 'complete and crushing certainty'; he saw Terry as the very definition of a 'goat', or a 'backwards child', and said so. To Tame, 'goats' were a species apart. As Welby, who was also dubbed a B student, says: 'It seemed at the time that his judgement was not so much of your performance but of your nature. Goats are not sheep having a bad day – they are entirely another kind of thing.'

Being placed among the goats impacted Terry in several ways, some positive, some not. None of them was the intended result of segregation. Terry never received the special and specific attention from teachers that streaming promised. Nor were the lessons usually suitable for his level, and he often found himself either ahead or behind the rest of the class. Tame's view of education focused almost fanatically on the basics of reading, writing, and arithmetic ('the three Rs'). As Goldman observed in her book, he was accustomed to 'riding roughshod over parents' and teachers' wishes' on the subject, and Terry always struggled with such a nuts-and-bolts approach, responding more positively when his imagination was engaged. A few years later, when reading and writing had become a passion, the 'rithmetic would still be lagging behind.

But goathood had unexpected benefits: it lit a bonfire under both mother and son. Eileen Pratchett was not about to let her only child languish on the B pile just because an uppity headmaster said so. She was determined that Tame's decision wouldn't become a self-fulfilling prophecy. Eileen took Terry's reading into her own hands, initially with the endless patience of a natural teacher, and later – when Terry's tendency to get distracted got in the way – by resorting to bribery, promising to pay him a penny for every page of a book he could read aloud to her.[5] She also

---

5. Terry would later point out that this early financial outlay was a sound investment for his parents, since he was able to buy them a comfortable house in affluent Hay-on-Wye when they retired. Encouraging your son's literacy pays off when he grows up to be a multi-millionaire author.

found a local teacher to help fill in the lessons denied to the B classes at Holtspur.

While the lessons at school remained dry (and, appropriately enough, tame), Eileen's knack for spinning a yarn was able to keep Terry engaged and interested. He fell in love with learning, and those lessons nudged the first snowflakes in the avalanche of knowledge he acquired across a lifetime of unending research, done mostly for the sheer joy of finding out something new. Additional homeschooling, however, wasn't without its drawbacks. Eileen did her job too well. On one horrible occasion, the class was asked to explain where rain came from. When Terry confidently replied, 'the sea', the other children, who all knew the answer was *obviously* the sky, erupted into laughter. Rather than be impressed with a child who already knew the cycles of evaporation and precipitation, Terry's teacher joined in with the jeering. His lifelong anger with poor teachers is rooted as much in that one event as it was in Tame's earlier prediction. The incident kickstarted Terry's competitive streak. As school progressed he regularly found himself ahead of the other goats: he was a dreamy and introspective kid, yes, but he was also clever and enjoyed being top of the class, a position he probably wouldn't have managed had he been placed among the sheep.

As Terry's school career progressed, two interests would start to dominate his spare time. The first was the night sky and a love of all things astronomical, and the second was reading for pleasure. The two would dovetail neatly and the combination of these passions would start a chain reaction that would shape the rest of his life.

Astronomy came first. Terry traced his love of stargazing to the age of 9. Brooke Bond tea, which had a long tradition of including collectable cards in its packaging, had launched a series called Out Into Space, capitalising on the escalating space race between Soviet Russia and the United States. Previous card collections featuring wildflowers or British birds hadn't really sparked much interest, but this was different. The first card Terry found was number nine, 'Planets and their Moons'. The pictures on the front were basically coloured blobs with labels, but the text on the reverse was fascinating. Terry read the words 'Ganymede', 'Callisto' and 'Titan' for the first time, absorbing their distance from Earth and sizes in relation to Jupiter and Saturn. It was mesmerising.

The next step was to collect the remaining eleven cards, and the family embarked on a prolific period of tea-drinking in order to secure the full set. Each card contained a ropey illustration and some solid scientific facts: the phases of the moon, the order, comparative sizes and orbits of the planets, the rotation of the earth, and so on. Terry was fascinated and decided that a career in astronomy beckoned. His parents bought him a telescope; it was very cheap, and the lens somewhat blurry, but the skies above the Chilterns were clear, and it was a good enough piece of kit to make out, albeit fuzzily, the rings of Saturn, and the moons of Jupiter, and provide fantastically detailed lunar views.

It wasn't until he was 10 years old that finally, after years of patient teaching and the odd bribe from his mother, Terry read a book of his own volition. It was Kenneth Grahame's *The Wind In The Willows*, a much-imitated classic following the exploits of talking animals who drive cars, dress up as washerwomen and have adventures. Crucially, it was given to Terry by a friend of the family, known as 'Uncle Don', during a trip to London; it wasn't mandated by a teacher, and his mother wasn't paying him to read it. It had been handed to him casually and thus bred no resentment or obligation. He read it in a single sitting, starting on the drive home in his father's old Jowett Javelin by the glow of the roadside sodium lights, concentrating so as not to lose his place when the car went into shadows. When he finished, he returned to the beginning and read it again. He was entranced by Grahame's weird reality – where some animals spoke and drank tea and others were mute, and pulled carts. It was a direct line back to that visit to Gamages department store, when a world of wonder had opened up to him, and a line forward to his career as a writer.

Terry became, almost overnight, a voracious reader. He read without discernment; fiction, fact, reference … anything he could get his hands on. No-one had bothered to tell him that some books were intended for children and others for adults. To Terry, everything was fair game. He read T. H. White's *Mistress Masham's Repose* and was delighted that it took another book he'd picked up, Jonathan Swift's *Gulliver's Travels*, and treated it as if it were true. He read *Just William*, *The Moomins* and *Jeeves and Wooster*. He read his way along his grandmother's treasured bookshelf, discovering Charles Dickens and G. K. Chesterton, and when that was exhausted he headed for the newly opened public library.

Terry's entry in *Who's Who*, the regularly updated guide to influential Britons, lists his place of education as 'Beaconsfield Library'. It is not an exaggeration. Many years later a plaque would be unveiled outside the building celebrating his life. His daughter, Rhianna, released a statement to mark the occasion, saying, 'Dad was born in Beaconsfield, but Terry Pratchett the author was born at Beaconsfield Library. This was the place Dad got his education.' Terry entered his local library with the enthusiasm of a ravished orangutan given the keys to a banana plantation. He read everything from children's books to dictionaries, consuming fact and fiction alike, constantly filing the information away as he began to build a picture of the world far more vivid than the one he was being taught at Holtspur School.

One of his first stops was the astronomy shelves, where he rapidly added to the knowledge he'd acquired from collecting tea cards. Most of the books on space contained an introductory chapter exploring various myths about the universe that had been discarded in favour of proper science. In one such book he came across an old belief common in many cultures: that the world is a flat disc, carried through space on the back of a huge turtle. A version of this idea specific to Hindu mythology added four giant elephants that stand on the turtle's shell and hold the disc of the world on their backs.

The film critic Mark Kermode often talks about a trope, found in the cheaper sort of movie biopics, he calls a 'Chubby, hmm?', referencing the scene in *The Karen Carpenter Story*[6] where an off-hand comment about the singer's weight clumsily foreshadows her anorexia. In the straight-to-DVD version of Terry Pratchett's life, *this* is that moment. There should be a light bulb switching on over his head. Or at least a shot of a young boy staring into the distance and rubbing his chin, thoughtfully. In truth, the ancient disc-shaped world was just another fact, another image, another piece of trivia to be carefully filed away for later recall, and at the time the young Terry thought very little of it.

The biggest revelation he took from the books on astronomy was that the study of stars involved a lot of difficult maths, something Terry struggled with, and he soon abandoned it as a career choice. The

---

6. He credits the writer Jon Ronson with the phrase, though it's Kermode who popularised it.

stargazing, however, led him to the science fiction section, and science fiction led him to fantasy. Over the years, fantasy led him to mythology and ancient history, which led to modern history, and back to science again. Every book, every story, every fact added something new to the pile. There's a scene in Terry's 1992 novel *Small Gods* where Brutha, the illiterate hero with a photographic memory, 'rescues' a library's worth of information from destruction by simply looking at the pages of the books it contains until he has the accumulated knowledge of the ages floating around in his head ready to be written down later. Terry's experience in Beaconsfield Library was less dramatic but just as immersive.

Eventually, his reading habits started outpacing the library's lending limits; he was only allowed to borrow two books at a time and it simply wasn't enough. The solution was simple – he asked the librarian for a job. At just 10 years old he became the Saturday boy, working for free, filing, stamping and carrying books in return for the opportunity to write out his own library tickets. The library's filing system had two drawers: one of books currently out on loan to the public, and another of books currently borrowed by Terry Pratchett. He claimed in an interview with *Science Fiction Review* in 2004 that, at one point, he had 143 library books on loan at the same time.

H. W. Tame had written off Terry Pratchett as one of life's losers by the time he was 6 and then provided a school programme that did everything possible to ensure that prediction was right. Despite Terry's voracious reading habit and Eileen's careful tutelage, he would spend his entire primary school career in the B class. Tame never revised his opinion.

In 1958, around the time the family moved to a council house in Holtspur – this time possessing modern amenities such as electricity and running water – Terry and the other goats took their eleven plus exam. It was Tame himself who delivered the results, walking around the classroom, stopping at each child's desk, one by one. When he got to Terry his announcement was met with silence from the class. Terry was the only child in the year to prove the headmaster wrong. He had passed.

Chapter 2

The Young Writer

The summer of 1959 saw Terry prepare for the next phase of his education. He had decided against attending a local grammar and instead he applied for a place at the technical school in the nearby town of High Wycombe. Though he'd comfortably passed the eleven plus, Terry had *hated* his lessons at Holtspur. He may have recently caught the reading bug and was enjoying learning about the world, but that was on his own terms. He had always been a practical-minded rather than academic child. He loved crafting and building with his father, and the two usually had a project on the go. He was also a skilled artist who could draw and paint and could have trained to be a draughtsman or graphic designer. A practical education was always going to appeal more than an academic one.

The all-boys Wycombe Tech offered the same lessons as most schools – English, Maths, Science, History, Games and so forth, but while a grammar school might include scholarly learning with Classics and Latin, the Tech specialised in hands-on, creative skills, with a syllabus which included Woodwork, Metalwork, Technical Drawing and Art. A school uniform was naturally required (complete with compulsory cap and tie, which pupils were forbidden from removing until they had arrived home) but here, in addition to the standard blazer, school tie and rugby kit, boys were required to supply a boiler suit.

Despite the emphasis on practical skills, Wycombe Technical High School was a fairly typical late-1950s establishment: lessons could be dry and discipline was strict. While the cane was restricted to the headmaster's office, where unruly boys received 'six of the best', any teacher was free to whack a misbehaving pupil with whatever they happened to have to hand; which meant bits of spare wood, metal rulers and T-squares, and for those who caused trouble in PE lessons, a rubber-soled gym shoe. During Terry's time at the school, a boy was beaten so hard with his own

T-square it actually broke, and he was forced to stay behind for several evenings to make a new one. The sports master was especially tough on the boys. While a doctor's note might excuse them from Games, it meant they would spend the lesson shovelling coal in the boiler room instead. One former pupil, Stuart Rooksby, writing on a website set up for school alumni, remembers throwing young Terry a sixpence to do his shovelling for him.

Headmaster Harry Ward, who had taken on the post in 1958, was a keen disciplinarian. A harrowing experience during his war service had left him defensive, short-tempered and uncompromising. Just like Bill Tame, Ward would soon take a dislike to Terry Pratchett.

Terry's career at Wycombe Tech did not begin in the most auspicious of ways. The Pratchetts took their summer vacation at the same time each year, meaning their son once again missed his first day at a new school. For the second time in his life, he began an important phase of his education on the back foot. From that first day,[1] until the day he left, he felt that he was playing catch up.

He established himself quickly as a mid-table kind of student; too bright to be struggling at the bottom of the class and too disinterested to shine at the top. He was, by his own admission, a 'weird kid', and was seen as something of a troublemaker and class clown; quick with a smart reply, clever enough to be funny but not wise enough to know when to keep his mouth shut. It could make him, occasionally, annoying to be around. His character is clearly on display in a 1961 school photo: Terry is sat cross-legged with the other shorter boys, cheerfully mugging for the camera, his sense of humour and twitchy inability to be quiet radiates from the image.[2] Such quirks would land him in trouble with teachers and school bullies alike. He was an obvious target for the thugs that prowl every playground; a smart mouth did him no favours with bigger lads, who already targeted him for being short and having a mild speech impediment. One bully took against him regularly and viciously, until Terry eventually lost his temper, ran at him across the room and barrelled headfirst into the boy's midriff. The bully found himself on

---

1. Which was actually the second day.
2. There's a line in Pratchett's novel *Men At Arms*, that says there's always one kid sat at the front of a school photo, pulling a stupid face. He should know. It was usually him.

the floor, his head bleeding after landing heavily against an iron fireplace. Terry tended to be left alone after that.

Formal education continued sluggishly. He absolutely hated Maths, and could never get the hang of algebra or equations. He was unfocused in English and if he could engineer it, absent entirely in Games, where he was always among the last to be picked for teams (though he did enjoy playing hockey, which his father had played during the war in India – his nippy frame and surprisingly adept way with a stick made him a dangerous opponent). A reluctant and occasionally unlucky sportsman, he once spent two months with both of his arms in plaster after breaking his wrists in a trampolining accident.

Subjects that had the potential to fascinate him, such as Science and History, were sacrificed on the altar of bad teaching. He learned about the 1815 Corn Laws, but all that really penetrated was a vague sense of a government getting one over on the poor in some way.

His real education continued to be extra-curricular. His mother paid for him to have touch-typing lessons, reasoning that his bookish tendencies meant he was probably on course for a desk-bound job. Most of his really effective book-learning was self-administered in Beaconsfield Library, where he stayed on as a Saturday boy. He buzzed through library books at a pace that would have surprised his English teachers. In those early years, he demolished the works of P. G. Wodehouse, Jules Verne and Arthur Conan Doyle. At one point he was simultaneously reading Henry Mayhew's *London Labour and the London Poor* – a series of Victorian articles about social reform – and Tove Jansson's *Moomintroll* children's series.

One writer whose work Pratchett would come to love, and later be greatly influenced by, was G. K. Chesterton, a favourite of his paternal grandmother. The twenty-first century has seen Chesterton's impact fading and he's remembered mostly for the *Father Brown* series of novels; parable-filled tales of a Catholic priest with a sideline in solving crimes. In the years that followed the First World War, however, he was seen as an intellectual heavyweight;[3] a known wit and essayist, famous

---

3. And a literal one. At his peak he weighed upwards of 20 stone. P. G. Wodehouse once described a sudden noise as 'a sound like G. K. Chesterton falling onto a sheet of tin'.

for his numerous columns, poems and novels. Chesterton had lived in Beaconsfield in the years before his death in 1936, and was much celebrated in the area. 'Granny Pratchett', as Terry called his grandmother, even lived on Chesterton Green, and remembered seeing the great author strolling around the town, a large man with a high-pitched voice. Terry's love affair with Chesterton began with Granny Pratchett's copies of *The Napoleon of Notting Hill* and *The Man Who Was Thursday*. (He would tell *Interzone* magazine in 1991 that the two novels contained some of the most emotive plotting of the era, while in a 2014 interview with *The New York Times*, he would nominate the latter as a book that should be read by every president and prime minister.) Before long he was racing through every Chesterton in the library. He was the first creative figure to turn Pratchett from an admirer, into what we now think of as a 'fan'.

His influence cannot be overstated. Terry got his taste for pithy oneliners and satirical asides from Chesterton and the Beaconsfield connection showed him that although authors might be extraordinary people, they walked among us in ordinary towns.[4] He was particularly impressed when his grandmother told him of a London-bound express train that was once held back at Beaconsfield Station so that Chesterton could file his latest piece for *The Strand* magazine. Terry was astonished that a writer could wield so much respect and influence. Most importantly, Chesterton taught Pratchett about the power, the durability and the importance of fantasy.

Pratchett's interest in the fantastical side of literature actually predates his discovery of *The Wind In The Willows* and the glut of reading it inspired. His first taste of the life fantastic came at 9 years old when a boy he met on holiday loaned him a *Superman* comic. Within a few days he was running faster than a speeding deckchair, and leaping tall sandcastles with a single bound, a red towel tucked into the collar of his shirt and his underwear on the wrong side of his trousers. He purchased the latest issue for the drive home – which at 6d cost most of a week's pocket money – but it was stolen by a little girl he'd met and whom he'd become attached to during the trip, breaking his schoolboy heart as a

---

4. Beaconsfield was also home to Enid Blyton. Pratchett wasn't especially influenced by her work, though he did parody it ruthlessly in his later career.

result. Nevertheless, the torch had been lit. *Superman* led to a dalliance with *Batman* comics and other superheroes of the golden age of comic books, all with their own in-built playground games and make-do outfits.

He would lose interest in Americanised comic book worlds as he grew older, finding Superman too boring and Batman too fanciful. Something had sparked his imagination though; a yearning for the escape that came with the unearthly. It was only a matter of time before that hankering for the fantastic collided with an interest in the night sky inspired by those Brooke Bond tea cards. Handily that collision would take place just in front of the science fiction shelves in Beaconsfield Library. Science fiction, usually shortened to SF by enthusiasts, became an all-consuming passion.

If Terry's reading had been restricted to the contents of the public library, his descent into fully fledged fanatic might have taken much longer. There is only so much SF two smallish rooms and a mezzanine can contain. There would certainly have been H. G. Wells, Jules Verne, Robert A. Heinlein, John Wyndham and Edgar Rice Burroughs. There may also have been Isaac Asimov, Ray Bradbury, L. Ron Hubbard, Arthur C. Clarke and E. E. 'Doc' Smith. It's unlikely there would have been much more.

A chance discovery after school changed everything. Terry happened upon an unobtrusive shed on a wartime bombsite in the Frogmore area of High Wycombe: the sign above the door said 'The Little Library'. Never one to pass up a chance for new books, he went in to investigate. The shop had a beaded curtain covering the entrance and was run by a little old lady who, in between knitting and drinking tea, made her living supplying high-quality pornography provided in plain brown envelopes to a steady stream of embarrassed-looking men. In order to maintain a veneer of respectability – and so its owner could rightfully claim to run a bookshop as opposed to being a mere peddler of smut – The Little Library also bought and sold a large selection of British and American science fiction, much of it sourced from the US Air Force base situated near the town. Terry, then 12 years old, had little interest in what he thought of as the 'pinker shelves', but was breathlessly excited by the cache of otherworldly delights he had discovered in the crates on the floor. He quickly became The Little Library's only juvenile regular.

The Little Library finally gave Terry access to a depth of material that could satisfy a fanatic. Here he discovered the pulp paperbacks of Fritz Leiber, A. E van Vogt and Henry Kuttner, and the distinctive custard yellow or violent magenta jackets of the Victor Gollancz publishing house, the publishers of Hal Clement, Algis Budrys and Harry Harrison. Terry sank gratefully into all of them, immersing himself in a universe of black holes, lost civilisations, and planetary conquests. Every time he went into The Little Library, which was around three times a week, there was something new to pick up. Possibly the lady who ran the place made sure to renew her stock, having grown quite fond of the short, awkward boy who showed no interest in her primary product but would drool at the sight of a Harry Harrison novel he hadn't yet read.

Arguably more important, and certainly more affordable than the novels, were the anthologies, magazines and amateur fanzines, published in the UK or shipped over from the US. A subculture of SF fandom had been active in Britain since the 1930s, built around periodicals and a succession of short-lived associations and societies, and was enjoying a new flush of life in the post-war years. Terry picked up magazines with names such as *New Worlds, Science Fantasy, Astounding, Galaxy* and *Analog*. They contained some news and editorial content but were mostly comprised of short stories and serialised novels. Here he found a new generation of writers, including Michael Moorcock, Brian Aldiss and J. G. Ballard. Most of these publications carried classified ads for mail-order fanzines, written by amateurs and usually hand-typed and duplicated. Pratchett sent off for zines such as *Aporrhēta, Zenith* and *New Frontiers*, each one containing more stories from newer writers alongside yet more classified ads and letters. These led to yet more fanzines, more stories and, eventually, to the British Science Fiction Association, and other fans. Terry had not only uncovered a whole slew of new writing; he had made contact with a subculture he felt he could belong to. Much later, when he wrote the Discworld novel *Going Postal* he would channel his discovery of fandom into Stanley, the obsessive collector of pins,[5] and the specialist pin-collectors shop, found under a massage parlour, selling smudged and misspelled fan magazines.

---

5. Or 'pinhead', a reference which will please fans of the *Hellraiser* books.

Terry's reading was not restricted exclusively to space adventures obtained from a porn shop. His father told him about a second-hand bookshop in the nearby village of Penn.[6] There he found a treasure trove of material, and would regularly attempt the perilous cycle home with an overstuffed carrier bag full of books dangling from each handlebar. The SF selections were decent enough, but they were outshone by the collection of humorous writing on offer, which Terry, already primed by Chesterton and Dickens, devoured. One of his prize finds was several bound volumes of *Punch*, the satirical magazine founded by Henry Mayhew in the 1840s. He later claimed that, by his early teens, he had read every issue of *Punch* published between 1841 and 1960, gorging on columns and stories by Geoffrey Willans, Mark Twain, Jerome K. Jerome and Alan Coren. These would join Chesterton in establishing his wry, satirical and occasionally silly sense of humour, as well as a pervading interest in the Victorian era – and especially Victorian London – that would stick with him throughout his life.

At school, Terry was by all accounts (and not least his own), an unremarkable pupil, but that didn't mean he wasn't constantly learning – and learning fast. His version of academia was entirely self-taught, and he picked up information in the form of handy facts and nuggets of trivia, rather than the school-approved method of drilled-in dates and definitions. Every book he read contributed to his education, either by adding to the sum total of his knowledge or by honing his tastes and interests. Though he wasn't always conscious of it, his reading was also helping him to develop a creative voice which, once unleashed, would be impossible to contain. Many books, of many genres and types, dissolved in the crucible of his developing intellect; like nuggets of gold, dug from the ground, ready to be cast into bars. Or, just possibly, into a ring. For there was one book[7] that, for a while at least, would rule them all.

Terry had heard of J. R. R. Tolkien's *The Lord of the Rings*, of course. By 1961 it was already a publishing sensation. 'Frodo Lives' graffiti wouldn't begin appearing in San Francisco for another year or so, but the

---

6. The family actually moved to Penn for a short while, but it's difficult to determine when this was. It certainly wasn't for long, as they were living in Holtspur by the time Terry was in his teens, and they lived in Forty Green for most of his childhood.
7. Technically, three books.

first person to commit that particularly Tolkienian act of vandalism had probably started on chapter one, at least. A few of the boys at school had already read Tolkien's masterpiece and had talked it up, but Terry had yet to get his hands on a copy.

On the last Saturday of the year, having trudged through the freezing December weather to his job at the library, Terry was presented with a late Christmas gift. The librarian, knowing how excited his young volunteer would be, pushed three large books, bound together with string, across the counter. *The Lord of the Rings* had finally arrived. The following day would be New Year's Eve and Terry, now 13, would spend the last night of the year babysitting for some friends of the family. He decided to save his latest prize for the evening, when the adults had left for whatever party or pub in which they'd see in 1962, and the children had gone to bed. Settling himself down, he began to read … 'This book is largely concerned with Hobbits …'.

That evening, and the day that followed were one of the most profound literary experiences of Terry's life. He read until he could no longer keep his eyes open, and fell asleep with the book splayed across his chest. He made short work of *The Fellowship of the Ring* and moved straight onto *The Two Towers*. By the following evening, he had read his way to the end of the appendices in *The Return of the King*. Without much of a pause, he picked up *Fellowship* and started all over again … 'This book is largely concerned with Hobbits ….'.

It's not unusual for a boy of a certain age to resonate with Tolkien in such a way. It's an experience common to anyone who stumbles into fantasy as an impressionable adolescent. *The Lord of the Rings*, for all of its faults – and there *are* numerous faults – is an evocative and engrossing book. As a professor of Anglo-Saxon who had spent his own adolescence reading ancient languages and mythology, Tolkien, a man who found Shakespeare a little modern for his tastes, was channelling the very earliest literature. He distilled that experience into his own work, and his book effortlessly connected to a tree of storytelling stretching back 1,000 years. It gives *The Lord of the Rings* a mythic weight that feels beguiling and impressive, especially to someone who hadn't been exposed to this sort of epic fantasy before. Discovering *The Lord of the Rings*, like discovering extreme music, religious fundamentalism and sex, will always impact most profoundly on impressionable teenagers.

Terry had read some fantasy before, but, well, *The Lord of the Rings* is not just 'some fantasy'. In many ways, it's *the* fantasy. *The Lord of the Rings* is to the genre of fantasy what The Beatles is to pop music: a gear shift in the culture. A year zero. For Pratchett it was a revelation in much the same way that *The Wind in the Willows* had been a few years earlier; he felt an immediate relationship with Tolkien's world. The dark woods and idyllic landscapes of Middle Earth felt familiar to a boy who had grown up in the Chiltern Hills – unsurprising, since the Hobbit's homeland of The Shire was inspired by the West Midlands countryside of Tolkien's own childhood, less than 80 miles away. Later he would describe the experience of reading the book for the first time in immersive terms. That evening the trees of Fangorn began at the edge of the living room carpet, and the light in the room took on the dappled, greenish feel of a forest canopy.

Terry quickly became a Tolkien fanatic, the kind who would happily spend classes dreamily drawing Dwarf runes and writing snatches of Elvish in his exercise books. As late as 2014 he still said Tolkien was his favourite fantasy author, and for much of his life he would re-read *The Lord of the Rings* every year, in springtime. In 1967, at the age of 19, he even wrote to the great man to thank him for his latest novella, *Smith of Wootton Major*, a curious parable-cum-fairy-story which the notoriously deadline-averse Tolkien had written when he was supposed to be working on revisions to *The Lord of the Rings* for his American publishers. It stands out among the author's usually rather impersonal work. Tolkien, then 75, described it as an 'an old man's story, filled with the presage of bereavement'. Despite being much younger, Terry felt a connection with the tale, akin to that he had experienced reading *The Lord of the Rings* for the first time. Professor Tolkien was overjoyed to receive his letter and replied within days, saying it was the first correspondence he had ever been sent about that particular work, and that Terry 'evidently feel[s] about the story very much as I do myself. I can hardly say more.'

Terry was developing an unstoppable thirst for heroic fantasy that matched his enthusiasm for space adventures. It would be years before he could resist any book with a dragon on the cover. He bought all seven of C. S. Lewis' 'Narnia' novels in one go, racing through them one after another (he found them rather dry and preachy), and went on to immerse himself in E. R. Edison's *Zimiamvia* books, John Ruskin's *The King of the Golden River*[8] and the works of George MacDonald, L. Frank Baum and H. P. Lovecraft, among dozens of other fantasy authors of the Victorian era and early twentieth century. It was this love of 'sword and sorcery' that led him to research ancient history and mythology. Ultimately, he was just looking for more stories about swords, armies and kings. The better ones even had magic. All of this stimulated his imagination and furthered his education far more than his actual lessons, which he continued to find dull and unrewarding. In September 1963, he even ranted about his school's disinterest in the finer things in life (by which he meant books about spaceships and wizards) via the letters page in *Vector*, the official magazine of the British Science Fiction Association, signing his letter 'Master Terry Pratchett', which at the time struck editor Roger Peyton as somewhat archaic.

It was perhaps inevitable that a boy so obsessed with *reading* otherworldly stories would eventually try his hand at *writing* them. One of his first pieces of creative writing was an ahead-of-its-time mashup between the worlds of Tolkien's Middle Earth and Jane Austen's *Pride and Prejudice*, which saw hapless Mr Collins' rectory attacked by Orcs.[9] According to Pratchett, it was passed around the class and was a hit with the other boys, desperately in need of something to liven up Austen's delicate, stuffy version of England. That particular work has long been lost but thankfully, due to one attentive teacher, Terry's next stories would get substantially more exposure; indeed, at the time of writing, half a century later, three of them are still in print.

Janet Campbell-Dick was Wycombe Tech's only female teacher and usually oversaw Technical Drawing and Art. However, in 1962 the English department found itself short-staffed and she was asked to cover classes for Terry's form. She was astonished to find there was no standard syllabus and was told to choose a book for the class to study based on how many copies were in the store cupboard. Campbell-Dick was having none of it, picking work on merit and teaching it with a fiery passion. A particular favourite was traditional Scottish narrative poetry, such as

---

8. A title that Terry would borrow for a Discworld character many years later.
9. Alas, we do not know what Lady Catherine de Bourgh had to say on the matter.

the ballad *Sir Patrick Spens*, which she would recount, lapsing into her native Scots accent.[10] 'Mrs C-D' became one of the school's most popular teachers, and one of the few that could bring their subject to life, always emphasising the emotional expression to be found in art of all kinds.

It was Campbell-Dick who set the class the task of writing a short story as a homework assignment. Terry submitted a piece called *Business Rivals*, a sharp tale about an advertising executive asked by the Devil to improve Hell's reputation and get more visitors through the door. Mrs Campbell-Dick was impressed and awarded the story twenty marks out of a possible twenty, selecting it to be typed up for the school magazine, *Technical Cygnet*. *Business Rivals* was a hit with the other kids, though it further lowered Pratchett's standing in the eyes of Harry Ward, the headmaster, who objected to its subversive tone and said so in an assembly, giving the story the most effective marketing possible and causing a hitherto unknown rush on the school mag.

The success of *Business Rivals* had a galvanising effect on young Terry: confirming thoughts he'd been having privately. He could write. He was *good* at writing. He wrote several more stories for *Technical Cygnet* – though *Business Rivals* remained the strongest – and experimented with different styles and genres. Of the surviving ones, *Look For The Little –Dragon?* revisits the character of Crucible from *Business Rivals*, a curious first-person account of the landing of a dragon on London's war office, which is either an on-the-nose parody of, or else a straight homage to, Arthur Conan Doyle's *Sherlock Holmes* stories. *The Searcher*, which appears in the same issue, is the tale of a man who investigates the origins of curious stories only to find himself the subject of one. *Solution* is a short mystery about a crashing plane; while *The Picture* is an even shorter musing on madness and art. Many have twists in the final sentence which, if we're honest, betray an author a little too pleased with his own cleverness; a trait not uncommon in bright teenagers. Still, the five stories are more than promising, especially considering Terry was 13 and 14 when they were written.[11] Here is a young writer playing with

---

10. Her husband believes that some of the flavour of her recitations lives on in Pratchett's Scots-influenced characters, the Nac Mac Feegle.
11. Three of which, *Business Rivals* (in its rewritten form as *The Hades Business*), *Solution* and *The Picture* would be published in their original form in *A Blink of the Screen*, a 2012 collection of Pratchett's short fiction.

form and ideas as he tries to land on a style that suits him. Arguably, it would be another twenty years before he found it.

Emboldened by his success, Terry rewrote and expanded *Business Rivals*, brushing up the prose and imagery, though not adding a great deal to the plot itself. He retitled the story *The Hades Business* and persuaded his aunt to type it up for him, before taking a remarkably precocious step for a 14 year old – submitting it for professional publication. A few years of obsessive SF fandom meant he knew exactly where the story should be sent.

John 'Ted' Carnell was the editor of both *New Worlds* and *Science Fantasy*, two periodicals of which Terry was a regular reader. Both were produced by Nova Publications, a company set up by SF fans, of which Carnell was a board member, and whose address was included in each issue. For Terry, it was an obvious target. Carnell was impressed enough with the piece to include it in the August 1963 issue of *Science Fantasy*, writing in his editorial that *The Hades Business* was 'not a perfectly written story by any means' but that 'for a fourteen-year-old it is outstanding', going on to say it was better than seventy-five per cent of submissions he usually received. In an introduction to Terry's story, he noted that the young writer had 'great potential for the future'. Carnell would be the first in a long line of professionals to take a chance on Terry Pratchett's future potential. Unlike his teachers, such figures were usually proved right.

Science Fantasy was the less popular of Nova's two periodicals but still had a circulation of around 5,000, and was well respected in the SF community. Terry was paid £14 for his troubles, money he invested in his future career, purchasing a reliable second-hand Imperial 58 typewriter from his typing teacher.[12] He also saved up for a copy of the reference work *Brewer's Dictionary of Phrase and Fable*, which he had read was an invaluable resource for a writer, and the latest edition of *The Writers' and Artists' Yearbook*. He may have been only 14, but he was now a published science fiction author. It was time to start behaving as such.

One of the things published SF authors were supposed to do was attend conventions. Terry attended his first science fiction convention in

---

12. Later, when he worked out what it was worth, he suspected his parents may have quietly thrown in a little extra.

1964, after some fast talking about the 'educational value' of such events to his parents.[13] Eastercon was (and indeed, is) an annual gathering of SF fans and personalities held over the Easter weekend somewhere in the UK. The 1964 Eastercon took place in the Bull Hotel, Peterborough. As this was the second year the town had played host, the event was dubbed, with a sense of humour typical of the SF fan, 'Repetercon'.

SF conventions in the twenty-first century are big business, with Comic Con events across the world attracting huge names and tens of thousands of fans, and being used as launchpads for giant, tentpole movie franchises. British conventions are modest compared to those in the US, though London's annual MCM event boasts more than decent numbers, with cult celebrities and thousands of attendees in costume. Matters were somewhat calmer in 1964, and Repetercon had only 151 attendees, including guests (Pratchett was number eighty-five on the list of delegates).

Repetercon and the events that followed, including 'Brumcon' and 'Yarcon',[14] took place amid something of a changing of the guard in British SF fandom. Nova Publications, run by enthusiastic fans rather than savvy business types, was sliding into trouble and both *Science Fantasy* and *New Worlds* were picked up by a new publisher, with new editors installed. Younger names were beginning to make their mark on the scene, not only Terry, but also Ed James, Christopher Priest, Michael Moorcock and J. G. Ballard. The sense that British authors were having a 'moment' was capped by the selection of London as the host for the 1965 World Science Fiction Convention, aka 'Worldcon'. It was the first time the event had left the US.

For Terry, these conventions were a revelation. He found himself among peers, people with as good an encyclopaedic knowledge of Aldiss and Harrison as his. He made new friends, including writers Ed James, Roger Peyton and Dave Busby, who would remain part of his life for the next half century, and indulged, naturally, in a lot of underage drinking and high jinks. Later he recalled watching someone trying to throw an

---

13. The main educational value was in learning what beer tasted like, but that's still an education of sorts.
14. The reader is left to crack the cunning code that reveals the location of these two events in their own time.

inebriated Charles Platt, the young editor of the fanzine *Beyond*, out of a window at a convention in Birmingham. A contemporary report of the same con, written by teenage fans Beryl Henley and Archie Mercer, notes that 'Terry Pratchett was doing something incredibly funny in a corner, only we can't quite remember what.'

That's not to say Terry was wildly popular at these events. Platt remembers him as 'mildly amusing, ironic, and a bit twitchy. Not an easy person to talk to.' This chimes with the view we have of him at school: overcompensating for his shyness with his sense of humour in a way that could grate occasionally.

Even among this nerdiest of crowds Terry was something of an outsider and held himself apart from all the petty squabbles and schisms that are par for the course in dedicated fan communities. The old guard was suspicious of the newcomers, the London 'new wave' writers thought the earlier generation of fandom was provincial and dull, while the contingents from Birmingham and the north thought the London new wavers pretentious and depressing.[15] 'Terry Pratchett was completely outside of this foolishness,' says Platt. 'He just enjoyed reading books and seemed mildly amused by the bad blood in our microcosm. I think ironic detachment was his default state.'

Yet Terry accumulated a certain amount of notoriety and interest, if not necessarily respect, at these events. *The Hades Business* had been widely noted in the SF community, partly because it was a decent and original work, but also because Terry had managed to land a published story in one of the genre's holy tomes at such a young age. He even started to worry that he'd peaked too early, fearing he would be pegged forever as a '14-year-old writer' – he was displaying that mixture of cockiness and self-doubt unique to creative teenagers. His presence at Brumcon[16] in 1965 was even advertised in an edition of the long-running SF newsletter *Skyrack*, alongside big hitters Brian Aldiss and Ted Tubb. By the 1966 Eastercon, held in Great Yarmouth, he was being invited to sit on a new

---

15. The Londoners, meanwhile, considered their cousins in the north to be oafish and uncultured and referred to the 1965 Birmingham Eastercon ('Brumcon') as 'Bumcon'. This might account for why someone attempted to throw Londoner Charles Platt out of a window.
16. You're thinking of it as 'Bumcon' now, aren't you?

writers' panel which, according to convention rumour, also included Harry Harrison under a pseudonym. All of this played into his self-image: he was an author, a writer. It was becoming part of his identity.

Christopher Priest, who would go on to great acclaim with his multi-award-winning book *The Prestige*, and would ultimately write Terry's obituary for *The Guardian*, remembers encountering him in London the following year, and seeing both his awkwardness and growing credibility first hand:

> An American editor called Judith Merril visited London. She was on a mission to discover and understand the 'New Wave' of science fiction, which in some terrible way she associated with 'swinging London'. She was utterly wrong about that, and the anthology she eventually published was something to cringe about. But she was a pleasant woman, and she started making contact with the many young writers then working. I was one of them, and Terry was another. One evening we met Judy for a meal and then a general conversation back at her rented apartment. Terry had brought along a friend, who had published one story (nothing since then).[17] I remember he and this friend sat side by side, chirping like sparrows, an endless stream of silly puns and jokes. Completely inoffensive, and Judy obviously found them charming and amusing, but for me, it was a waste of time. I was always dead serious about writing. We were all very young still.

Terry's most significant encounters had come a year earlier, at the 1965 London Worldcon. Firstly, he had found himself chatting to American author James Blish about the quality of English breakfasts. He was thrilled. The giants of science fiction didn't just walk among the ordinary folk as G. K. Chesterton had, they stomped about complaining to you about the absence of waffles as if you were their equal. This point was hammered home thanks to a chance encounter with British SF legend Arthur C. Clarke in the lavatories. Terry would tell this story many times throughout his career; in some versions Clarke was at the urinals, in

---

17. It's likely that this is Dave Busby.

others he was grunting in a cubicle. Either way, Terry was able to shake hands with someone he had previously thought was an unreachable icon of the genre. We can only hope Clarke washed his hands first.

Worldcon took place a few weeks before Terry was due to return to school after the summer break, having achieved a respectable five O-Levels. His plan was to stay at Wycombe Tech for the next phase of his education, and he applied to study English, History and Art at A-level. The Terry Pratchett that returned to High Wycombe that year, however, was not the same as the one who had sat his exams the previous term. This Terry Pratchett had walked with giants, and though he would drop out of active, convention-going fandom over the next few years as study, work and girls soaked up his time, he was beginning to realise that he could have a place somewhere, in some way, among such titans himself.

Chapter 3

The Journalist's Apprentice

Terry returned to Wycombe Tech after the summer break of 1965 unaware he was entering his final few weeks in full-time education. His dislike of school had turned into a simmering resentment, though the idea that he could bail on academia and throw himself into the real world wasn't one he was taking seriously just yet. He wasn't sure what awaited him on the other side of A-Levels, but it was unthinkable not to take them. Still, ideas about his future had begun to form; a professionally published story under his belt and several more in the school magazine, alongside the lessons in touch typing that his mother had paid for, had given him confidence in his abilities. Writing wasn't just the only thing he was good at, as he would later claim in an interview with the BBC,[1] it was something he was *very* good at, and knowing this gave him a clear focus. All those other vague ambitions, the astronomy and the electronics, had fallen to the wayside. Writing was the only way he could see himself spending his life.

Terry began to research a career in the written word. He read several books on the subject[2] and learned quickly that penning sci-fi stories was unlikely to provide a reliable living. Luckily his skill with words left another path available: in September he wrote to the editor of his local newspaper, the *Bucks Free Press*, optimistically claiming he was going to graduate the following year with three A-levels[3] and asked if a job would be available in the summer.

There's an idea that recurs in Discworld novels about 'the trousers of time', those moments when two possible futures open up and you're forced to pick a leg. History bifurcates: go one way, and your life will be

---

1. This was not quite true, he was also a skilled artist and had a sincere love and aptitude for technology.
2. His answer to pretty much any problem was to find a book about it.
3. 'I was pretty certain I'd have at least passed History and English' he said later.

completely different from the other. The young Terry's only real 'trousers of time' experience so far had been choosing High Wycombe Technical School over the local grammar. He would always claim it was his first real mistake. He was six years older now and teetering on the edge of adulthood. The trousers had become much bigger, and the stakes much higher. Against all biological and metaphysical expectation, another leg was about to open up.

Arthur Church, the respected editor of the *Bucks Free Press*, replied almost immediately: he had no idea if a position would be available months down the line, but the paper was looking for a trainee reporter right now. Would he be interested in interviewing for the role? Terry jumped at the chance.

The interview took place on a Saturday afternoon. Terry, a man always keen to self-mythologise, would tell people he'd turned up in his school uniform. It's a curious detail. After all, the Pratchetts weren't so badly off that David wouldn't have owned a tie his son could borrow, and since it was Saturday it's not as if he was coming straight from class. That said, using your uniform for job interviews was common at a time when not everyone owned a smarter get-up. A *Free Press* alumna, Janice Raycroft, who would be mentored by Terry in the early 1970s, remembers attending her own interview at the paper in her grammar school-approved skirt and school tie.

Whatever his attire, the young writer clearly made an impression, receiving a job offer from Church on the spot. Terry was fond of telling people that his new boss had remarked, 'I like the cut of your jib!', usually adding that this was 'the last recorded use of the phrase in Britain' or 'this was the last time anyone was heard to say this without being arrested.' Forty-five years later, during a lecture at Trinity College, Dublin, he admitted he wasn't certain whether Church had ever really uttered the line or if he'd added that detail himself to spice up the anecdote. The story had grown with the telling. Terry Pratchett stories often did.

The trousers of time had opened: should he endure another year of school and leave in the summer with the safety net of three[4] A-levels in his pocket? Or roll the dice, turn his back on Wycombe Tech and see if

---

4. Or, more likely, two.

he could cut it as a reporter? The decision was made substantially easier thanks to one last insult from headmaster Harry Ward. Terry had been appointed the school's student head librarian, an unpaid position which he, a self-described 'library boy', worked diligently at, staying behind every Thursday evening to tidy up and repair books. Traditionally the head librarian was also made a prefect, and having 'school prefect' on your CV could be invaluable; it indicated trustworthiness, someone who had gone above and beyond in their academic career. It could swing the balance on job offers and university placements. Ward was adamant that Terry Pratchett, a student who wrote weird fiction, had once been caught stealing an old encyclopedia out of a bin and brought in scurrilous magazines such as *Mad* and *Private Eye*, would never become a prefect at his school. He prevented the appointment. Terry saw it as a wholly malicious act, for which he never forgave his headmaster.

In his 2010 speech at Trinity College, Terry claimed he walked into school on the Monday following his interview, handed back his textbooks and left, somewhat satisfyingly, via a visitors' entrance which only teachers and prefects were allowed to use.[5] The story has a neat symmetry and obeys what on Discworld is often called 'the law of narrative causality'.[6] The truth is likely a little less narratively tidy. For starters, David and Eileen Pratchett were on holiday at the time and their son respected them far too much to make a decision without their approval. Besides which, at 17 he legally needed his father's consent to embark on an apprenticeship. On their return, Terry was surprised how quickly his sensible, practical parents came round to the idea. David was simply relieved that his son wasn't going to spend his life looking at the undercarriage of a motor car,[7] while Eileen had lofty visions of Terry editing *The Times*.

Pratchett began his three-year apprenticeship in journalism in the September of 1965, on a wage of £8 and 10 shillings per week. Alongside on-the-job training, he worked in his spare time to achieve his National Council for the Training of Journalists (NCTJ) qualification[8] and an

---

5. And also, presumably, visitors.
6. Where reality obeys the rules of a story, rather than the inconvenient logic of the real world.
7. Technically untrue, Terry insisted on doing his own car repairs even when he became a wealthy man.
8. He claimed he got the top grade in the country.

A-Level in English. While his former headmaster was undoubtedly happy to see the back of him, other students felt a Pratchett-less school was a sadder one. The head of the Debating Society wrote in *Technical Cygnet* to say, 'Regrettably, Pratchett's premature departure has meant the loss of one of our great characters.'

The *Bucks Free Press* had been part of the local landscape since its founding in 1856. Every Thursday the bulky paper was forced through letterboxes across South Buckinghamshire, dispatched from its premises in High Wycombe to local towns such as Amersham, Princes Risborough, Beaconsfield and the dozens of villages and hamlets that orbited them – a patch Terry knew intimately. This was standard local paper stuff; twenty or so stories to a page, often barely more than fifty words apiece, covering everything from murders to the fortunes of Wycombe Wanderers FC, via flower shows, village fetes, traffic accidents and a week's worth of local weddings. Typically, half the pages were given over to classifieds and ads; the lifeblood of any local rag. Journalists were assigned a patch, and cub reporters were assigned a journalist to shadow. On arrival, the young Terry was attached to a reporter called Mr Alan and dutifully followed him into the field, notebook in hand.

Most people's first day at a new job involves being shown where the kettle is and trying to find a handy way to memorise about a dozen strangers' names. On Terry Pratchett's first day he saw a corpse. Or at least, that's the tale he would repeat countless times. One of the first stories Mr Alan covered that day was the discovery of a body; a homeless man had fallen into an animal latrine on a farm and drowned in pig manure. This wasn't the serene and peaceful close of a life ended well, this was an obviously, horribly and vividly dead body. The sight taught Terry three things: how undignified death could be, how many colours the human body could turn, and the extent to which a 17 year old could vomit on his first day at a new job. It's hard to imagine a more formative experience for a new reporter.

The details of this encounter are tricky to nail down. Searching through issues of the *Free Press* from September of 1965 yields only one story that matches Terry's description: the death of an elderly tourist from Glamorgan, who was found at the Abbotswood Estate, Bourne End. Frustratingly, the dates don't quite match – the body was reported in the

3 September edition but found the previous week, before Terry says he started his stint. What's more, the Abbotswood Estate isn't a farm, nor is a tourist a 'tramp', as Terry often described the unfortunate man. A report in the 23 July edition has a family discovering a body in a river, but this was a well-heeled civil servant, and besides, the *Free Press* didn't start advertising for a trainee journalist until 13 August. A woman's body found in a dyke was reported in the 29 October edition, but again this doesn't fit the facts as Terry told them later. In fact, there is no death reported in the *Bucks Free Press* during 1965, either as a recent discovery, coroner's report or classified family notice that matches the details. Was this another story that grew in the telling? The gruesome body was certainly real and the visceral effect it had on the young writer is clear, but the 'first-day' element is such a satisfactory narrative detail that you can't help but suspect Terry embellished it, just a little. On the other hand, the story could well have been spiked, been deemed outside of the *Free Press's* jurisdiction or reported in a way that was unrecognisable from Terry's original description. Whether it happened on his first day or not, the sight of that unfortunate man would stay with Terry for the rest of his life, surfacing grimly as hints in his books. Later, when the subject of death was very much on his mind, that first glimpse of a body served as an example of how horrible a man's sudden demise could be when compared to more peaceful alternatives.

If Beaconsfield Library is where Pratchett got his real education, the *Bucks Free Press* is where he obtained his PhD.[9] He credited several mentors at the paper with instilling in him a discipline and work ethic that would be carried into his career as an author. Experiences and lessons were soaked up by his sponge-like personality, to be dripped into his novels many years later.

Since 1956 the *Free Press* had been overseen by Arthur Church, the well-liked but rather old-fashioned editor who had tempted Terry away from school with the prospect of a real job. Church himself had joined as a cub reporter in 1928 at the age of 16, and would likely have seen something of himself in the young writer. It wouldn't be the last time he would extend a lifeline to a teenager desperate to prove themselves; under Arthur Church, the *Free Press* trained a succession of successful

---

9. Figuratively speaking. As discussed, he actually got an NCTJ and an A-Level.

and capable journalists. He stood down as editor in 1976 but continued to write a column right up until 2000, just a year before his death from lung cancer at the age of 89 – an astonishing seventy-two years of service. Church was 53 when Pratchett began his apprenticeship and was already a man out of step with the more progressive 1960s. Dressed in tweeds and smoking a pipe he bore a passing resemblance to J. R. R. Tolkien, a fact that couldn't have been lost on his new SF-obsessed staffer. Just as Tolkien distracted himself from a changing world by obsessing over his imaginary one, Church blotted out the wider modern era with a laser focus on his beloved South Bucks, only agreeing to run pictures of the Apollo 11 landings after thinking it over carefully and deciding that 'the moon shines on High Wycombe too'. Devoted to journalistic ethics and besotted with his hometown, Arthur Church was an ideal mentor. In a 1992 feature in the *Free Press*, he would say Terry 'was a great lad, a little eccentric but very ambitious. George Topley forecast he would go far and gave him a great deal of encouragement.'

Chief reporter George Topley was, after Church, the staffer who had the most influence on Terry. If Church's example was about being right in the sense of being *correct*, Topley's was about being right in the sense of being *just*. Terry considered Topley to be an excellent journalist and a consummate moralist who, in his youth, had attempted to stow away on a boat to Spain and fight against the fascists in the civil war, but boarded the wrong vessel and found himself in Hull.[10] From Topley, he learned how to *use* the truth; how to be *right* in a way that went beyond simply being correct. It was Topley who helped stoke and sharpen the anger at injustice and unfairness that would mark much of Terry's best writing. He helped hone his moral edge. George Topley would later inspire the character of William Stickers in Terry's children's novel *Johnny and the Dead*, a passionate campaigner for social justice who also attempted to fight the fascists in Spain and, just as Topley did, found himself on the East Yorkshire coast. In tribute, or possibly as revenge on his old mentor, a stickler for grammar who would throw incorrect copy back at hapless young writers, Terry gave William Stickers the ultimate indignity for a journalist: forcing him to spend eternity with a misspelt headstone.

---

10. Pratchett admitted later that he didn't know if this was literally true, or a metaphor for his journey.

Other mentors included sub editor Johnny How, a short, chubby man who was an expert at hiding the dirtiest jokes in the most innocent of copy and who nicknamed Terry 'Steed' after the dapper oddball from the TV show *The Avengers*; and his tall, thin colleague Ken 'Bugsy' Burroughs who dealt harshly with mistakes and impressed on new reporters the vital importance of deadlines and the need to turn your copy around no matter what. Burroughs would later sing Terry's praises in the pages of the *Bucks Free Press*, telling the paper in 1992 that he 'obviously had talent right from the start. He had an original mind.' How and Burroughs would head to the pub together at lunch, a fine old industry tradition, looking for all the world like Buckinghamshire's answer to Laurel and Hardy.

Life at the *Bucks Free Press* was never easy. Cub reporters were expected to hit the ground running, do as they were told and – crucially – own their own typewriter, or else buy a clunky second-hand one from the company and pay for it in instalments deducted from their weekly wages. Terry's trusty Imperial 58, purchased two years earlier with the money from his first story, meant he was ahead of the game. The hours were long, frequently absorbing evenings and weekends, and the trainees were given the dullest and most menial jobs. Pratchett found himself zipping around the area on a succession of cheap, wobbly motorbikes to coroners' inquiries, local council meetings and magistrates' courts; doorstepping mugging victims, and writing up flower shows, parish council decisions and new Rotary Club chairmen. On Thursdays, after the paper had gone to print, he had the task of clearing and filing the spikes, the traditional sorting system of the newspaperman: literal metal spikes at the end of every desk used for discarding notes and unused copy in a way that could be easily retrieved. Boring work, on the one hand,[11] but essential to a young man trying to understand how a newspaper works. He'd write short bedtime stories for younger readers, often working on them at home, polishing them up for subbing on Monday morning. There was also studying to be done, with days off and evenings allocated to NCTJ coursework, brushing up on journalistic ethics and defamation law and trying to get close to the required 100 words per

---

11. And dangerous for the other one, as many a careless office junior has discovered.

minute in Pitman's shorthand necessary for jotting down quotes and court reporting.[12]

It was a job, though not a very well paid one, but more than that it was an experience, instilling instincts and ethics that would serve him well in the future. He learned quickly that there could be no such thing as writer's block with a looming print deadline: a handy trait in an author. He was also taught to accept editing with good grace, an instinct possibly even handier.

This went beyond learning a trade, though. It was an education in *people*. The local paper is an important part of any community, plugged into life at every level. He got to know the local police and authorities and saw first hand how citizens responded to trauma and joy.

Odd experiences stuck in his head, like the time a coroner's court heard about the demise of an old man who had burned to death, complete with the strange and unrelated detail that he had a rice pudding in the oven at the time; or when a man in Beaconsfield declared himself, apropos of nothing, the town crier, an idea people loved so much they made it official and bought him a uniform. Terry interviewed a pleasant couple who spent each evening watching a weird, glowing ball journey across the sky and below the horizon, only to discover their UFO was actually the setting sun. Each new story taught him something else about the odder corners of humanity. Sometimes the person he observed most closely was himself, such as on the harrowing occasion he covered a minibus crash on New Year's Day – the horror tinged with a guilty excitement that he had a sure-fire splash – only to find another trainee's younger sister was killed in the incident. His reaction was to lock himself in a toilet and laugh his head off because sometimes life is so absurdly horrible that laughter is the only pressure valve available.

The *Bucks Free Press* was an environment in which the teenage Terry Pratchett could thrive. Away from the pettiness of school, by doing work he saw as engaging and important he found himself growing every day.

---

12. Though still a required part of most journalism qualifications, the use of shorthand has declined with the popularity of firstly, dictaphones and, later, recording apps on smartphones. When he became famous enough to be interviewed himself, Pratchett would often accuse journalists using some device to record their chat of 'cheating', before asking them questions about legal and ethical practices in journalism in an attempt to catch them out.

A background in journalism was a major source of pride for Pratchett throughout his life. He rarely gave an interview without mentioning it, often using his experience as a way to needle and tease reporters sent to speak to him. He would call out interviewers when he realised they were pushing him into a neat conclusion about fans, critics or awards, pointing out that he knew exactly what they were doing: finding the shape of the story. He knew because he'd done it himself.

To him, there was a purity to journalism. It was writing with a purpose and it informed the way he would later see the role of an author; you turned facts and opinions into digestible chunks of words, got as many people to read them as you could, and ideally got paid for your trouble. His new role also came with certain responsibilities, both to people and to the truth. He would later describe the strange power he felt when given a notebook and pencil, understanding its influence on and responsibility towards an eager readership. It was a power that he was both proud of, and suspected he didn't actually deserve.

Terry Pratchett was a natural journalist. He completed his apprenticeship with aplomb, becoming a fully qualified member of the *Free Press* team in 1968. It was a pivotal year in his life.

A little earlier he had met Lyn Purves at a party. She was an art student, studying Illustration at the prestigious Chelsea College of Art, and she came from a more affluent background. Her parents had built their own bungalow[13] in the slightly posher Gerrards Cross, while Terry was still very much the council estate boy from Forty Green. Lyn's father, R. F. Purves, was an electrical engineer and secretary of his local church. In an interview with *The Times* in 2011, Terry said the gulf in class gave their romance a flavour of *The Lady and the Tramp*. His apprentice wages meant it was difficult for him to impress during their courtship; he could afford a taxi from Lyn's house to a restaurant, for example, but not from his own house to Lyn's. He would order a cab to the Purves bungalow and race it there on his rickety motorbike, which he'd hide in a field around the corner, clambering out of his leathers to reveal his best suit. When the meal was done he would have the cab drop his date at home and then drive around the corner, where he would pay the driver and retrieve his bike. Lyn and her parents were none the wiser.

---

13. Or at least had someone build it for them.

They married on 5 October 1968, at Gerrards Cross Congregational Church. Terry's best man was fellow sci-fi fan and budding writer Dave Busby, and he gifted a silver ring to Lyn's bridesmaid, Amy Colton. The wedding photos would be the last time that Terry was ever pictured clean shaven. He grew a beard on his honeymoon, liked the way it looked and kept it, at various lengths, for the rest of his life.

Naturally, the ceremony was acknowledged in that week's *Bucks Free Press,* under the headline 'Gerrards Cross Bride for *Free Press* Man'. The couple would remain devoted to one another for the rest of Terry's life. Many years later, attendees at a Discworld convention were told of their guest of honour: 'He will flirt like a champion but don't worry … you will never find a more married man.'

As well as marriage and qualifications Terry would achieve another milestone in 1968. That year the *Midweek Free Press* was launched – a slimmer sister paper to the *Bucks Free Press*, published on Tuesdays and less concerned with the minutiae of South Bucks life, with more scope for features, pictures and personalities. Terry was given his own column, though he had to write it under the byline 'Marcus', presumably so he could be rotated away from the role and replaced should the need arise. It was an unnecessary precaution. Terry was the only person to write 'Marcus's' column, and the feature was retired when he left the paper in 1970. The *Midweek* allowed Terry to flesh out his prose style and, ironically, it's under the guise of Marcus that the voice he would become known for – that of wry humourist – emerges. As Marcus he plumbed the odder corners of life in the county, delighting in time spent among stage magicians or self-styled witches.

The Marcus columns gave him an opportunity to use another of his creative skills as they were often accompanied by a cartoon, signed 'TP'. Again you can see the combination of sharp and silly: a story about child-focused movie screenings in which adults can only attend in the company of children is illustrated by a queue of OAPs looking imploringly at a little boy in the hope he will take them in. An image of a sneering Concorde accompanies a piece featuring an imaginary conversation regarding noise complaints about Heathrow Airport, and an article about the future of local rail lines is illustrated by bowler-hatted business types frantically pumping a hand-cranked rail trolley, representing the future of economy travel.

It was while writing as Marcus for *Midweek* that Terry sent a letter to Roald Dahl, dated 25 April 1969, expressing admiration for his work and requesting an interview for his column. Dahl, then 52, was at this point primarily known as a writer of inventive and rather nasty short stories for adults, though his two recent children's novels, *James and the Giant Peach* and *Charlie and the Chocolate Factory* were both gaining fame, and his scripts dramatising his friend Ian Fleming's novels *Chitty Chitty Bang Bang* and *You Only Live Twice* hinted that a future in screenwriting was on the cards. When Terry arrived at Dahl's Buckinghamshire home for his interview, neither man could have known that the other would become one of the most successful English novelists of the twentieth century.

Considering the juicy potential of these two great literary minds coming together, Terry's feature – published on 21 May – contains no great revelations, though it's not a bad read. With the benefit of hindsight, knowing what the two men would go on to achieve, the chat becomes much more interesting. Many of Dahl's quotes could easily have come from Terry himself in later interviews, arguing that art as a concept is overrated and that humans are, by and large, decent enough – except for the ones that aren't. Terry, meanwhile, is full of praise for the older man and his abilities, though it says something about Dahl's level of fame that Terry has to specify that his subject is probably best known to his readers as 'the husband of Oscar-winning actress Patricia Neal'. Terry, who would later spend much of his spare time tending exotic plants as a hobby, makes a point of mentioning the flourishing orchids in Dahl's greenhouse.

It's tempting to say that Terry took something from this meeting that would inform his future, either in his ethical approach to writing or inspiration as a children's novelist – he had already written dozens of short stories for the paper by this point – but that may be looking for significance that isn't really there. Real life is rarely as satisfying as the type of narrative either man could spin. Still, it's a nice footnote in Pratchett's own backstory, one that – due to being written by an unknown hack called Marcus in a spin-off from a smallish regional newspaper – few have read since it was first published in 1969.[14]

---

14. At the time of writing the official Roald Dahl website lists the two men's correspondence but concludes 'tantalisingly we don't know if a meeting ever took place'.

In his five years at the *Bucks Free Press* Terry said he went from boy to man. He had learned a trade, got married, and grown up. It was time to take a new step. In September of 1970, Terry and Lyn moved to a cottage in Rowberrow, Somerset, in the south west of England. It was an area they would fall in love with and one that would inspire much of his later writing, especially the rural landscapes of his 'Witch' books and the Tiffany Aching young adult series.

Terry had been offered a role at the *Western Daily Press*, the Bristol-based newspaper serving a number of counties in the south west, including Gloucestershire, Wiltshire, and Somerset, selling around 76,000 copies a day, six days a week – a substantially bigger patch than South Bucks. This was a different type of journalism: a daily newspaper is a beast that needs constant feeding, is more serious in tone, less personal and more frequently involved in issues of national and international importance. Terry started at the *Western Daily Press* on 28 September and filed his first story the next day; a report on the assassination of Egyptian president Gamal Abdel Nasser. It was a far cry from flower shows and parish council meetings.

Despite the hard news focus, the *Western Daily* still had scope for Terry's more personal features, this time printed under the more recognisable byline of Terence Pratchett. The evolution of his comic tone of voice continued through these more character-led pieces. In a story entitled *The King and I or How the Bottom Dropped Out of the Wise Man Business*, published on Christmas Eve, Pratchett attempts to buy gold, frankincense and myrrh during a shopping spree in Bristol. It proved an unsuccessful quest, but a very successful piece of comic writing. An accompanying photograph saw the author dressed as King Herod.

He filed several first-person pieces in his time at the *Western Daily Press* which showcased his warmth and wit as a brilliant observer of the minutiae of ordinary life. Sadly, though, there's more to the cut and thrust of a daily newspaper than whimsical attempts to recreate the Nativity, and as a straight reporter Terry never quite lived up to editor Eric Price's standards.

Terry's new boss could not have contrasted more with genial, polite Arthur Church. Eric Price had come from Fleet Street, having spent time at the *London Evening Standard*, the *Daily* and *Sunday Express* and

The Star as well as major regionals including the *Manchester Evening News*. His vision was to apply the techniques of Fleet Street to regional reporting, making sub editing[15] into a fine art, hacking and slashing as he punched up copy and inserted provocative headlines. It's an approach he executed to great effect: at its peak, with Price at the helm, the *Western Daily Press* was selling upwards of 80,000 copies a day. This ruthless, no-nonsense approach was also applied to his staffing; one colleague, Ian Beales, writing for the *Press Gazette* on Price's death in 2013, recalled many a luckless reporter or sub being sent packing before their first shift was even complete. Staff members were terrified of Price, who would hurl expletive-ridden commands across the newsroom, shout down anyone that crossed him and sack people on the spot. He had a habit of gabbling instructions quickly and expecting them to be obeyed to the letter. Anyone unwise enough to ask him to repeat something would be met with an angry 'why don't you just fucking listen?'

Another journalist working at the *Western Daily* at the time was Tony Bush, then a cub reporter of 21. He remembers Price's management style as terrifying but effective:

> It was a tyrannical regime, he would shout at you, swear at you, and slam his hand down on the desk. He was inspired, and he did inspire everyone else, but people were also afraid of him. He was a hell of a taskmaster and set a ferocious pace. Even today I still have a hard spot on the second finger of my right hand, where I just kept writing, writing, writing. It was constant.

A few weeks of yelling and bullying was too much for Terry, who vowed to give Price a piece of his mind. The more reserved Bush, who had arrived at the paper slightly before Terry, remembers cautioning him to 'do be careful, dear chap'.

---

15. Sub editors or 'subs' are the unsung heroes and detested villains of the print industry. Their job is to take the stories written by reporters, columnists and writers, and proofread them, edit where necessary and add headlines and subheadings, crucially making sure the words fit the allocated space on the page. The good ones polish and improve, the bad ones butcher and usually take the jokes out. If you're reading this, then we got a good one.*
* This is a dirty trick to play on a sub.

After several days of getting his nerve up Terry finally got a chance to stand his ground when Price came storming through the saloon-style doors of the newsroom ('marching like a guard officer', remembers Bush). Knowing it was now or never, Terry got to his feet, turned to face his boss and, jacked up on nerves and adrenaline, promptly fainted. Price took one look at the prone, bearded figure on the floor and demanded that 'someone get this body out of here'.

Nevertheless, young reporters benefited professionally from working for Price. 'I never wrote a decent headline before I went to the *Western Daily*,' remembers Bush. 'Afterwards I never wrote a bad one.' But working under such pressure began to take its toll. 'It was like Colditz', says Bush who, like Terry, daydreamed of escaping to somewhere more sedate and civilised, eyeing jealously the nearby *Bath Evening Chronicle*. Bush jumped ship to the rival paper within six months, receiving an offer of a job on the subs desk. Terry, meanwhile, was eventually fired by Price in April 1971. As he said himself in his Trinity College lecture, he just didn't have 'the killer instinct' for that sort of journalism. Price, however, would later say that Terry Pratchett was one of the best writers he had worked with.

His sacking from the *Western Daily Press* marked the end of Terry's time as a reporter. Ultimately, it was not a life he wanted to continue. He had become jaded, sick of asking widows and mothers how they felt about their loved one's death, bored of chasing stories. His time working under Eric Price had underlined for him where his strengths were. In 1971 he returned to the *Bucks Free Press*, this time as a sub editor, away from the coalface of reporting, where his gifts for sparkling copy and fastidious accuracy would be put to good use, and where he could devote more time and energy to the writing he was doing in his spare time.

Chapter 4

The Carpet People and Other Stories

T hroughout his time working in journalism, Terry had been developing his skills as a fiction writer. Back in September 1965, the same month that he began his apprenticeship at the *Bucks Free Press*, Terry sold his second science fiction short, this time to *New Worlds*, now under the editorship of Michael Moorcock, whom Pratchett knew distantly through SF fandom. With Moorcock at the helm, *New Worlds* had become the go-to periodical for SF's so-called 'new wave', with a circulation of 18,000. Terry's contribution, *Night Dweller* – a gloomy tale about a doomed mission to the edge of the solar system – appears in the November 1965 issue.

Few Pratchett fans have read this story, which has never been republished in English (though curiously it has in German), meaning completists must track down an original copy. Those that do so occasionally feel short-changed (literally – copies can go for around £170). Writing in *Book Collector* in 1995, the critic M. J. Simpson called *Night Dweller* 'simply *awful*', which is rather a harsh review. True, there's a bleak and ponderous tone to the story that's rare in Terry's work – even his juvenile writing has quite a light touch – but there's also an evocative, chilly atmosphere that takes some skill to achieve. Moorcock's editorial praises the story for the way it describes space in 'a new and somewhat poetic light', and there's a hint of H. P. Lovecraft in Terry's sinister and faintly queasy nods to a wider mystery. *Night Dweller* is especially interesting in the context of his long career – in fifty-one years of writing it is the only work he ever published that betrays no sense of humour at all. He had a long way to go before he found his voice. Still, having two stories published at such a young age – alongside some of the established names in the genre – can't have done the young writer's growing confidence any harm, though it would be many years before he dabbled in straight science fiction again.

At the beginning of 1965, Terry had started writing the full history of a fictional ancient Mediterranean civilisation called *The Tropnecian Empire*, a parody of ancient Rome. Most of the stories were never published and survive only in fragments kept by Terry's friend, Ed James, whom he had met at his first Eastercon. James was studying History at Oxford at the time, and the two corresponded regularly via letters and postcards, which – with absolutely no regard for posterity – Terry had a habit of dating inaccurately as '1929' or '2037'.[1] James would contribute his own suggestions, and the two worked up a reasonably detailed and very silly Tropnecian history together. The pair eventually found themselves too distracted to take the concept any further, but James believes many of the ideas, including an increasingly crowded Pantheon of Gods, would feed into Terry's later writing. A section quoted by James in *Terry Pratchett: Guilty of Literature* could stylistically have come from any Discworld novel. A distinctly militaristic Roman society, which bore many of the hallmarks of the Tropnecian parodies, would also surface in a much earlier story – the tale of a microscopic world found amid the dust and hairs of a carpet which he had first started to develop while still at Wycombe Tech, and which would find a home in the *Bucks Free Press*.

For years the paper had featured a small column in the corner of page five called Children's Circle, credited to 'Uncle Jim', a byline like 'Marcus' which could be passed around various writers. For the next five years, it would be Pratchett's alone. It consisted of a short bedtime story, usually serialised over several issues, and a list of boys and girls with birthdays that week. Children could 'join' the circle by sending in their name and date of birth, meaning they'd get a timely 'happy birthday' from 'Uncle Jim'. Writing stories for Children's Circle was one of the most loathed jobs at the paper so its current occupant, a writer named Marion, was keen to palm it off on the *Free Press*'s latest trainee. Terry, who loved writing fiction and adored children's stories, relished the opportunity.

It was a neat fit. Terry was a skilled storyteller, and Children's Circle needed those skills. In recent months the column had followed the babyish tales of Boo Boo Bunny, Frances Frog, Hereward Hedgehog and

---

1. Ed James writes about these in the updated edition of the excellent book, *Terry Pratchett: Guilty of Literature*.

Peter Piper the stoat. Every week the animals tumbled through a series of what could only generously be called 'adventures': they learned to swim, shampooed their fur and went to the shops. Occasionally someone would get very briefly lost. Years later the talking rats of Pratchett's 2001 young adult novel *The Amazing Maurice and His Educated Rodents* would encounter similar characters in a book-within-a-book called *Mr Bunnsy Has An Adventure*, a story full of cute animals wearing waistcoats, called Oily the snake, Howard the stoat and Ratty Rupert the rat. Pratchett's main target here is probably Beatrix Potter, but it's not a huge stretch to imagine that the stories penned by his Children's Circle predecessor served as inspiration.

The final story published before Pratchett took on the mantle of Uncle Jim was a morality tale, with Boo Boo watching, horrified, as Lester the deer smokes a cigarette. Pledging to help his friend kick the habit, Boo Boo makes up fake 'French' cigarettes and tricks Lester into puffing on one; Lester is promptly sick and vows never to smoke again. Had *Book Collector*'s M. J. Simpson read this he might have looked a little more favourably on *Night Dweller*.

On 8 November 1965, Terry Pratchett began a five-year stint writing Children's Circle, with part one of a story he would later call *Tales of the Carpet People*,[2] a serialised version of a piece he'd been working on at school. It opened with a neat through line from the previous week's story – an unseen hand knocking cigarette ash onto the carpet and starting a fire.[3] Children turning the page might have felt a little conflicted when, despite the warnings of two consecutive Uncle Jim stories, they found an advert for Park Drive cigarettes.

The leap in quality from Boo Boo Bunny and his funny fags is pronounced. Gone was the insipid morality and cutesy lives of woodland animals; instead readers were treated to an imaginative adventure set among the hairs of a carpet populated by tribes of tiny people to whom the fibres were a forest, and a dropped matchstick a mountain. According

---

2. Children's Circle stories weren't printed with titles, though some would gain them when they were published in collections of Pratchett's short fiction.
3. Perhaps it was Lester the deer. The story was reprinted nearly fifty years later in a collection of Pratchett's children's writing called *Dragons at Crumbling Castle*. The detail about the cigarette ash has been omitted from the later version – presumably for health and safety reasons.

to Pratchett, the idea of a miniature society that lived in a carpet came to him, as many good ideas do, in the pub. A friend had jigged enthusiastically across the floor during a particularly animated discussion, leading him to joke, 'Be careful, you'll disturb the carpet people.'[4] Whether or not a light bulb appeared above his teenage head is unreported.

The story establishes a long-running theme in Pratchett's work: that of tiny characters living in a full-sized human world. It begins with the tribes of the carpet and continues with the 'nomes' of the *Bromeliad* trilogy, an early version of which, starring Rincemangle the Gnome, would appear in a Children's Circle story in 1973 during Pratchett's second stint at the *Bucks Free Press*. More gnomes crop up in a 1966 story about a submarine built from a walnut and powered by an elastic band; its centimetre-high crew use their craft to ram menacing ducks from below with a hawthorn spike. Another Uncle Jim piece, published in the summer of 1969, featured characters even more microscopic than the inhabitants of the carpet: the citizens of rival cities called Grabist and Posra, situated on a floating speck of dust visible in a beam of light on a sunny day. Later, the Discworld series would be full of gnomes, 'pictsies' and other tiny species, most notably the 'wee free men' of the Nac Mac Feegle, who arrived in 1998's *Carpe Jugulum* and became mainstays of the Tiffany Aching books, featuring regularly in the series right up to Pratchett's final full novel, *The Shepherd's Crown*.

During that first visit with his mother to Gamages department store in London, 5-year-old Terry had imagined the place swarming with tiny gnomes who came out when the humans weren't looking – an idea which would later manifest itself in his children's novel, *Truckers*. There's a passage in his 1987 book *Equal Rites*, the first of many Pratchett stories with an isolated child as the main character, in which the heroine, Eskarina Smith, describes the plastered ceiling of Granny Weatherwax's bedroom as a 'fantastic upside-down landscape that she had peopled with a private and complex civilisation.' It's a game fairly common to imaginative only children and Terry, whose devouring of the contents of the local library

---

4. Writing on his website, Colin Smythe, Terry's agent of many years, wonders whether this could have been a bit of typical Pratchett tale-spinning, as the writer would have been too young to drink in pubs at the time; though that has rarely stopped young men in small country towns giving it a go.

had introduced him to Mary Norton's *The Borrowers* and the Lilliputians of Swift's *Gulliver's Travels*, would never quite shake his fascination with hidden worlds of tiny people.

Armchair psychologists might point to Pratchett's height – at 5ft 8ins he was a short man and had been small for his age as a child – as one of the inspirations behind a long line of diminutive characters with big personalities, living in a world designed for those much larger. The influence of his own height is not an issue he appears to have discussed publicly, and he may well have found the theory laughable. Though, of course, that doesn't mean there isn't something in it. Terry himself had another explanation – in 1993 two primary school children writing for the junior publication *Young Writer* asked him why he wrote about small people. He claimed it's because he found characters who see the world from different angles to be interesting.

The first *Carpet* serial is notable for a few reasons. Not only was it Terry's first foray into children's writing and his first fictional piece for the *Bucks Free Press*, it was also easily his best published work so far, and one of his first attempts to create a self-contained world.[5] It was also wonderfully imaginative; a proper adventure filled with weird beasts and warriors. Pratchett sets out a fairly standard fantasy quest story: the people of the village of Fallen Matchstick, which nearly burned down due to that carelessly dropped ash, must leave their homes because the carpet is beginning to fray. A mysterious hermit tells them of a land far away, where they can be safe. The villagers, led by Snibril (a hero noted for his imagination rather than for bravery or cleverness) and Glurk the hunter, fight their way across the long inches of the carpet in search of their new home, surviving attacks by vicious 'snargs' and warring armies keen to claim the promised land for themselves. What really impresses is the deft way Pratchett, even at 17, handles his premise. The story is full of beautiful details that hint at a wider and darker world beyond that of the small lives of its characters, like the distant 'carpet drums' that pass word of the travellers across the land. The reader is given a sense of history, of fallen empires, and the faint, quiet menace to be found in the concept of

---

5. A *flat* world at that.

the fraying carpet.[6] The storytelling owes more than a little to Tolkien, who peppered *The Hobbit* with similar hints towards grander tales. Like Dickens before him, Pratchett proved to be a master at serialising his work, exemplified by the sudden emergence in the dark of glowing, red eyes at the end of part three of the story. Uncle Jim's readers remained on the edge of their seats for another week. It's remarkably rich stuff for a tale published in the neglected children's column of a local newspaper, from the pen of a 17-year-old trainee.

Terry took the role of children's writer extremely seriously, and devoted hours of his own time to his stories. It's especially admirable when you consider that, as an apprentice with studying to do on top of his day-to-day duties, he had very little spare time to give. The Uncle Jim stories were as important a part of the young Terry Pratchett's education as the lessons in journalistic rigour and professionalism he received. Here was another chance to hone his craft, and this time he had no mentor other than his own imagination and the work of his favourite authors. Just like the more grown-up sections of the paper, Children's Circle was a furnace that needed constant fuel, and Terry had to grind out content week after week. He wrote over seventy stories for the *Bucks Free Press*, and when his career took him to the *Western Daily Press* and, later, the *Bath and West Evening Chronicle* he would continue to write fiction, both children's stories and later humorous pieces aimed at the paper's adult readership.

The Children's Circle meant Pratchett could stretch his writing in a number of directions.[7] *Tales of the Carpet People* was a serious adventure story, despite the occasional comic aside, but elsewhere his sense of humour led from the front. Almost all of the stories are shot through with silliness to some degree or other, usually very playful and occasionally extremely daft. You can sense a young writer learning when to let loose, and when to rein in and let the story take him forward. Those early stories also included the tale of Professor Whelk, a scientist who

---

6. Part Two opens by telling the reader that the carpet itself was beginning to fray. The literal fabric of the world was unravelling. Children's Circle readers had come a long way from Boo Boo Bunny.
7. At least, numerous directions appropriate for an audience of 5–10 year olds. Which is more directions than you'd think.

dreamed of going to Mars, and *The Tropnecian Invasion of England*, the only published fruit of Terry's collaboration with Ed James.

By February 1966, Pratchett had settled on an irreverent and silly tone full of wordplay and askew references, influenced partly by Spike Milligan and the Goons, partly by *Punch* magazine, but mostly by his own imagination. *Hunt The Snorry*, as it was later titled, tells the story of Colonel Vest, a 'little-game hunter' who leads an expedition in the search for a never-before-seen creature, the eponymous Snorry. The hunting party consists of ninety-one characters from various walks of life, chosen so that the party has as wide a skill-set as possible. The band trek through jungles (complete with thickets of 'tapioca trees') until eventually they all start sneezing, at which point a passing tapioca collector informs them that 'snorry' is a local word for the common cold, and they had, indeed, succeeded in catching it. It is a deeply silly tale, and typical of Pratchett's early humour.

The Children's Circle stories are linked by a handful of recurring themes. Many take place in a fictional middle England market town called Blackbury, which would later serve as the setting for Pratchett's trilogy of young adult novels *Only You Can Save Mankind*, *Johnny and the Dead* and *Johnny and the Bomb*. Blackbury allowed Pratchett to set up and then send up a typical small town familiar to his readers, creating a blank canvas for some fantastically odd concepts. The people of Blackbury bake giant Christmas pies and indulge in sports such as 'egg dancing', which involves a boxing ring and two dancers trying to avoid stepping on eggs. They have a park full of statues of Victorian prime ministers that come to life at night and commute on time-travelling buses or via a time-travelling television. What's more, the town has an apparently rich history of very silly people echoing down the ages.

Another mini-theme is the 'British Wild West': a series of stories set in the Welsh border town of Llandanffwanfafegettupagogo, a nod to the real-life village of Llanfairpwllgwyngyllgogerychwyrndrobwllllantysiliogogoch.[8] Pratchett's premise is that Britain had its own 'old west', just across the border between England and Wales. A coal rush, rather than a gold one,

---

8. The direct translation of which, 'St Mary's church in the hollow of the white hazel near to the fierce whirlpool of St Tysilio of the red cave', could double as one of the unexpectedly beautiful goblin names in later Discworld novels.

had turned Llandanffwanfafegettupagogo into a frontier boomtown, with all the old west features this implied. Just as the Discworld series would subvert fantasy tropes (and Shakespeare, folklore, mythology, opera, fairy stories, Hollywood, rock music, China, Australia, ancient Egypt, ancient Greece, religious dogma, racism, the patriarchy and a thousand other themes),[9] the 'Wild West of Wales' stories were Pratchett's send up of the Western genre, still going strong in the mid-1960s with shows including *Bonanza*, *Rawhide* and *Gun Smoke* broadcast regularly on tea-time television. There's a sheriff that moseys into town, but he's a British bobby with a proper policeman's helmet and is known throughout that land as 'the fastest truncheon west of the river Severn'. Cowboys are 'sheep boys', horses are replaced with bicycles, and the menacing outlaws have names such as Dai Evans, Dai Orribly and his brother, Dai Too. Children's Circle readers would be more than familiar with the clichés of Westerns and Wales. The jokes squeezed from their juxtaposition are not subtle, but it's fun to see Pratchett begin to flex his parody muscles.

What's fascinating about these stories, aside from how good they are given the youth of their author and the context of their publishing, is how many ideas, techniques and themes common in later books are present in embryonic form. The plots of two novels, *The Carpet People* and *Truckers* both originate here, while Sergeant Bunyan from Llandanffwanfafegettupagogo, feels like a precursor to Discworld's Commander Vimes, a lone voice of sane justice in a world going slightly mad. We can also see Pratchett feeling his way around names and sounds; Rincemangle, the department store gnome, has a clear link to Terry's first really successful character, Rincewind the Wizard, who would emerge ten years after his diminutive namesake in 1983's *The Colour of Magic*. The word 'Ogg' crops up as the surname of an ogre, long before it would later attach itself to Granny Weatherwax's irascible sidekick in the Discworld novels, while the colour of magic itself, the 'greenish-purple' octarine, makes an appearance in one story where magic turns the ground 'purply-green'.

---

9. Discworld, as we'll see later, left no trope unturned.

From the very start of his literary career, Pratchett was subverting the fantasy genre. Wizards make an early appearance,[10] with Merlin himself popping up in one of the first *Bucks Free Press* stories, a quite lovely Arthurian time travel adventure.[11] Venerable, pointy-hatted and rather silly wizards of a type familiar to Discworld fans quickly become an established theme in Terry's work, starting with a ridiculous mage called Fossfiddle, an adventurer having problems with his magical seven-league boots in a 1966 story later reprinted as *Dragons at Crumbling Castle.*[12] Though a minor character, Fossfiddle establishes the archetypal Pratchett wizard, a blueprint he rarely deviated from in fifty years of storytelling. Wizards are knowledgeable but lack common sense, and magic is an entirely unreliable way of getting anything done that causes more problems than it solves, be it Fossfiddle accidentally turning a door into a pink meringue in *Dragons at Crumbling Castle* or Rincewind, two decades later, being transported to the mysterious land of Fourecks in *Interesting Times* when his colleagues attempt to zap him home. Pointy headwear, across the board, is extremely important.

Even if these tales were devoid of witches or wizards, they would still be a recognisable template for Pratchett's future writing. At the centre of most of his stories is a moral code that is absolutely Pratchettian: think for yourself but work together, be imaginative but don't rely on shortcuts, be sensible and clever and use bravery as a back-up plan, and above all things be decent. That's as true of Me, the deserter ant in a 1970 Children's Circle story, who runs away from the nest and at one point sacrifices himself to save his new friend,[13] as it is of Tiffany Aching refusing help and facing down the Cunning Man alone at the climax of 2010's *I Shall Wear Midnight*.

---

10. The character of Pismire, who features in the first *Carpet People* adventure would later be developed into a wizard of sorts, but at this point is described only as a hermit.
11. Arthurian legend and time travel would be blended again many years later in Pratchett's 1995 short story *Once and Future*.
12. Seven-league boots are referenced fairly often in Pratchett's work, bleeding from his short stories into the early Discworld novels of the mid 1980s. Though an age-old folklore staple, common in more traditional fantasy stories, the boots – which allow the wearer to step several miles in a single stride – rarely crop up in modern literature. The fashion world can be extremely fickle.
13. Don't panic, he survives.

Life, as has been discussed, occasionally drops a 'trousers of time' moment in your lap, as it were; those crucial forks in the road of our personal universe where a new possible future is created – just so long as you're lucky enough to tumble down the correct leg. In 1968, the year of his marriage and graduation as a qualified reporter, Terry Pratchett once again found himself staring the bisecting pantaloons of destiny full in the crotch, though this time it was the casual choice of his mentor that pushed him towards a whole new life. Arthur Church had sent Terry to interview Peter Bander, the editor of an upcoming book that speculated on the future of the education system entitled *Looking Forward To The Seventies*, produced by local publishing house Colin Smythe Limited. Had the assignment been given to another reporter Pratchett's future could have been very different.

Bander found a sympathetic ear in the young journalist – Pratchett's interview, published in the *Bucks Free Press* in May of 1968, is extremely complimentary. It's hardly surprising that Terry, who'd bailed on a school he hated just three years earlier, would be smitten with Bander's pleas for education reform; even so, his enthusiastic tone is uncharacteristic for the *Free Press* at the time, which tended to avoid overt political opinions outside of columns and editorials. He praises Bander's book as vital and timely.

Peter Bander (later Peter Bander van Duren) and his business partner, Colin Smythe, were the co-owners of Colin Smythe Limited. They make a fascinating duo. Bander, who added a form of his mother's maiden name – von Duren – to his surname in 1976, was a German-born devout Roman Catholic who had previously worked as a teacher in Borstal prison and in a fairly rough inner-city London school. By 1968 he was working as a senior lecturer at Wall Hall College, Aldenham, and had already written two books on morality in education, *One for the Road* (1966) and *Two for the Road* (1967). He would go on to write several respected titles on the obscure world of Roman Catholic heraldry and later became a Knight of the Order of Saint Gregory.[14]

Colin Smythe, meanwhile, hailed from Maidenhead, and had studied at Trinity College, Dublin, as Irish universities didn't require A-Levels

---

14. Comparisons to the 'Elucidated Brethren of the Ebon Night' in Pratchett's *Guards! Guards!* are probably entirely coincidental.

at the time. He returned to the UK in the mid-1960s and started the publishing company which bears his name in 1966, with Bander as co-director. After giving a lecture on the Irish dramatist Lady Gregory for the Yeats Society's summer school in 1968, he began publishing works by classic Irish writers of the early twentieth century, including Lady Gregory herself, George Moore and George William 'Æ' Russell. That year Colin Smythe Ltd also published a childrens book, *Katya and The Crocodile*. He is an acknowledged expert in Irish literature and folklore, and books on those subjects would make up much of his company's output for the next fifty years.

Smythe and Bander can be considered establishment figures and experts in traditionally worthy areas of history, society and literature, which makes it all the more interesting that they shared a fascination with the paranormal. In 1971 they published one of the first ever English language books on electronic voice phenomenon, or EVPs: the theory that the voices of ghosts can be captured on tape. Two years later the pair would collaborate on their own newspaper, *The Psychic Researcher and Spiritualist Gazette*, in partnership with the Spiritualist Association of Great Britain, edited and printed by Bander – who also ran a printing firm – with Smythe serving as features and reviews editor. The monthly publication reported sightings of ghosts and UFOs, explored saints and miracles and ran book reviews and classifieds which advertised the services of mediums, psychic healers and spiritual writers.

Pratchett soon became a regular in the offices of Colin Smythe Limited, with Bander and Smythe feeding him stories for the *Free Press*. It's not surprising that the three got on well: the pair were not much older than Pratchett, their politics aligned (at least on the matter of education, though probably not on religion), and the book-obsessed younger man, who soaked up facts and trivia like a sponge, would have been excited to spend time with two such interesting figures who were publishing fascinating work. Pratchett also shared their interest in the paranormal and wrote occasionally about witchcraft, folklore and UFOs in his Marcus column. And, of course, having the ear of a bonafide publishing house will always appeal to a budding writer. At one point he even asked Smythe for a job, though ultimately his heart was in writing, not publishing. In December 1968 Pratchett finally, inevitably, broached the subject of his first novel.[15]

In between new Children's Circle tales and zipping around the county reporting on court cases and humorous vegetables, Terry had been quietly working up his *Carpet People* story into a full-length children's book, taking the sketch of that first adventure and expanding the world and the characters. The longer version was considerably deeper, darker and more exciting than the original story, though the bare bones of the tale were already present in that first Uncle Jim serial back in 1965.

How long had he been working on it? Writing in the 2009 US Discworld convention programme, Smythe says *The Carpet People* was written when Terry was 17, the year he started work at the *Bucks Free Press*. He's referring to the novel, rather than the short story. It's an interesting note. That first Uncle Jim serial feels like a self-contained tale; not the first chapter of a longer story at all. The full-length version of *The Carpet People* is an expansion of that story, rather than a continuation of it. The two finish in roughly the same place, with the villagers safe in their new home and Snibril leaving them to start a life of adventures. Did Pratchett write further adventures, and then later discard them; choosing to expand the first chapter into a full book instead?[16] The presence of a second *Carpet People* story published in the *Bucks Free Press* in 1967 – a totally separate tale in which Snibril and Bane journey on a ship across the shiny linoleum floor that begins where the carpet ends – supports that theory.[17]

Further muddying the waters is a claim in *The Psychic Researcher and Spiritualist Gazette*, for which Pratchett would contribute a brilliantly funny cartoon strip, that his first novel had been written 'at the ripe old age of fifteen', suggesting he sat on the story for two years prior to

---

15. This version of events is pieced together from biographies, interviews with Pratchett and essays written by Smythe. Pratchett told this anecdote too, though in typical fashion was fond of a simplified account of the story in which he looked up local publishers in the phone book and sent the first one he found his manuscript, which they agreed to publish. This is the version he used most often in interviews. Which begs the question, 'How many people read this and copied the technique, and did it work for any of them?'
16. George Lucas claims he did this with *Star Wars*, although his producer, Gary Kurtz, always denied it.
17. This would make the second story a carpet offcut.

starting at the *Bucks Free Press*. It would account for the difference in tone between *Tales of the Carpet People* and later Uncle Jim stories, and it's backed up by doodles of characters and words such as 'snarg' found in a school notebook from 1964, the year Pratchett turned 16, alongside the words 'The Carpet People' in a Tolkienesque runic font. The ideas were obviously percolating, but it's unlikely he'd yet written the story published in Children's Circle. *Tales of the Carpet People* is light years ahead of *The Hades Business* and *Solution*, which date from Terry's school years, and it seems odd that he would try to sell *Night Dweller* when something as strong as *Tales of the Carpet People* was in his back pocket. We also know (or at least Pratchett always maintained) that the idea for the carpet tribes came to him during a pub argument ... the further back in time we go, the less likely that becomes: even country landlords have to draw the line somewhere. The most we can say for sure is that Terry had been working on *The Carpet People*, comfortably the strongest concept he'd come up with, on and off, in some form or other, for years.

Regardless of when it was written, the manuscript handed to Colin Smythe just before the Christmas of 1968 was for a finished novel, and was certainly good enough for Smythe and Bander to agree to publish it pretty much on the spot. 'It was far too good and original for us not to recognise that Terry had a successful writing career ahead of him,' wrote Smythe. A contract was duly signed on 9 January 1969, with an agreed advance of £250, though as Terry was only 20 and still technically a minor – despite being a married man with a respectable career – he would have to wait another four months to confirm the agreement legally.

It was Terry himself who created the next delay. He was unsatisfied with the current version of the story, which isn't a surprise as he had started writing it in his mid-teens (in a 2014 interview with *The New York Times* he would describe his first draft as the worst book he'd ever read). He wrote to his publishers asking for more time for revisions. By this point, tinkering with *The Carpet People* must have been a difficult habit to break. For the rest of his life, Pratchett was unable to resist an opportunity to fiddle with his first book, rewriting it substantially for reissue in 1992 and even tweaking the original Uncle Jim version for its inclusion in the *Dragons at Crumbling Castle* collection in 2014.

Smythe and Bander agreed to the revisions, and – having seen Pratchett's cartoons in the *Bucks* and *Midweek Free Press* – asked if he would also provide illustrations for the book. He was initially reluctant, thinking his time was better spent elsewhere, but was eventually brought around to the idea, though not before a few false starts – at one point even suggesting *The Carpet People* would work best as a comic strip. The work proceeded slowly through 1969 and 1970. Pratchett still had the day-to-day business of reporting to occupy his time, not to mention his Children's Circle and Marcus columns and then his move with Lyn to the south west and a demanding new role at the *Western Daily Press*. Nevertheless, he was able to complete his final draft, including some thirty illustrations, in time for a Christmas 1971 release, almost three years after submitting the original manuscript to Colin Smythe.

The Carpet People was finally published on 16 November, with a print run of 3,000 copies, around a dozen of which had illustrations hand-coloured by the author. Both Smythe and Bander wanted to write a synopsis for the jacket and, as neither was willing to back down, the book was eventually published with two blurbs: one on the inside front flap, and one on the back.[18]

The release was celebrated with a launch party in the carpet showroom of Heal's department store in London,[19] featuring a carpet-themed cocktail called Essence of Underlay and a selection of nibbles which, according to Colin Smythe in the 2018 Discworld Convention programme, included 'Stewed Snarg with Master Mushrooms, Fried Tromp and Green Glebe Salad, Smoked Weft-borer and Purple Groad, Chrystobella Cheese, and Sugar Crystal Cake'.

Pratchett chatted to journalists, read from his book and did some drawing for children in attendance. Photos from the event show a good time generally being had by all, with Pratchett himself looking delighted. He had every reason to be: on his first attempt, at the age of just 23, Terry Pratchett was a published novelist.

---

18. A review in *Teachers World* singled one blurb out as 'exceptionally badly written', though sadly doesn't specify which.
19. Remarkably for a central London business, Heal's is still trading in the same Tottenham Court Road location. At least at the time of writing. In this economy, you never know.

Chapter 5

There and Back Again

On 1 March 1972, regular readers of the *Midweek Free Press* would have been delighted to spot a new column by Marcus, whose witty editorials had been absent from the paper for over a year. It heralded the return of Terry Pratchett to its sister paper, the *Bucks Free Press*, which officially took place a month later. Though primarily employed as a sub editor – one of those 'indoor jobs with no heavy lifting' he was so fond of – he happily took up the pens of both Marcus and Uncle Jim once more. It's a shame Arthur Church didn't let Pratchett publish Uncle Jim stories under his real name; after all, hiding Terry's latest tales behind a pseudonym wasted all the potential kudos generated by having a genuine children's author writing Children's Circle.

The Carpet People sold respectably enough, though it would take more than a decade to shift all 3,000 copies, and Bander and Smythe never felt the need for a second printing. Pratchett's debut earned a decent handful of reviews, especially for the first novel by an unknown 23 year old. Complimentary essence of underlay and stewed snark turned out to be an effective marketing ploy.

The responses were broadly positive. Peter Grosvenor of the *Daily Express* called the book 'extraordinary' and 'strangely gripping'. Other reviewers were keen to praise its originality and Pratchett's skill as a world builder ('one of the most original tots' tomes to hit the bookshops for many a decade' according to *Smith's Trade News*.) Writing in the *Irish Times*, Rosemary Doyle said the book was 'a new dimension in imagination', adding that 'the prose is beautiful'. Not every response was positive. The Indian newspaper *The Sunday Statesman* thought the book 'too sinister and heavy' for younger readers, and noted that – possibly unfairly given Pratchett's intended audience – 'most Indian children do not live in homes with heavy carpets anyway'. Margery Fisher of *The Sunday Times* worried that the wealth of races and ideas might be too complex for some younger readers. Several reviews mentioned the obvious influence of Tolkien.

They had a point. A lot of *The Carpet People* is wonderfully inventive and original; not least the central premise of a microscopic society that lives in a carpet, with characters substantially smaller than Dwarves, Hobbits, Lilliputians or Borrowers. There are flashes of real beauty here, too. The scene where dozens of animals feast on a single grain of sugar is an image that stays with the reader, and not just because it's illustrated on the front cover. However, other aspects are less original. Pratchett once described his debut novel as '*The Lord of the Rings* of the microscope', and that's a pretty accurate assessment.

As previously noted, the impact of *The Lord of the Rings* on young Terry was profound. To borrow a phrase from *Equal Rites*, reading *The Lord of the Rings* was 'a half brick in the road of history' for many burgeoning fantasy authors.[1] Later he would learn to reject, ridicule, twist or update the conventions of traditional fantasy, with pretty spectacular results, but that sort of thinking was for an older man. *The Carpet People*, in all of its various drafts and rewrites, was written in the shadow of Tolkien by an unabashed fanboy and *The Lord of the Rings* is coded into its DNA. The similarities are so strong you do wonder how Pratchett managed to get away with them ... until you realise that almost every fantasy author at the time was rewriting *The Lord of the Rings* and *The Hobbit*, and most with substantially less elegance.

The parallels are pretty clear, even without a microscope. Snibril is Frodo, the plucky dreamer pulled from a quiet existence into a terrifying quest. Pismire is Gandalf, the twinkly eyed yet wise and occasionally fierce wizard. The Wights are the Elves; wise mystics fleeing the land, the hardy and war-like Deftmenes are the Dwarves, while the Mouls are a combination of Orcs and Black Riders, right down to their 'mocking screech'. There's a young Wight daughter who may as well be called Galadriel, a wise elder who, if you squint, is Elrond, and just when our naive heroes need him, along comes a road-battered warrior with a mysterious lineage. Pratchett calls him Bane, but the mould he's popped

---

1. Actually, most editions of *The Lord of the Rings* are thicker and heavier than the average house brick.

from is labelled 'Strider'. At the start of the book Snibril is taken with the idea – just like Frodo and Bilbo – that all roads are one great connected stream that can sweep a person off to adventure. When that road finally carries him to the ancient city of Ware, we find an old tree at its centre. If Gollum had turned up demanding his birthday present, no-one would have been that surprised.[2]

The homage is forgivable. Pratchett was still very young and almost all first-time novelists struggle to keep their influences in the background. What's more, the world of Middle Earth was all-pervading at the time. Fantasy has been around for as long as literature itself, but *The Lord of the Rings*, as discussed, is very much a 'year zero' for the genre as we see it now. Tolkien's work begat role-playing games such as Dungeons and Dragons, and gradually a sort of open-source tool kit for fantasy worlds emerged, where Orcs were ugly, Elves were beautiful,[3] wizards were wise and young farmhands had unavoidable destinies. That Pratchett had the sense to rename everything, miniaturise it and set it among the dust and hairs of a carpet means his originality probably outweighs his borrowing.

The Carpet People was a success. It may not have bothered the bestseller list, but the book did well enough for Smythe and Bander to welcome either a sequel or a fresh story. Press was limited, but the reviews were respectable and broadly positive. Critically and commercially, surely that counts as a success? *The Carpet People* was also a creative and symbolic win. Pratchett had published a novel at 23, and people had liked it. It proved his writing was versatile and rich; the published version of *The Carpet People* is as far from the Uncle Jim stories as *they* are from *Business Rivals*. It had been an educational success too: Pratchett had learned to draft and redraft; he had learned how time-consuming and frustrating writing can be when the end result is a book, rather than a short story. And, most importantly, he had learned what he was capable of.

Terry and Lyn returned to Buckinghamshire a few months after the release of *The Carpet People*. They had rented a small house in High Wycombe, handy for the Gomm Road offices of the *Bucks Free Press* where Terry was to take on the sub editor position. His second stint at

---

2. Pratchett saved this particular cameo for *Witches Abroad*, many years later.
3. And their collective noun had an elegant 've' in it, replacing the vulgar 'f' associated with Santa's little helpers.

the paper was a different experience to the first. He wasn't a trainee, or a newly qualified reporter, he was an old hand, albeit one who had been absent for the last year. For those who had joined the team in the years before he left, he was as much a part of the furniture as Ken Burroughs or George Topley. What's more, a new generation of trainees had been taken on and history was repeating itself, especially in the case of 16-year-old Janice Raycroft, whose route into journalism will seem naggingly familiar. She had arrived in the newsroom via an interview with Arthur Church – in her school uniform, no less – leaving school the following Friday and presenting herself at the *Free Press's* High Wycombe offices the next Monday. Raycroft had been so desperate to get into journalism she'd applied for a job in accounts and talked her way into working as Church's secretary until a trainee reporter position opened up. Arthur Church had, again, recognised talent and drive in a young writer and thrown them a lifeline.

When Raycroft became an apprentice reporter, Terry was one of the few who was openly pleased: others had wanted Church to hire a more experienced journalist. Pratchett became a champion and mentor for the *Free Press's* newest recruit, realising how much her story mirrored his own. It's an early example of what Pratchett referred to as 'paying forward', something he would do throughout his life. He was aware that others had stuck their neck out to get him where he was: mentors and supporters such as Ted Casson, Arthur Church, Colin Smythe and Peter Bander, and authors including Brian Aldiss, Michael Moorcock and Arthur C. Clarke. Either directly by their actions, or indirectly by being open, accessible and attentive, these people had helped him to his current position, and throughout his career, he would endeavour to do the same. Later, as a famous author,[4] he would write innumerable replies to budding writers who'd asked for advice in letters and emails. He was a constant presence on the sci-fi convention circuit, giving talks and appearing on panels. Towards the end of his life, he even took an occasional teaching gig at Trinity College, Dublin. It was all about paying forward, rather than simply paying back. Each generation of writers planting a seed for the next. Janice Raycroft recalls how she was one of the first people to benefit from his generosity:

---

4. Spoiler alert.

I was dubbed 'The Nipper' and Terry really took me under his wing at this stage, alongside another junior reporter, Robert House. Becoming a reporter meant I could move from the secretary's desk to one across the room in the reporters' ranks. The empty desk was opposite Robert's and the NUJ [National Union of Journalists] actually discussed whether two junior reporters should be allowed to sit facing each other instead of being cub reporters attached to seniors. We stayed put, supported by Terry who regularly appeared from the adjoining subs' room to chat about stories we were working on, providing advice on sharpening our intros and adding colour to pieces without straying from the facts. He gently and quietly steered us in the right direction.

Both trainees would benefit from Pratchett's support, with Robert House taking on Children's Circle when Terry eventually moved on from the paper. Raycroft remembers Terry coming to her aid on more than one occasion:

Once I'd got my feet under the table I made a faux pas and Terry saved me. Walking into the subs' room to deliver one of my masterpieces for the youth page, which Terry subbed every week, I made some cocky comment about how easy their jobs must be, whereas we had to actually go out and find the stories. The subs were mostly much older men, all answering to formidable chief sub Ken Burroughs.

Burroughs exploded and put me in detention. While everyone else went to lunch, I would have to sit in this smoky hole and not leave until I'd subbed the youth page. If I had to stay all night, so be it. He handed me a type chart and ems rule[5] and off they all went for an hour ... or two. I was sitting alone in misery when Terry sneaked back and swiftly 'dictated' the answers to the mystery [of subbing the page] before vanishing again.

When the venerable subs returned I apologised, appeared to be writing the last scribbled instructions to the typesetters, and was then allowed to escape.

---

5. In publishing 'ems' is a unit of measurement used for the width of a column.

Though he had been involved with the paper for almost a decade, Terry felt closer to the younger generation of reporters. The younger staffers would tease the old guard relentlessly behind their backs, though rarely cruelly. The funniest encounters and wildest flights of fancy were written down and pasted in 'The Book', a red accounts journal filled with jokes and observations from Pratchett, Raycroft, House and others. The Book, alas, has been lost to the mists of time.[6]

Terry continued to expand his creative portfolio beyond the pages of the *Bucks* and *Midweek Free Press*. Smythe and Bander had roped him in as a cartoonist for their new venture, *The Psychic Researcher and Spiritualist Gazette*. He developed a regular comic strip entitled *Warlock Hall*, which followed the escapades of the government's 'first official psychic research facility'. The cartoons are uniformly excellent, showing how much progress he'd made since his early Marcus doodles in the *Midweek*. They're also very funny, regularly throwing out jokes that would comfortably sit in any Discworld book, and wouldn't be out of place in the pages of *The Beano*. *Warlock Hall* ran for seventeen issues.

Meanwhile, *The Carpet People* was making its way out into the world via bookshops and libraries. Smythe had even secured a release in Germany, where the book was translated under the title *Alarm im Teppichreich* (literally *Alarm in the Carpet Kingdom*). The German publishers, Sauerländer, decided against Terry's own illustrations and commissioned Swiss artist Jörg Müller to create a set of slick and rather stylised (and, indeed, quite *stylish*) images. The German edition is a beautiful piece, complete with maps of the carpet and the city of Ware, though Müller's illustrations do take one or two liberties with the text, especially revealing the mysterious and powerful Fray to be the careless foot of a giant man. Sauerländer's edition actually outsold its English counterpart.

Smythe and Bander were keen to print a follow up, as they felt instinctively that their young author would only get better as he matured. Initially, Pratchett had planned on writing a sequel set elsewhere in the world of the carpet with completely new characters. His publishers were delighted and a contract was signed for another *Carpet People* tale. In

---

6. Which is a shame for anyone studying Pratchett's work, but probably just as well for the young journalists writing in it, whose careers wouldn't have benefited had their superiors had a look.

the end, it wasn't to be. Pratchett had lost interest in his microscopic Middle Earth, and after writing almost seventy children's stories across seven years, he was ready to write for adults again, especially since he had now joined their ranks. He laid out his reasoning in a letter sent to Colin Smythe in 1973, arguing that though 'a second book would probably be as intrinsically good as the first' it would also 'somehow take away the mystery of the carpet'. He came to his decision, apparently, following a conversation with a friend,[7] who persuaded him that writing a sequel without having had a detailed overarching story in mind from the very start, somehow 'exploited' the original work. Smythe was unimpressed. In an essay he contributed to *Terry Pratchett: His World*, the companion book to a 2017 exhibition dedicated to Terry's life, he called it 'odd advice'. You can see why Smythe might be a little peeved; after all, a sequel would have been much easier for him to market and sell than an original story with a different target audience. You can also sympathise with Pratchett. He'd been laying that carpet in his mind since at least 1965; it was now 1973, and you couldn't blame him for wanting to set his sights higher than a few millimetres.

The Carpet People wasn't the only thing Pratchett left behind in 1973. Eight years after beginning his apprenticeship he was ready to leave the *Bucks Free Press* – and Buckinghamshire – for good. His first stint at the paper had lasted five years and had taught him to be a fine reporter. His second lasted just over a year, and this time – through the training was less formal – he was taught the dark arts of the sub editor. He learned about kerning, decks and ems, about punching up copy and writing headlines. The bulk of his time was spent up to his elbows in the guts of language, working and moulding it into its best form, until he felt ready to take his skills elsewhere. In September 1973, Pratchett took a sub position at the *Bath Evening Chronicle*, a busier paper, published six days a week. Unlike his experience at the *Western Daily Press*, which had been a steep

---

7. Modern sci-fi fandom often refers to a phenomenon called 'head canon', a theory about events in a fictional universe, usually offscreen, that the reader or viewer has decided to believe for themselves. In my personal head canon of Pratchett's life, this friend is the same one whose drunken pub ranting inspired the idea for the carpet tribes in the first place. It would be satisfyingly neat, wouldn't it?

and short-lived learning curve, *The Bath Chronicle*[8] was a good match for Pratchett. Though still a daily paper, the *Chron* had a circulation of just 35,000 – less than half that of the *Western Daily* – and therefore had a more personal relationship with its readers. It was also based in a smaller city, and had more of a rural focus which suited Pratchett down to the ground; a halfway point between the relentless nature of the *Western Daily* and the local feel of the *Bucks Free Press*. He would stay in the role for five years.

Terry and Lyn returned to the cottage they'd purchased in Rowberrow, in the Mendip Hills, and Terry finally said goodbye to the *Bucks Free Press*. Before they left, the Pratchetts hosted a party in their small town-centre home, where Janice Raycroft fell in love with the baby tortoises Terry and Lyn had been raising in their garden. She begged them to let her keep one but was told she was too irresponsible. ('He dug in for several minutes about it', she recalls.) Years later, Raycroft would become a successful newspaper editor and something of a legend in the industry, with responsibility for several different titles. She would never meet her old mentor again in person, but did receive one last message from him:

I was at Hounslow overseeing a portfolio of West London and Surrey papers owned by Trinity Mirror when one of the news eds said someone was going down to a book signing by Terry. I revealed I'd worked with him 'back in the day' – there are not many weekly journalists who can claim such an illustrious mentor. The reporter who met Terry told him this … his reply was: 'Tell her it doesn't matter how many newspapers she runs, I still wouldn't trust her with a tortoise.'

The pace of the *Bath Evening Chronicle* suited Pratchett far better than the cut-throat environment of the *Western Daily,* while challenging him more than the familiar world of the *Bucks Free Press*. He was reunited in the subs' room with his old colleague Tony Bush, and the pair resumed a close friendship alongside another *Western Daily* refugee, Peter Phipps

---

8. Technically it was called the *Bath and Wilts Evening Chronicle* until 1974 when it became the *Bath and West Evening Chronicle*, before reverting to *The Bath Chronicle* again a decade later. It's known locally as the '*Chron*'.

('a lanky streak of lamppost', according to their ever-tactful former boss Eric Price).

The *Chron* was edited by Pat Wheare, a very different character from the old-fashioned Arthur Church, or the dynamic but terrifying Eric Price. Wheare, the son of Sir Kenneth Wheare, an Australian academic who became a rector at Oxford University, was boyish and likeable and set the tone for the familial and convivial atmosphere that marked that era of the paper. The *Chron*'s staff was a tight-knit team consisting of old pros knocking on the door of middle age, and young guns attracted by the excellent training programme provided by the owners, Westminster News. Wheare's mentorship kickstarted the careers of several notable newsmen, including Adam Raphael, the award-winning investigative journalist who served as *The Guardian*'s Washington correspondent and went on to present BBC's *Newsnight*, and Michael Cole, the former royal correspondent who worked as a spokesman for Mohamed Al-Fayed at the time of Princess Diana's death. Terry was less interested in using the paper as a springboard to bigger and better things and was happy to settle into his new role with the anticipation of a long stay.

Former staffer, Martin Wainwright, remembers a friendly, energetic newsroom atmosphere, full of laughs and pranks:

The fun in the office was chiefly had by the young reporters who drank and socialised a lot and played the usual games of trying to sneak words of the week or whole phrases into stories, or to say 'golly' in an uncontrived way when the office was visited, as it often was, by Mrs Robertson of the local jam-making dynasty[9] who was a big player in Bath's cultural scene. The office was very open and was constantly playing host to visitors who called in unannounced with what they hoped were stories, from the endlessly optimistic Gilbert White of the World Government Party to an amateur vet with a supposed cure for swine vesicular disease who carried with him a fold-out diagram of the insides of a pig.

Terry, naturally shy and working on the more sedate subs' desk, tended to stay away from this sort of journalistic horseplay, though the subs had

9. Robertson's jam was famous for using the extremely politically incorrect 'gollywog' in its marketing.

games of their own. Occasionally, he and Tony Bush would be dragooned into working a Saturday shift in order to cover the sport, something the extremely un-sporty Terry loathed. The sports editor would head out to report on the town's football and rugby teams, leaving the young subs to deal with his deputy, a middle-aged Navy veteran called George Singer who would spend the day discreetly pouring whiskey into a plastic beaker. As the reports came in, Pratchett and Bush would amuse themselves by writing increasingly daft headlines, sending them down to the sports desk for approval until, eventually, goading the now quite drunk Singer into an apoplectic rage. The older man would storm up the stairs to the subs' office, glasses askew and smelling of scotch, to yell at the 'young buggers' who had distilled Bath's tense game against Canterbury into 'Canterbury tale may have sad ending' or 'Shocker on the cards for Wife of Bath'.[10] Pratchett and Bush would wait until he left the room and then dissolve into laughter.

As well as subbing copy for the main paper, Terry was given the responsibility of editing the *Keynsham Weekly Chronicle*, a hyper-local version of the *Chron* whittled down to stories relevant to the small town of Keynsham, midway between Bath and Bristol. 'Editor' is rather a grand (though literally accurate) title for this particular role, which involved cribbing relevant stories from the past week and compiling them into a new edition, but the appointment still shows the level of trust and responsibility he enjoyed.

He was also a regular contributor to the *Chron*'s features and arts sections. He wrote book reviews and several longer pieces, usually focused on rural activities or the countryside. His review column, which would appear on Saturdays in the Weekender section, ran for over five years. What is clear from the Weekender reviews is that Pratchett was still a voracious reader, which is impressive when you consider the demands of his job, the fact that he was working on a new novel in his spare time and that, by 1976, he had become a father. He also had an hour's drive every day to and from his cottage in the Mendip Hills to the offices in Bath. A new role as a literary critic gave someone with little time to visit the library a constant supply of new material to read.

---

10. They eventually compromised on 'Ding dong tussle at Canterbury'.

Pratchett proves himself a fine critic. His reviews are always strongly opinionated, and he could be cutting when required, but he never eviscerated a book undeservedly, and his views were always well-argued, even when they were hilariously damning. He managed to avoid the common critical traps of soft targets, nasty swipes or cheap laughs, and when he praised something he did so with great sincerity.

The books he selected for his Weekender column tell us a lot about his interests and worldview at the time. Skewering claims of otherworldly phenomenon was a particular favourite, and he treated works about Aztecs communing with aliens, or the lost city of Atlantis sparking the birth of human civilisation, with withering scorn. His own interest in the paranormal meant he gave short shrift to anything he felt cheapened the rational examination of such phenomenon. He often reviewed books on witchcraft and folklore – on one occasion praising two works by twentieth-century witch Sybil Leek; *Diary of a Witch* and *The Complete Art of Witchcraft*. The latter points out the impracticality of dancing naked – as witches are rumoured to do – in chilly rural England; a gag he would recycle when he wrote about witches in the Discworld books. He was delighted by Katharine M. Briggs' *The Folklore of the Cotswolds*, which played into his fascination with the myths of the rural south west. A 1974 book called *The Leaping Hare*, another delve into rural English folklore, received a particularly enthusiastic write-up. The seeds of Pratchett's Tiffany Aching story *I Shall Wear Midnight*, one of his absolute best, can be found within its pages. He was dismissive about a book called *Home Farm*, which he felt cashed in on the craze for *Good Life*-style self-sufficiency without teaching the reader anything useful about country living, but was impressed by Peter Singer's 1975 book *Animal Liberation*, which was one of the first mainstream titles to promote veganism. He approached it with skepticism but found himself surprisingly moved – though not to the point that he embraced a plant-based lifestyle or joined his wife in her vegetarianism.

Elsewhere Pratchett praised or skewered books on international politics, gardening, history, satire, and even *The Lord of the Rings*, reissued in a single volume in 1976, (a review he had presumably been desperate to write since he was 13). His fundamental mistrust of the establishment shines through in an enthusiastic recommendation for Victor Marchetti and John D. Marks' *The CIA and the Cult of Intelligence,* while he expertly pricks accusations of journalistic bias in his review of *Publish It Not: The Middle East Cover-up,* an examination of the way Israel and the Middle East crisis was misrepresented in the British press. The reviews all add up to a fair summary of Pratchett's intellectual interests and opinions.

Since the majority of his work involved the careful pruning and presentation of other people's writing, these bonus reviews, stories and columns were an opportunity for Pratchett to flex his creativity, indulge his interests and inject some of his own personality into the paper. By 1976 he was writing regular comic pieces, and was coming into his own as a humourist. Though technically works of fiction, these were a far cry from the daft adventures of the Children's Circle, and were usually digs at recent news or askew looks at local and, especially, rural life. They were often character pieces, more satire than story. Pratchett riffs like an observational stand up while talking about lengthy post office queues in 'There's No Fool Like an Old Fool Found in an English Queue', while 'Kindly Breathe in Short Pants' takes aim at spurious government departments with the appointment of a 'minister for fresh air'. Petty bureaucracy was an evergreen Pratchett target. The year 1977 even saw a rare foray into poetry, with a piece entitled *The Glastonbury Tales,* a tightly rhymed mini-epic about his experience picking up hitchhiking hippies bound for the Glastonbury free festival.[11]

A favourite technique of his was the 'comedy list'. One of his columns saw him offering replies to fabricated questions from a list of 'readers' seeking advice, mostly because they'd seen something on the telly that had scared them into thinking they were going to be sucked into a black hole, or that the woods around their house were going to walk to Scotland, like in *Macbeth.* One 'letter' was from a young mum whose soldier-obsessed 4 year old had accidentally joined the Army (Pratchett advised her not to worry, as her young Ronnie would be treated well and get his own special army toothbrush).

---

11. Despite his long career and prolific output, Pratchett published very few poems. The ones he did write almost always used tight rhyming and worked-out rhythms to get laughs. Many characters in his books take swipes at poets and poetry, suggesting it wasn't an artform he was especially fond of.

His knack for puncturing stereotypes had become more sophisticated since the days of Dai Orribly and the Wild West of Wales. A piece from June 1977 listed the type of people who actually lived in the south-west countryside (retired Solihull bank managers, BBC producers 'with wives called Jo', artisans with only one car, sociologists) as opposed to the type of people one would expect to find (old men called Seth, witches, 'buxom wenches', scrumpy cider). In October 1977, he combined his satirical and critical writing into a spoof book review column, listing the worst books of the year 'in the hope that no-one would actually write them', including *Chariots of the Vets* by Eric Von Herlot; *The A. A. Book of Squashed Animals* by Rupert Vest; *The Sunday Mimes Guide to Self-Sufficiency* by Galadriel and Bimbo Bucket and *Noddy and the Cost Accountants*.

One of his best pieces from this period was a rambling, spoof letter to Prince Charles written around the time of the Queen's Silver Jubilee under the headline 'Course, SHE always knows where her lot are'. Pratchett assumes the voice of an 'Elizabeth Kray, (Mrs)', who feels the need to write to the Prince of Wales about her family's various squabbles. It's brilliant comic writing, the kind of thing you could easily hear performed as a monologue by Victoria Wood or Alan Bennett, with a tone of voice Pratchett would later use for the Discworld witch, Nanny Ogg. Nanny even borrowed the names of Mrs Kray's children, with the letter referencing 'our Darren' and 'our Shane'.

These pieces show a sharpening of Pratchett's comic voice. Fifteen years' worth of reading, listening and watching the very best in English satire and comedy, from Wodehouse and Chesterton, to *Punch* magazine, Spike Milligan and the Goons was drifting together to form a style that was uniquely his own. Terry held a vast trove of English humorous writing in his head, as recalled by the writer David Langford, who would meet Pratchett a few years later at an SF convention where the latter was promoting *The Colour of Magic*. It was the start of a life-long friendship. Langford found himself deeply impressed by Terry's encyclopedic knowledge of British humour:

Before Novacon was over I'd heard Terry chatting eruditely about the surreal whimsy of the 'Oddly Enough' newspaper column by Paul Jennings – who got in well ahead of Douglas Adams with new definitions of place names, a 'Bodmin' being 'one sixtieth of a man-hour'. We shared happy memories of the humorous tomes by W. C. Sellar and R. J. Yeatman that unlike *1066 and All That* are now forgotten: *Garden Rubbish*, for example, with its unforgettable descriptions of the bit of a suburban garden that its owner tries in vain to hide away, the 'Unpleasaunce'.

Terry had an alarming ability to quote this stuff from memory, and I tried my best to keep up. Until, at the end of some conversation about the folly and wickedness of publishers, he wandered off saying in an unusually high voice, 'But there you are, my dear fellow, they will do these things, they will do these things.' I knew I was missing something and tried to look knowing, but it wasn't until the day after that I remembered the quote from an eccentric barrister in Henry Cecil's courtroom comedy *Brothers in Law*. Score one to Terry Pratchett.

Chapter 6

Dark Sides and Disc Worlds

P ratchett's next book was well underway when he jumped ship to the *Bath Evening Chronicle*. He was turning over 3,000 words a day during a holiday in August 1973, according to a letter he sent to Smythe updating him on his progress. It was an early glimpse of how prolific he could be without a day job to distract him. He estimated he had, at most, 20,000 words left to go, plus revisions. The emerging book, *The Dark Side of the Sun*,[1] was far removed from anything he had written so far, and light years away from *The Carpet People* in tone.

This second novel, which nearly underwent a name change due to another book with a similar title,[2] recalls the classic science fiction he fell in love with as a teenager. It's an unashamed planet-spanning space opera, set in the far future and featuring interstellar travel, alien races, strange nobility and a quest to uncover the origins of life. Textbook sci-fi stuff. But this wasn't the work of a genre-obsessed teen; Pratchett had spent much of the last decade learning to write, and learning to write with knowing humour. *The Dark Side of the Sun* isn't an out-and-out comedy or parody, but it is shot through with typically Pratchettian touches and puns such as the legend of the 'prodigal sun', a biblical text known as 'the *Newer* Testament', and the discovery that scientific jargon was invented by God to prevent scientists understanding each other and unravelling His secrets. There's also a living planet called The First Sirian Bank which TALKS IN SMALLCAPS. These are solid Terry Pratchett concepts, establishing a style he'd still be using thirty years later. He plays with words and phrases that he would recycle in later work: a celebration called 'Hogswatch', a tribe called 'the Klatch' a reference to 'small gods', and the idea that a 'billion to one chance' will be successful

1. A title almost certainly chosen for its resonance with Pink Floyd's *Dark Side of the Moon*, which was released that year.
2. The Pink Floyd pun was rather low-hanging fruit.

'nine times out of ten', all of which would turn up in very different forms in the Discworld series, still the best part of a decade away. Here Joker is the name of an alien race – it would surface again many years later in Pratchett's *Long Earth* books, co-written with Stephen Baxter, as a word for weird or untrustworthy parallel Earths.[3]

The plot is slightly convoluted, but it romps along well enough. A young prince called Dom Sabalos is about to become the figurehead of a wealthy merchant family in charge of the planet Widdershins (another word that would be recycled on the Discworld). Dom decides to take his fate into his own hands after learning that every event in his life had been predicted by his late father using a science called 'probability math'. He sets off with a wise-cracking robot, a long-suffering tutor and a pet swamp creature called Ig on a mission to find the homeworld of the Jokers, the ancient beings that created life in the universe, and the one race in the galaxy mathematics can never predict.

The Dark Side of the Sun borrows just as heavily from the shared tropes of hard sci-fi as *The Carpet People* does from epic fantasy, but while the latter's debt to Tolkien was blunt to the point of obvious, here Pratchett weaves his influences in a more subtle way. His first book took old clichés, gave them a fresh coat of paint and passed them off as new. His second saw them deployed as homage, acknowledged with a knowing wink. He never slips into outright parody – that would come later – but the backdrop of Dom's quest is one Pratchett knew his audience would be familiar with. He was writing for fellow SF nerds and relying on a shared universe of references, films and books. Pratchett had devoured science fiction since his early teens, he'd read the classics, the trashy pulp and the amateur work published alongside his own in monthly periodicals. He had been to conventions and met Arthur C. Clarke in the loo. He was a devotee of the genre and absolutely encyclopedic in his knowledge.

Key to both *The Dark Side of the Sun* and Pratchett's next book, *Strata*, is the concept of 'forerunners', defined by the *Encyclopedia of Science Fiction* as 'a bygone alien race which once dominated the galaxy but ... has mysteriously vanished, generally leaving behind numerous

---

3. Look, we'll get to that, okay. And maybe sooner than you'd think.

relics of its "Old Technology" which may serve as tempting McGuffins.'[4]
The term was coined by Andre Norton in her book *Storm Over Warlock*,
published just as Terry was discovering SF in the early 1960s. A similar
concept can be found in the work of E. E. 'Doc' Smith; in the movie
Forbidden Planet and, notably, in the hard sci-fi of author Larry Niven.
Niven, in particular, sits in the background of both *The Dark Side of the
Sun* and *Strata*, which take place among galactic communities of planets
and races that nod to the 'Known Space' universe, the setting for most
of Niven's work.

Pratchett's second novel also shares several elements with Douglas
Adams' *The Hitchhiker's Guide to the Galaxy*. There's a planet-spanning
SF setting, the use of 'probability' to drive both plot and spaceships, a
quest for 'founders' which turn out to be hiding in plain sight all along
– Trillian's white mice in *Hitchhiker*, Ig the swamp creature in *Dark Side*
– and an affectionate teasing of genre. Pratchett and Adams would be
mentioned in the same breath for most of their respective careers, so it's
interesting to note that *The Dark Side of the Sun* predates *Hitchhiker* by
several years, though it's extremely unlikely Adams ever read it. Adams'
book delivers its concepts and jokes with more panache and a substantially
more defined voice than Pratchett's, who was still very much learning his
craft, but Pratchett had the honour of getting to them first.

The Dark Side of the Sun was completed in time for Smythe to tout the
book around the 1974 Frankfurt Book Fair in search of a US publishing
partner, but the ensuing negotiations and revisions delayed release by a
further two years. Pratchett's second novel wouldn't reach shelves on
either side of the Atlantic until the blazing summer of 1976.

In the meantime, Terry had a life to be getting on with. For most of
the 1970s, his career as a novelist took a backseat to his work at the *Bath
Chronicle* and his duties as a husband and, later, a father; writing fiction
was a hobby, and he saw it as an escape from his daily grind at the paper.
Every night he would write 400 words before he went to bed, staying
up until he'd met his goal. Sometimes he would be grinding out those
words into the wee hours, other times they flowed freely. Crucially, he

---

4. McGuffin is a word coined by Alfred Hitchcock to describe some hidden object or person
   the desire for which moves the plot along. For example, in the quest for the Holy Grail the
   McGuffin is the grail itself.

would never write more than his target of *exactly* 400 words, however the muse took him. He would deliver a new book to Smythe and Bander every five years or so, more or less at his own pace, and they commissioned him on the basis of one contract at a time, rather than signing a multi-book deal. No-one, with the possible exception of Colin Smythe, was expecting Terry Pratchett to ever make a serious living from writing fiction.

Terry was 25 when he and Lyn moved into their home in Rowberrow, a tiny village near the slightly larger Shipham, in the idyllic countryside of the Mendip Hills. The house was known as Gayes Cottage,[5] and the Pratchetts would live there until 1993. The cottage was one of half a dozen smallish, detached old houses, situated on a winding lane barely large enough for one car to overtake another. Its walls were painted a pale pink, and Terry's friend and colleague Martin Wainwright remembers it being thatched, though he now wonders if that's just his memory playing tricks. ('Was it thatched?' he says, 'I like to think so.') Visiting the area today you can hardly blame him for being fuzzy on this detail. It's not clear if Gayes Cottage had a thatched roof in the 1970s – certainly none of the buildings on the lane are thatched now – and Colin Smythe's only surviving photograph of the building shows a tiled roof, but it feels like the sort of place that *ought* to have a thatched roof. Rowberrow is tiny and beautiful, the chocolate-box definition of an English country village. It's the kind of place you suspect might one day be bought in its entirety by a wealthy American tourist and shipped, brick by brick, to the middle of Missouri.

Terry and Lyn slipped comfortably into rural life. There was a fashionable trend for 'self-sufficiency' in Britain at the time, a result of the hippy values of the 1960s trying to root themselves in a more pragmatic age. This would give rise to the popular mid-1970s sitcom *The Good Life* and a slew of manuals about how to live off the land. The Pratchetts kept goats in their front garden, ducks and chickens in the back, and beehives at the end of their yard.[6] They would grow their own vegetables, and

---

5. It is vitally important, as I have learned the hard way, to make sure you spell 'Gayes' correctly if you plan to Google this in a public space.
6. A hobby Terry took very seriously. In 1976 he even wrote to *Undercurrents* magazine, a publication dedicated to 'radical science and alternative technology', to complain that an

sometimes Terry would rise at the crack of dawn to gather mushrooms in the hills for breakfast. He'd used the advance for *The Dark Side of the Sun* to buy a greenhouse in which to grow huge, knobbly tomatoes and cultivate exotic, carnivorous plants.

Technically the goats were there for milk; the chickens for eggs; the bees for honey; the veg patch for dinner and the carnivorous plants for fun. Really though, those were just excuses. Terry and Lyn kept bees, goats, chickens, vegetables and Venus fly traps for the same reason they also had cats, birds and tortoises: because it was satisfying to do so. Lyn was an art teacher, and Terry a journalist. They had demanding, time-consuming jobs that required them to be alert to the wider world, as bleak as it could sometimes be. A life at home that involved growing herbs, tending goats and, in the evening, writing stories, would have been a welcome and even necessary respite. Their home represented a quiet, self-contained corner in which to ignore the world beyond their garden gate. Terry even claimed that they didn't own a television, going as far as to tell the *Bath Chronicle*'s chief sub, Gerald Walker, that he'd never watched TV in his life, as Walker explains:

> Terry came home for dinner once and we watched a TV programme. He claimed it was the first time he had watched television. The programme centred on some contestant answering twenty questions about space. As the contestant floundered, Terry would jump to his feet and answer each question correctly before sitting down again. Whether it was true or not that this was the first time he had watched TV I shall never know, but he certainly showed an unusual measure of excitement.

Terry played up to his image as an eccentric, hippy-ish hermit, telling his colleagues that he made his own clothes from wool he'd collected from barbed wire fences in the fields around the villages. While he did have a tendency to wear huge, hooped jumpers that certainly looked hand-knitted, the idea that his wardrobe was comprised of items spun from the discarded wool of Mendips sheep is about as likely as someone

article on beekeeping in the previous issue had been misleading and to offer his own tips.

with such a profound knowledge of science fiction claiming to have *never* watched television in the era of *Doctor Who*, *The Prisoner* and *Star Trek*. Later, Pratchett wrote a piece for *SFX* magazine in which he said he'd seen William Hartnell's debut episode of *Doctor Who* when the show was first broadcast in 1963. He could never leave an anecdote alone if there was a chance he could give it a spin and make it more interesting.

This was a calm and largely content period of Pratchett's life. He was a well-liked member of the *Bath Chronicle* team, and would sit at his desk sketching the other subs expertly on notepaper and presenting them with neat portraits or scribbled snatches of poetry, haikus and little sayings. Most of his colleagues regarded his eccentricities with fond acceptance, though some could find his sense of humour contrived and a little grating. Newsman, Martin Wainwright, shared Terry's sense of adventure and the pair would embark on expeditions, such as an eleven-hour voyage rowing a two-man canoe up the River Avon from Chippenham to Bath, – immortalised in a 1975 *Bath Chronicle* feature entitled 'Yo Heave Ho and Mind the Bananas Adrift in the Bilges' – or a gruelling attempt at the 48-mile Lyke Wake Walk across the North Yorkshire moors.

One element of his working life at this time presents a mystery. In an introduction to one of his *Bath Chronicle* pieces reprinted in *A Blink of the Screen*, a 2012 collection of his short fiction, Pratchett writes: 'My place of work was a shed – your actual fairly cheap garden shed – which was so ramshackle that if I moved a useful piece of wood in one corner, I had a direct view of young pigeons in a nest. Sometimes I used to feed them.'

He mentioned the 'shed on the roof' again in the introduction to another *Bath Chronicle* piece in *A Slip of the Keyboard*, published the following year. According to Terry, his shed was situated on a flat roof atop the *Bath Chronicle* building, opposite a window into which he could see the tele-ad sales girls working. This is curious, because neither Gerald Walker nor Tony Bush have any memory of the paper using a garden shed as a workspace.

'What I would say, is that Terry hived himself away in a corner of the subs' room not far from the wire[7] room,' says Bush. 'Has he, I wonder, in his mind erected a little shed around his desk and substituted "tele-ads" for "wire room", perhaps on the basis that general readers may not have any knowledge of a wire room?' Gerald Walker, who sat opposite Pratchett for much of his time at the paper, is similarly baffled: 'I spent forty-one years on the *Bath Chronicle* but I am afraid I missed the garden shed,' he says. 'I should have been more observant.'

Both men take this story in good humour, though neither can seriously explain where it comes from. Did Terry's shed exist? Given the testimonies of his colleagues, almost certainly not, or at least not in the way he described it. Was Terry making it up? Not necessarily. Thirty-six years lie between the *Bath Chronicle* piece and its introduction in *A Blink of the Screen*. Perhaps Pratchett, like Roald Dahl, worked in a shed at home, and had misremembered its location. Perhaps the shed was actually something he used at his earlier job at the *Bucks Free Press*. After all, thirty-six years is a long time and human memories, even Pratchett's (who was usually pin-sharp on details even later, when in the grip of Alzheimer's,) are fallible. That said, it's worth noting that a 'shed on the roof' is quite literally a piece of Pratchett whimsy; it appears in his 2004 Discworld novel *Going Postal*, in which a gang of unscrupulous types use a pigeon loft on the roof of the Ankh-Morpork Post Office as a hideout. He may simply have lifted the idea, consciously or not, and applied it to his own life, in a reversal of typical writers' practice. Either way, it's a fun detail which, like the thatch on the roof of Gayes Cottage, or the sci-fi obsessive who had never watched television, we can choose to believe or not.

It was 1976 before *The Dark Side of the Sun* finally appeared on the shelves, published in the UK on 15 May and in America a few months later; courtesy of gigantic US publishers St Martin's Press. St Martin's editor Leslie M. Pockell, who was something of a publishing legend, had happened upon Colin Smythe reading one of *Dark Side*'s best action scenes aloud at the Frankfurt Book Fair and was impressed enough to take

---

7. Wire dispatches are news reports sent out to multiple newspapers from a central service such as Reuters or Associated Press. These days it's done through email, and doesn't need its own room.

a punt on a largely unknown English science fiction author. The initial print run for both countries was a combined 2,421, slightly less than that of *The Carpet People*. The jacket illustration was once again painted by the author and depicted one of the robotic insects from the planet Laoth, which featured only briefly in the story but served as a symbolic reminder that nothing in the *Dark Side* universe was truly natural. It was another impressive piece of artwork from Pratchett; bright and eye-catching and much less cartoonish than his previous book. Terry knew exactly what a decent SF jacket should look like, and it was surely no coincidence that the predominantly yellow design echoed the classic Victor Gollancz books of the 1960s. It would be the last time Pratchett would illustrate one of his novels himself, which is a shame; he was a talented artist and knew his own work better than anyone.

The Dark Side of the Sun also received a British paperback release – something *The Carpet People* had missed out on – licensed to the Anglo-American publisher New English Library (NEL). Pratchett was delighted – NEL specialised in precisely the type of pulpy SF he loved. The new version reached shelves in the spring of 1978, with an enlarged print run of around 15,000. That same year NEL also published paperbacks by Michael Moorcock, Frank Herbert, Robert A. Heinlein and A. E. van Vogt – exactly the sort of company Pratchett would want to keep. The bright yellow jacket of the first edition was replaced by a new design by sci-fi illustrator Tim White, who had a less charming, edgier take on Pratchett's robotic wasp. The resulting volume, though slim, looks every inch the classic pulp SF.

Reviews for either edition were scant, but they were broadly kind. A write-up in *The Oxford Times* praised the book for its 'unexpected conceits and original inventions', astutely recognising that 'if Mr Pratchett's tongue is frequently in his cheek, his parody of the science fiction idiom is always deft, knowledgeable and good humoured.' Slightly less impressed were Pratchett's former colleagues at the *Western Daily Press*, who described the work as a 'good-ish mainstream sci-fi yarn, into which the author has crammed everything but the solar stove.' The *Western Daily*'s review, which doesn't carry a byline, correctly pegs Pratchett's sophomore novel as slight, if good natured. However, it does conclude with a prescient note of optimism, a prediction of 'an excellent future for the author if he can only bring off the difficult feat of curbing ever so slightly the riotous imagination which enables him to write sci-fi in the first place.'

Despite its long gestation, *The Dark Side of the Sun* was by no means the most significant milestone for Terry in 1976. On 30 December, Lyn gave birth to a baby girl the couple named Rhianna, their first and ultimately, only child. The birth was not an easy one; both mother and daughter needed immediate medical attention. Rhianna spent her first night on Earth in the intensive care unit of Southmead Hospital in Bristol. Terry found himself something of a spare part, as new fathers often do on such occasions, and as doctors were confident that everything would be okay, he was sent home for the night to get some rest.

Terry found himself overwhelmed by the reality of fatherhood and the bond he'd felt with his daughter as she curled her tiny hand around his finger. His emotions that night were magnified, and his memories sharpened. Having eaten only a bag of Maltesers all day, he found some stewing steak in the fridge and cooked it with onions. He would remember it as one of the most delicious meals of his life. Winter was especially cold that year, and there was snow in the hills; that night Terry slipped in the driveway and landed face first on the ground, but was so elated he barely felt it. Many years later he would describe that night as a perfect memory, and the one he hoped his Alzheimer's could never take from him. The next day he returned to Southmead to find his daughter recovering. It gave him a renewed faith in medical science.

In 2014, with her father's health declining, Rhianna, now a games writer and journalist, included an account of her birth in the script for the video game, *Rise of the Tomb Raider*, in the form of a letter to the game's iconic lead character, Lara Croft, from her father, Richard:

> Before I even held you, I almost lost you. Yet you fought back … I went home that snowy night [and] cooked myself steak … drunk [*sic*] half a bottle of whiskey, tried to make snow-shoes out of tennis rackets and fell asleep with the cat. I was so damn happy.

The years that followed Rhianna's birth were happy ones. Terry deduced that by taking a small pay cut, he could drop his time in the office to four days a week, still get all the subbing done and finish any writing on his 'spare day' at home. This meant he could spend more time at home with his family, an experience he treasured as he watched his daughter grow. It also gave him more time to write.

He had been working on his next novel, *Strata*, since delivering the manuscript for *The Dark Side of the Sun* in 1974. By the time Rhianna was born he was nearing the completion of his second draft, though she would be nearing her fifth birthday before it reached the shelves.

Though not a sequel, *Strata* syncs nicely with the themes in *Dark Side*. Again it's a space opera, set among a community of planets and races that nod to Niven's Known Space concept. Again there are founders at the heart of the story – ancient beings who created the known universe. *Strata*, though, takes the ideas further, establishing founders for the founders, a string of alien races that come and go over millennia, bequeathing ancient tech to their successors. As before, it's a universe where everything has been, on some level, 'created'. It also closes with an ingenious twist about the origins of life on our own Earth.

Strata gets even closer to full parody than *Dark Side*, though it stops short of being what you'd call a comic novel. Pratchett had attended a talk by Larry Niven in the early 1970s, in which the author had discussed his novel *Ringworld*, set on a ring-shaped artificial planet. Niven's talk got Pratchett's mind racing. What if, rather than a ring, the planet was a disc? And what if the inhabitants didn't realise they lived on a fake world? And since a flat earth is common in ancient myths, what if those inhabitants were primitive and barbarian and would, as Arthur C. Clarke once famously said, mistake technology for magic?[8] In *Strata*, Pratchett gives us his first, prototype 'discworld', and just like the one that would make his fortune, peopled it with fantasy archetypes.

This was his most interesting and satisfying novel yet, and a noticeable acceleration in his writing. The alien races feel more vivid and better defined than those in *The Dark Side of the Sun*, and the universe is richer and yet easier to understand. *Strata* makes some fascinating narrative leaps, taking a left turn halfway through the novel when it moves away

---

8. 'Any sufficiently advanced technology is indistinguishable from magic' was one of Clarke's 'three laws', the other two of which are almost never quoted anywhere.

from hard SF and into fantasy as the plot starts to gather pace, and the jokes get bigger and funnier. *Strata* has one foot in *The Dark Side of The Sun* and one in his next book, *The Colour of Magic*.

There are problems though. Pratchett's writing was still evolving (and would continue to do so for the next thirty years), and *Strata,* though bursting with ideas, is hampered by the limitations of its author. The main issue is character. The book's central protagonist, Kin Arad, is a woman in her prime; sardonic, controlled and quite sexual (the blurb for the paperback edition even describes her as 'hot-blooded'). She is a universe away from the man who created her; it's unlikely Pratchett had ever met *anyone* like Kin Arad, and as such she never feels wholly real. Pratchett would get better at writing outgoing, confident women, but his skills weren't yet up to the job of reaching so far outside of his experience. He was better with dysfunctional, damaged characters who were just a tiny bit pathetic. This hadn't been a problem with *The Carpet People*, whose principal cast were stock fantasy types, simplified for children. Ultimately, they just needed to be likeable. Dom, the hero of *The Dark Side of the Sun*, might think of himself as a capable adult but he has a naivety that makes him interesting. Dom's is a coming-of-age story. Kin Arad, meanwhile, has not only come of age, she's *been* of age for a few hundred years. She's not flawed enough to be interesting, and not developed enough to be relatable. Kin is basically *too cool* for someone as fundamentally oddball and nerdy as 30-year-old Terry Pratchett to handle. Some misjudged cracks about sexual favours and a few 'fner fner' sniggers don't help matters either. This sort of mishandling of strong women and sexuality was fairly common in the masculine world of hard SF that Pratchett had grown up with, and he can hardly be blamed for inheriting the problems of the wider genre. It's just a shame his own voice hadn't yet developed enough to get beyond them. Still, central protagonist aside, *Strata* is crammed full of ideas and was by far the most original work the author had yet delivered.

Pratchett's third book was published on 15 June 1981, a full five years after its predecessor. Once again British hardback sales were handled by Colin Smythe Ltd, with Smythe working with NEL for the UK paperback and St Martin's Press for the US release. The New American Library (NAL) obtained the paperback rights in America – Pratchett's first paperback release in the country. Tim White was once again on illustration duty; his image of lightning crashing down on a rain-soaked alien landscape feels too dark and serious to really represent Pratchett's energetic story. Far worse, however, is the design for the US paperback by fantasy artist Ken W. Kelly – who had illustrated the Science Fiction Book Club's *Conan* books – which features a clichéd image of a pert-bosomed Kin Arad on horseback, brandishing a sword. Pratchett's tone is represented best with the NEL paperback, published in 1982, which carries a strapline over White's image: 'Eat your heart out, Copernicus', it says, 'the Flat-Earthers were right.'

Strata was well received on its release. Reviews were scant, as they had been with his previous novels, but they were enthusiastic, especially in the literary magazines and SF press. Initial write-ups came from the British Science Fiction Association's *Vector* magazine, whose reviewer Chris Bailey gave it an enthusiastic thumbs up. *Kirkus Reviews* wrote, 'A well-handled, inventive, gleefully madcap flat-Earth jaunt' and *Library Journal* praised 'a satisfying blend of wonderment and adventure'. *Strata* would pick up plenty more positive notices on its journey to paperback and over subsequent editions.

Building on the small splash made by the *Dark Side of the Sun*, *Strata* helped establish a following for Pratchett's work that meant when he approached Colin Smythe with an idea for a collection of interlinked short stories called *The Colour of Magic*, his publisher was relatively confident that there was an audience waiting. There was much more flat Earth to come.

Chapter 7

The Colour of Magic

B
y 1979, as *Strata* neared completion, it was becoming clear to Terry that his time at the *Bath Evening Chronicle* had run its course. Rhianna was growing up, and it was getting harder to make a regional sub editor's salary stretch to meet his family's needs. Life at the *Chron* was changing, too. Pat Wheare had been replaced by former news editor Maurice Boardman, a brittle and more demanding character than his predecessor. Martin Wainwright had gone north to a new post in Bradford, and Peter Phipps had moved on from the subs desk, altering the office dynamic. After five happy years, it was time for a change. This was partly motivated by a growing feeling that, if he didn't leave soon, he would become one of the old staffers you occasionally saw about the place; former subs and writers for whom the *Chron* had been their whole life. In his 1993 book, *Men At Arms*, Terry would write about Captain Vimes, who contemplates leaving the City Watch and fears becoming a living ghost, haunting his old workplace because he didn't know where else to go.

The nail in the coffin came when Terry's old friend Tony Bush, with whom he had worked on and off since 1971, accepted a job with the Press Association. 'He had enjoyed the camaraderie,' explains Bush. 'I left to go to the Press Association and he felt a bit despondent. We were two friends having a lot of fun together. He often said, "It'll never be quite the same."'

Like many journalists eager for a less hectic and better-paid life, Pratchett decided to explore the possibilities offered in public relations. He applied for a job in the south-west offices of the Central Electricity Generating Board (CEGB), on a fairly appealing salary of around £13,000 per year. His newspaper friends were baffled. Martin Wainwright thought the job 'seemed to me to be the living death'. Tony Bush agrees: 'Working in public relations wasn't very Terry at all,' he says. 'I was so surprised. I mean, public relations? He was such an independent, sparky character, I couldn't imagine him churning out press releases for the establishment.' Both suspected that, aside from the extra money, Pratchett was looking for an easier job that would allow him more time to write. 'It paid quite a comfortable salary, he didn't have to think about it very much,' says Bush. 'I can almost imagine him churning press releases and then sitting back with his notebook and filling in ideas for his next book.'

Terry joined the CEGB in 1979, leaving the *Bath Chronicle* with good grace not, as he told the *Western Daily Press* in an interview in 1996, because he'd been sacked for a third time.[1] He was based in the company's Bristol offices and would stay for seven years – his longest period in any job – eventually being promoted to chief press officer. It would be the last 'real' job he would ever have.

Summaries of Pratchett's career often get this period slightly wrong, saying that he 'worked in the nuclear industry' or 'was a press officer for a nuclear power station'. He has even been mislabelled as a scientist or engineer. In truth, Pratchett was a desk-bound civil servant, working for the government. The CEGB was a nationalised organisation, charged[2] with meeting the nation's electricity needs. There was more to the CEGB than nuclear power, though it provided easily the most explosive[3] aspect of Terry's time there. Life at the CEGB wasn't quite as sedate as Pratchett may have hoped. True, he had a shorter commute, an increase in salary and access to a swimming pool, but he also had to work within the endless petty bureaucracy of the civil service, while attempting to calm the rising hysteria around the subject of nuclear power in the press.

In March 1979, just weeks before Pratchett joined the CEGB, a nuclear reactor at Three Mile Island power station in Pennsylvania went into partial meltdown, resulting in a radiation leak that caused 140,000 people to be evacuated from the area. The story made headlines around the world and led to serious questions about the safety of atomic power. The British press focused on the UK's expanding nuclear sector and questioned the disposal of toxic waste; possible reactor meltdowns

---

1. Pratchett had only been sacked from one job in his entire life. Funnily enough, that was from the *Western Daily Press*.
2. Sorry.
3. This one too.

and risks to public safety, while a growing environmentalist movement actively campaigned against atomic energy. It was amid this atmosphere that Terry Pratchett became a press officer with responsibility for the south west's three nuclear power stations.

At first his role was relatively easy; writing press releases, calling journalists and occasionally contributing to *Power News*, the industry newspaper published by the CEGB (he would eventually be named editor of the local edition). However, the civil service came with its own frustrations. Nationalised industries are, by their nature, heavily unionised, and the CEGB was no exception. Strict union rules meant that all typed material had to come from the women in the office's typing pool, which annoyed Pratchett as he was a proficient touch typist and had been used to the fast-paced environment of a newspaper. He would type out his press releases, send them down to the typing pool and wait for them to be typed out again. Eventually, he complained so much that he was given special dispensation to be allowed to bash out his own work.

Despite the serious subject, the power industry provided Terry with a wealth of you-wouldn't-believe-it anecdotes, which he trotted out regularly, over the years. A particular favourite was the time a visitor was found to have brought radioactive material *into* a plant. The man had been restoring wartime aviation equipment as a hobby and had found an old altimeter with a glow-in-the-dark face painted using radium. He had got this mildly radioactive material on his hands, setting off a Geiger counter designed to alert security to people taking radioactive material *out* of the building.

Much of Terry's time was devoted to playing down the risks in order to stop the press blowing them out of proportion. On one occasion a railway carriage carrying radioactive material was derailed as it jolted across the points in a shunting yard, causing no damage. However, British Rail's disaster protocols, as well as the guidelines for dealing with radioactive incidents, prompted a major deployment of emergency services, a rush of camera crews and not a small amount of panic.

Another memorable PR exercise involved Hinkley Point power station, on the coast near Weston-super-Mare. The station was situated close to an Iron Age burial site, known locally as 'the pixie mound'. During its construction, workers would joke that whenever anything went wrong the 'pixies' were responsible, and gifted a garden gnome 'pixie' to the manager when the job was complete. Over the years the staff at the station became oddly superstitious about that gnome, and matters came to a head when someone moved it from its customary home in a trophy cabinet. That night a freak flash flood knocked out two of the station's reactors, and the gnome was quickly found and returned. Word got out about the 'pixies in the power station', and, for weeks afterwards, the CEGB received letters from all over the world asking about sprites and fairies. To Terry's bemusement, he found many sensible, logical engineers and scientists weren't quite prepared to say for sure that the pixie curse wasn't real. It was his job to carefully manage press interviews and prevent the station from becoming a laughing stock.

For a novelist, and especially a humourist, such experiences were invaluable. Watching as petty bureaucracy and stubborn adherence to the rules scuppered common sense was a useful crash course in human nature. Pratchett often said he wanted to write a book about his experiences, though he let the idea go after reading his friend David Langford's 1984 novel *The Leaky Establishment*, based on Langford's own experience in the atomic industry.[4]

As Terry gained more responsibility, his role became substantially more stressful. He got used to being woken in the middle of the night by phone calls from panicked engineers, or having to call the *Western Daily Press* or *Bath Evening Chronicle* newsdesk to tell them of some minor issue that had occurred overnight, in order to be one step ahead of the rumour mill that would crank into action as soon as any repair work commenced. His job was to convince everyone that atomic Armageddon in the Bristol area was extremely unlikely and it became too much for Pratchett, who had given up frontline reporting a decade earlier to avoid this sort of frantic lifestyle. Gerald Walker recalls a phone call he received around this time:

He phoned me one evening and said he would like to re-join the *Bath Evening Chronicle*. However, he could not accept a salary lower than £13,000 a year. The next day I put this to the editor, Maurice Boardman, who rejected the application, saying such a high salary

---

4. Pratchett wrote the foreword for a new edition of the novel published in 2001, in which he cursed Langford for getting to the idea first.

would destroy the editorial pay structure. That night I phoned Terry with the decision. He commented: 'Pity. I suppose I'll now have to write some more novels.' That may have been the moment the idea of Discworld was born.

Walker was wrong. Discworld was well underway by the summer of 1981 when *Strata* finally made its way onto shelves. That said, it's true that Pratchett's time at the CEGB saw a noticeable jump in his writing. There would be a wait of just two years between the publication of *Strata* and his next work, *The Colour of Magic*, the shortest gap between Pratchett books yet.

Just as *Strata* had its thematic roots in *The Dark Side of the Sun*, his next book had its beginnings in the pages of *Strata*. When it was finished, Terry wrote to Colin Smythe and suggested that there was still some mileage in the concept of a flat world. Writing about a disc-shaped proto-Earth had triggered the old memory of the Hindu myth he'd found in an astronomy book when he was a boy – the flat world travelling on the backs of four giant elephants, themselves balancing on a huge turtle. He'd even referenced the image in *Strata*. The ridiculousness of the concept appealed to him. Here was something perfectly absurd that had once been taken deadly serious. And why not? If you knew no better, a flat world on a turtle was as likely as anything else. Playing with the ideas in Niven's *Ringworld* had led him, through a series of mental steps, to a new world of his own.

The idea of taking the absurd and making it serious chimed with another concept that had been percolating at the back of his mind. The late 1970s and early 1980s had seen a boom in heroic fantasy, a shifting of sands that had started with Tolkien and *The Lord of the Rings* in the late 1950s. Robert E. Howard's pulpy *Conan* novels had added their influence, as had Michael Moorcock's *Elric* stories. These helped popularise the trope of the gruff and brutal melancholy warrior stalking the land.

Multi-volume franchises appeared, telling overarching tales with complex backstories, many of which would eventually make *The Lord of the Rings*' wordcount look like *The Very Hungry Caterpillar*. Some were grand and eloquent, such as Stephen R. Donaldson's *The Chronicles of Thomas Covenant*, Terry Brooks' *Shannara* trilogy and Anne McCaffrey's long-running *Dragonriders of Pern* books. Other series were more grounded in their characters and language, if not their plots and themes. In 1982, David Eddings published the first novel in his extraordinarily successful *Belgariad* sequence, which would eventually run to twelve books. That same year Raymond E. Feist's *Magician*, the first of his *Riftwar Cycle* novels hit the shelves. Both writers brought a modern tone to stories which, at their heart, were as old as the hills. In both series, an impoverished orphan boy learns he has magical powers and a grand destiny. Two years later, Robert Jordan's *Wheel of Time* franchise began with *The Eye of the World*, telling the compelling and original story of ... an impoverished orphan boy, who learns he has magical powers and a grand destiny. It would eventually run to fourteen volumes. At the cinema, the *Star Wars* movies were redefining the language of the modern blockbuster with a story that – once you got past the spaceships and robots – was about ... an impoverished orphan boy, who learns he has magical powers and a grand destiny. It sometimes seemed like there was only one plot to go around.

In the background of all of this was the surging popularity of Dungeons and Dragons, the role-playing game which set characters and creatures cribbed from Tolkien into a generic fantasy world. Players are guided through the game by a dungeon master who sets challenges decided by the throw of many-sided dice.

Pratchett was no stranger to Dungeons and Dragons and played locally with friends, often acting as dungeon master. The game excited him, and he considered it to be an entirely new artform: here was a way to make fiction interactive and turn narrative into competition. Among the familiar gorgons, ogres and magic spells he would create his own characters and settings – including lavatories, which were probably unique among dungeon masters. One of his inventions was called the Luggage – an idea that popped into his head after seeing an American woman struggling with a large and unruly suitcase on wheels. The Luggage was an old travelling chest on hundreds of little legs in which players could store an infinite number of weapons or treasure. Pratchett added the stipulation that the Luggage would continue to walk in whatever direction it was facing unless told to stop or turn. It would also obey only nine commands out of every ten. Players invariably forgot these rules, until the point they needed to retrieve a sunsword to take down a level five demon, whereby Pratchett would cheerfully tell them the Luggage had walked off hours ago after they had forgotten to tell it where to go. If they *had* remembered to instruct the Luggage properly, there was still a chance it would refuse to hand over a desperately needed item.

Dungeons and Dragons emerged in the United States in the early 1970s and by the end of the decade was played all over the world. Its popularity boosted the profile of fantasy even further and cemented a subculture in wider SF fandom. It also calcified the stereotypes and conventions of fantasy in the popular imagination, creating a prefabricated toolkit of clichés, which in turn were churned into formulaic paperback novels and comic books of variable quality. Fantasy was eating itself, and it had become big business.

The more Pratchett saw of the popularity of bad fantasy, which felt like a tenth-generation facsimile of someone's impression of Tolkien, the more he wanted to mock it. *The Dark Side of the Sun* and *Strata* had both played with the tropes of hard science fiction, but they stopped short of being parodies. This time he would go further. For the first time in his career as a novelist, he could lead with the jokes and write something that was immediately funny.

He wasn't the first to take the po-faced and serious conventions of fantasy and twist them. Harvard students Henry Beard and Douglas Kenney published a parody called *Bored of the Rings* in 1969, which had great fun exploiting the more ridiculous elements in Tolkien's work. Pratchett was a fan of the book but felt there was a subtler way to expose the silliness in the genre. The humour in *Bored of the Rings* came from inflating Tolkien's terribly serious tone and making it ridiculous, but what if he were to approach parody from the other side? What happens if you take something as inherently ridiculous as a fantasy world and treat it realistically? How would real people react? Aragorn has taken the throne of Gondor, but what does that mean to the man in the street? Were the defeated Orcs all supposed to get jobs? Pratchett wanted to create a world where fantasy tropes have real consequences. He wanted to rip into the conventions of the genre and squeeze them for laughs, but with realistic characters and situations. The juxtaposition of mundane and fantastic would be laugh-out-loud funny. It would also, almost as a by-product, put relatable protagonists at the heart of the narrative. The flat world on the back of the sea turtle seemed – if taken seriously enough – the ideal setting.

This wasn't Pratchett's first stab at satirising the more ridiculous elements of a story by exposing them to a very British, literal-minded realism. In 1978 he had written a very funny column for the *Bath Chronicle* that took aim at the *Star Wars* phenomenon. The much-hyped movie had finally arrived in the area, and Pratchett was keen to see what all the fuss was about. His immediate take was to draft a series of memos to the Galactic Emperor from the Death Star's chief personnel officer, complaining that robots were taking people's jobs, that giant planet-destroying lasers were an impersonal way of conducting a galactic conquest, that the canteen served prunes too often and that the coffee machine didn't work. The approach could almost be a dry run for his next book.[5]

Since he wanted to puncture as many clichés as possible, and since he had a whole world to play with, Pratchett's instinct was to write a series of separate, though interlinked, tales. Despite objections from St Martin's Press editor Leslie Pockell, Colin Smythe was pleased with the idea and drew up a contract for a book of short stories which ultimately became *The Colour of Magic*, the first Pratchett book to be set on a turtle-borne planet he would call Discworld.

It consisted of four stories – 'The Colour of Magic', 'The Sender of Eight', 'The Lure of the Wyrm' and 'Close to the Edge' – each following the exploits of a failed wizard, Rincewind, and a naive tourist, Twoflower, through a sword 'n' sorcery adventure, allowing Pratchett to parody everything from Dungeons and Dragons to H. P. Lovecraft's occult horror, and the noble talking dragons of Anne McCaffrey's *Pern* series.

Pratchett had landed on a style that suited him absolutely. His vast knowledge and love of fantasy is at the book's heart, but it shares that with a front-loaded sense of humour that is equal parts playfulness, sharply observed satire and increasingly tortured puns. This a book written by someone who spent his teenage years obsessively reading on the one hand, *1066 And All That*, *Punch* and *Mad* magazines and on the other,

---

5. And predates Eddie Izzard's famous Death Star Canteen skit by over a decade.

The Lord of the Rings, Robert E. Howard and literally any book he saw with a dragon on the cover. On the Discworld, he could finally combine the two. He could let rip, allowing his jokes to run the full gamut from slow build set-ups and pratfalls to subtle wordplay that only a reader with specialist knowledge would even recognise. There's a bewildering tumble of jokes and references in the first few pages of *The Colour of Magic* alone.

'In a distant and second-hand set of dimensions', begins the first sentence of the first Discworld novel, 'in an astral plane that was never meant to fly ...'. It takes Pratchett just twenty words to land his first pun. It's followed quickly by a theory that life in the universe is the result of world-sized turtles mating, which is labelled 'the big bang'. This is such a giant, honking rubber-chicken of a pun, which should drag an audible groan from all but the most hard-hearted of readers, that it overshadows a much subtler one, just a few lines before, which suggests that the alternative to the big bang would be a turtle that simply continues ever onwards with a 'steady gait into nowhere'. This is only a joke at all if you happen to know that one of the alternative hypotheses to the big bang is called the 'steady state' theory.[6] A page later, and we're treated to an on-the-nose parody of Fritz Leiber's classic fantasy duo Fafhrd and the Gray Mouser. Our protagonist introduces himself by saying 'bugger off', all gods are called 'bastards' and we're slipped a pun on the seventeenth-century notion of an 'invisible college'[7] with the wizarding school of Unseen University. The gag rate would be dizzying but for the comfortable pace of Pratchett's prose, which slips each laugh past our defences and then moves on before we can be distracted by it.

We're also, very quickly, introduced to another Pratchett trademark: footnotes,[8] a device he would use in almost all subsequent books and short stories. Footnotes, usually associated with academia, are fairly common in fantasy and science fiction, often used to slot in context and minor details without disrupting the flow of the narrative. On the surface Pratchett seems to do this too, using footnotes as a handy depository for

6. Pratchett claimed in interviews that he didn't use puns as often as people thought he did, which shows either an uncharacteristic lack of self-awareness or a clever attempt at misdirection.

7. A self-bestowed and rather grand name for a collection of scholars who happened to be friends and helped each other out now and again.

8. Like this.

spare gags and asides. Often, however, his intention is quite the opposite. Pratchett uses footnotes specifically *because* they disrupt the narrative, in much the same way a stand-up comedian uses pauses and modulates their speech. The footnote drags the reader's eye down to the bottom of the page and back, interrupting their rhythm and throwing them off guard. Footnotes are a timing device. The form Pratchett establishes in *The Colour of Magic* has been much imitated,[9] but this aspect is often overlooked.

The success of *The Colour of Magic* is not just in its jokes, its references or the way it plays with form. Those aspects simply provide an entertaining backdrop. This might be the most demonstrably silly of his novels so far, but his fourth book marks the point when Terry Pratchett begins to really understand the characters he's writing about.

The plot itself is rather thin, as its author would be the first to admit: *The Colour of Magic* is an odd-couple road movie, featuring an inept, cynical and cowardly wizard, Rincewind, who finds himself acting as a guide to an innocent, trusting tourist called Twoflower, as they venture across the lands of the Disc looking for, well, nothing in particular. There is no McGuffin here. No epic quest, or great romance, no founders. The plot is secondary. Pratchett always maintained that the early Discworld novels are essentially plotless: the storyline was just an excuse for the parodies and references. Whether he truly believed that or not we can only speculate, but it feels unnecessarily dismissive. The plot is indeed secondary, but it's secondary to the characters rather than the jokes. Rincewind is Pratchett's first genuinely successful protagonist,[10] and the biggest contributor to *The Colour of Magic*'s success. Pratchett poured a lot of himself into the character; Rincewind's exasperation with the sheer bloody-minded idiocy of the universe is channelled directly from his creator. Years later, in an interview conducted in the online-only world of *Second Life* in 2009, Pratchett would tell fans that, deep in his heart, of all his characters, he related to Rincewind the most. The character works because, unlike Snibril, Dom Sabalos and *especially* Kin Arad, Rincewind is an underdog and an everyman. When faced with horrible

---

9. No, this is *homage*, it's not quite the same thing.
10. Successful as a literary device, that is. As a wizard he's a pretty miserable failure.

violence and the threat of death, most people do not throw themselves honourably into the fray: they get the hell out of there. Rincewind is the very distillation of Pratchett's central premise of treating a fantasy world literally. It's Rincewind's realist outlook that means someone with no knowledge of the tropes and conventions of fantasy – someone who is going to miss the references to Fritz Leiber, Anne McCaffrey and H. P. Lovecraft – can pick up *The Colour of Magic* (and most of the books that would follow it) and enjoy it. Rincewind works because he isn't Aragorn or Gandalf. He's (often quite literally) a bloke in the pub.[11] Pratchett partly based his reluctant hero on the character of Rodney Trotter,[12] the hapless and down-in-the-mouth younger brother from the BBC sitcom *Only Fools and Horses*. Ironically, when *The Colour of Magic* was finally adapted for television, the character would be played by David Jason, the actor who portrayed Rodney's older brother, Del Boy.

Twoflower, the cheerful 'Auriental' tourist, is less developed than Rincewind but works effectively as his foil. His hapless, trusting nature creates a classic double act, the dynamics of which are instantly familiar, whether our reference point is Vladimir and Estragon, Laurel and Hardy, Jay and Silent Bob, or Arthur Dent and Ford Prefect. One forever rolling his eyes at the other. It's this dynamic that drives the story. The jokes are just the icing on the cake.

The final piece of key characterisation comes in the form of the Luggage, borrowed from Pratchett's Dungeons and Dragons games, given a homicidal edge and dropped straight into Discworld. The sea chest on hundreds of little legs is, along with Great A'Tuin the world turtle himself, the most memorable image in the book and would become one of Discworld's enduring symbols, much to the annoyance of its creator who felt he'd exhausted the possibilities of a character that was, essentially, a suitcase with anger management issues, rather quickly.

Of course, there is still much about *The Colour of Magic* that doesn't quite hit its mark, and in later years Pratchett seemed almost embarrassed by the book and expressed a preference for *Strata*, which at least had a

---

11. Alright, yes, Aragorn and Gandalf actually spend a lot of time in pubs, but you really can't imagine bumping into them in a Wetherspoons in Nuneaton, can you? You'll find a Rincewind on every other table, ordering from the Curry Club menu.
12. Which is *amazing* considering his claim that he didn't own a TV.

plot. *The Colour of Magic* is an unarguably thin work; literally short (the first edition tops out at 204 pages, half the length of his longest novel, 2009's *Unseen Academicals*), and reliant on deliberately derivative plot devices to spin it along. Pratchett has fun at the expense of fantasy tropes, while also clearly enjoying writing a completely unabashed fantasy of a type he'd always loved. He does, occasionally, get carried away. Later Discworld characters would be called things such as Fred, Stan and Tiffany, while *The Colour of Magic* is peopled with Zlorfs, Hruns, Liesses and Druellaes. Characters eat candied sea urchins and drink a spirit made from freeze-distilled 'vul nuts', where later they would have a kebab and a pint of Winkle's Old Peculiar.

Not all of the jokes hit the mark. There's an extended gag about 'reflected sounds of underground spirits' – a tortured pun on 'economics'[13] – which takes the reader a couple of runs to get their head around; if they ever do. He even spells out the joke later in the book and as any comic will tell you, a joke that has to be explained is rarely worth telling. A throwaway gag about Twoflower's appearance also causes issues; the little tourist wears eye-glasses, but since the narrative is filtered through Rincewind's point of view, and spectacles are unknown in the city of Ankh-Morpork,[14] Twoflower is described as having an extra set of eyes. Many readers, including future Discworld illustrators Josh Kirby and Kirke Kangro, who drew the British and Estonian paperback art, read this literally and assumed the character *literally had four eyes*. Some fans didn't find out they'd been picturing Twoflower wrongly until his appearance in 1994's *Interesting Times*, with more accurate cover art and a less clumsy description. It was a sharp lesson for Pratchett in overestimating his audience, and one that he wouldn't make again.

Still, these are minor quibbles about a book that, nearly forty years later, feels incredibly fresh. It's a delight to find how very readable *The Colour*

---

13. Echo-gnome-ics. See?
14. There are various theories about the name Ankh-Morpork. Pratchett denied that it was a pun on Fritz Leiber's fantasy city of Lankhmar, or that the choice of words (an ankh being an ancient Egyptian symbol, and a morepork being a species of bird) had any meaning beyond a pleasing sound for two cities joined by a river, mirroring how the Hungarian towns of Buda and Pest became the city of Budapest. However the *London Evening Standard*'s Francis Spufford notes that 'morepork' is an obsolete expression for a ridiculous person, thus Ankh-Morpork could mean literally 'mystical nonsense'. It's exactly the kind of arcane detail Pratchett would know. It's as good an explanation as any.

of Magic is, especially coming after *Strata* and *The Dark Side of the Sun*, which can both feel a little convoluted and muddled at times. Pratchett's prose pulls you along for the ride as the story gallops ahead. Funny, easily digestible and, with the possible exception of *The Hitchhiker's Guide to the Galaxy*, unlike anything else floating around at the time; *The Colour of Magic* marked a watershed in Pratchett's writing and sounded the earliest rumblings of a publishing sensation.

The Colour of Magic was published in Britain on 24 November 1983. All 4,500 copies of the first edition were printed in the US to keep costs down, with just 506 earmarked for the UK due to a shrinking of the library market in the early 1980s. The first Discworld story has the distinction of having the smallest domestic print run of Pratchett's entire career. It's also the only Pratchett novel to enjoy a US release before arriving on British shelves, having been shipped to American stores several weeks early due to an error on the part of St Martin's Press. Meanwhile, the UK release, originally planned for 10 November, was delayed by a further two weeks as Smythe had hated the US edition's blurb and insisted it be covered with a sticker displaying positive reviews.[15] Both editions carried an illustration by a British art student called Alan Smith, depicting the Disc itself, atop the four elephants and a rather stoic looking Great A'Tuin swimming through space. It's an eye-catching and effective jacket design.

In 2013, Pratchett told *The Guardian* that *The Colour of Magic* had sold out on its first day in hardcover. Even by the standards of a Pratchett tall tale, this is a pretty ludicrous exaggeration – *The Colour of Magic* didn't attain immediate classic status, nor did it fly off the shelves. It would take three years for Smythe to sell all 506 of those first edition hardbacks. However, it's true that a buzz was beginning to grow. Reviews were very positive and, building on the critical acclaim of *Strata*, were starting to crop up in more respectable publications such as *The Scotsman* ('an exceptional gift of humour ... so much fun. Pratchett is very good indeed') and *The Times*. The latter's review may only have been thirty-two words, but, importantly, they were a *positive* thirty-two words. Slowly, reader by reader, critic by critic, fan by fan, word began to spread.

---

15. Possibly because it contained a sentence claiming that Rincewind's spells only worked 'half the time', when of course anyone who had actually read the story would know that Rincewind's spells didn't work *at all*.

Chapter 8

Tripping The Light Fantastic

Despite having written a cliffhanger ending for *The Colour of Magic*,[1] Pratchett wasn't planning another visit to Discworld straight away. He had intended to return to science fiction; and what's more, a harder, less frivolous take on the genre. He began work on a new story, a grand concept based around the discovery of 'stepper' technology that would allow people to travel between uninhabited parallel Earths, and the staggering effect that would have on mankind as land and resources became infinite. This epic storyline had its genesis in a real-life incident: a man trying to lead a horse through a front door, spotted by Terry on the way home from work one day. He began to ponder what set of circumstances could possibly make that a good idea, and decided that the horse was a test subject for interdimensional travel.

He began playing with the concept by writing short stories, only one of which, *The High Meggas*, has since been published in its original form, appearing in a collection of Pratchett's short fiction in 2012. It's an excellent bit of writing; a tense and exciting adventure story about a man called Valienté who is attacked by a mysterious stranger while camping in 'the high meggas', the name given to the quantum Earths more than a million 'steps' away from the original. There's some sardonic humour here but by and large, *The High Meggas* is the most serious piece of fiction he'd written since the 1960s; a solid action piece, bursting with more than enough intriguing ideas to power the multi-volume series he had in mind. There is probably a leg of the trousers of time where Terry Pratchett spent the 1980s working on those stories and became a cult SF author. Perhaps he never left the civil service to write full time, watching as his books slid out of print and were forgotten. Or perhaps the Valienté novels were a great success, and he became known as a writer of imaginative, hard science fiction, with the Discworld left as a curio

---

1. More of a cliff-dropper, really.

in his back catalogue. The trousers of time can be funny things. In *this* reality, however, word was spreading about *The Colour of Magic* and it was prudent to work on a sequel. The young man who refused to write a second *Carpet People* book, because it would 'cheapen' the original, had grown up. *The High Meggas*, and the other work done around the quantum Earth concept, was put aside. It would be thirty years before it was picked up again.

In the meantime, *The Colour of Magic* was in need of a paperback publisher. Colin Smythe had been unhappy with the way NEL had marketed *Strata* the previous year. The company had been bought by the much bigger Hodder and Stoughton, and the new owners had little interest in pulpy science fiction. Smythe turned to Diane Pearson, a veteran editor at publishing giants Transworld who was on the lookout for new authors for the company's paperback imprint, Corgi. A provisional deal was done, with only one minor hitch: NEL had a contractual first refusal on Pratchett's next book. Fortunately, as sales of *Strata* had been sluggish, NEL had little interest in activating an option for *The Colour of Magic*, and Smythe was free to take the book elsewhere.

Though the Corgi paperback wouldn't hit stores until January 1985, the respected Pearson was able to boost Pratchett's profile almost immediately by convincing Radio 4's *Woman's Hour* to broadcast an abridged serialisation. *The Colour of Magic* made its radio debut on 27 June 1984 and ran daily until 10 July. It was read by actor Nigel Hawthorne, then at the peak of his fame thanks to his role as the sardonic civil servant Sir Humphrey Appleby in the political sitcom *Yes, Minister*. The broadcast was a hit and contributed hugely to Pratchett's growing popularity. It also prompted a satisfying backtrack from NEL, who decided that they were interested in the paperback rights after all. Alas for them, that ship had sailed. Pratchett's relationship with Transworld, via its imprints Corgi and Doubleday, would last for the rest of his life.

Arguably the most significant contribution to Pratchett's career came with Corgi's choice of cover artist. Seeking an illustrator whose vision might chime with Pratchett's madcap style, the publisher chose jacket art veteran Ronald 'Josh' Kirby, who had worked for Transworld on various science fiction covers in the 1970s.

Born in 1928, Kirby had attended the Liverpool City School of Art, before heading to London to seek his fortune as a portrait artist. Falling into drawing movie posters to make ends meet, he enjoyed the challenge of commercial work far more than conventional fine art and quickly expanded into the publishing world. Kirby established his name as a jacket illustrator with Ian Fleming's James Bond novel *Moonraker*, although science fiction, especially fantasy-style sci-fi, suited him best. His back catalogue reads like a who's who of SF's greatest names: Ray Bradbury, Isaac Asimov, Ursula K. Le Guin, Brian Aldiss and hundreds more. Much later on, when Pratchett visited an exhibition of Kirby's work, he was surprised to find he had owned several books with Kirby covers since the 1960s; Kirby's work was so varied that many of his SF covers bear no resemblance to the distinctive style he became known for later in his career. A return to cinema artwork saw him create posters for SF and fantasy big-hitters such as *Return of the Jedi*, *The Beastmaster* and *Krull*, but it was probably his work for *Monty Python's Life Of Brian* that prompted Corgi to consider him for their latest signing, as it showcased his ability to distil comic concepts and parody into interesting design.

Kirby was surprised to get the call about *The Colour of Magic*; it had been years since he'd last worked with Transworld, and personnel in the art department had long since changed; however, he was delighted with the commission and enjoyed the book immensely. Pratchett's sense of humour chimed with his own, and he instinctively understood the fantasy conventions skewered in the text. He provided Corgi with a beautiful watercolour design,[2] depicting Twoflower running into the cellar of the Broken Drum tavern pursued by stony, axe-wielding trolls, and surrounded by a host of fantasy archetypes; all done in a distinctive, nobbly and exaggerated style that stopped just short of cartoonish. The only problem came with the extra two eyes given to Twoflower, thanks to a misunderstanding of Pratchett's joke. ('I didn't know it was supposed to be a joke!' Kirby told David Langford in the text accompanying his collection *A Cosmic Cornucopia*. 'I was used to fantasy and just accepted it

---

2. Which was unusual for Kirby, who usually worked in oils, hence the softer feel of his first Discworld piece.

as so.') Neither Pratchett nor Smythe saw the image before the paperback was published, and the mistake was never corrected.

Four-eyed tourists aside, Pratchett was delighted with the image and said that he hadn't really known what trolls on Discworld looked like until Kirby drew them. There may have been some fudged details (as well as Twoflower's literal double vision, Rincewind is depicted with a Gandalf-style long, grey beard, despite the text saying his beard is scruffy and brown – Pratchett had envisioned the character as weasel-like, and much younger), but Kirby had captured the spirit of the book absolutely. The pairing worked so well that Kirby was the obvious choice for the next Discworld novel, and became Pratchett's default jacket illustrator, providing cover art for every full Discworld novel and most of Pratchett's non-Discworld books, right up to his death in 2001. His style became synonymous with Pratchett's.

Corgi's ambitions were substantially higher than the 506 hardbacks Colin Smythe had shipped to libraries and shops in 1983. On 15 January 1985, *The Colour of Magic* paperback reached shelves with an initial print run of 26,000. A second printing would be necessary before the year was out.

The packaging was neat and striking, featuring Josh Kirby's artwork wrapped around both sides of the book, with the title and author's name floating in rectangular panels on the front cover and spine, overlapped by elements of Kirby's picture to give depth to the image. It stood out on bookshelves when only the spine was visible. Corgi would use the same concept for each of their Discworld paperbacks, only changing the look with the twenty-fifth book, *The Truth*, in 2001. It made Pratchett paperbacks look great when grouped together on a shelf and feel collectable – a masterstroke in understanding the fan mindset.

The paperback carried a strapline below the title, which read somewhat awkwardly: 'Jerome K. Jerome meets *Lord of the Rings* (with a touch of *Peter Pan*)'. The Jerome and Tolkien references were absolutely on the money, though the nod to J. M. Barrie's *Peter Pan* is an odd addition, especially considering how *right* Corgi got the rest of the marketing. Aside from a broad fantasy setting, there is virtually no crossover between Barrie's classic and Pratchett's parody. Pratchett, alas, had no say over the strapline, paperback publishers being rather a law unto themselves.

The blurb on the back cover declared the book to be 'The wackiest and most original fantasy since *The Hitchhiker's Guide to the Galaxy*', which is an understandable comparison, however much Pratchett (and indeed, Adams) might wince at the self-consciously I'm-dead-mad-me implications of the word 'wackiest'. Douglas Adams' sharp comedy was easily the most successful meeting of humour and science fiction on the market, and though Pratchett's fantasy parodies had a warmer and less Oxbridge, Pythonesque approach, the superficial similarities were plain enough. Pratchett said he was reading *Hitchhiker* while *The Colour of Magic* was gestating in his head, which inevitably spilled into his writing. He was such a fan of Adams' book, he once claimed to have rigged one of his doors to sigh and thank the person who had just walked through it whenever it opened or closed.

On 21 January 1985, Pratchett went to a Chinese restaurant in London to give an interview to a short-lived SF magazine called *Space Voyager*. After years of working as a journalist and a press officer, he was finally the subject of a feature himself. The interview was conducted by a 25-year-old, leather-clad, punky writer wearing a grey homburg hat, who had given *Strata* a glowing review the previous year, and was keen to talk about *The Colour of Magic*. He introduced himself as Neil Gaiman, a jobbing critic with aspirations to be a novelist and comic book author. The pair bonded immediately over a shared understanding of SF and fantasy, a mutual love of G. K. Chesterton, and a desire to explore every second-hand bookshop in Soho. It was the beginning of a long friendship and five years later it would bear fruit in a significant collaboration.

Pratchett would later learn to be guarded in interviews, preferring to spin out the same set of embellished anecdotes and pithy, quotable oneliners. He'd interviewed plenty of people in his career as a journalist and knew how to get his point across and swerve any awkward questions. He rarely gave details about his personal life and was careful to say nothing that could get him into trouble or be misconstrued. Back in 1985, however, sitting down with Gaiman, it's clear he had yet to apply many of these skills. He gives away jokes from his next book, freely admits to the influence of Douglas Adams (something he'd play down in later years) and makes an uncomfortable gag about journalists having a 'rapist's mentality' in the way they operate.

The accompanying photograph, taken in the Soho branch of comic store Forbidden Planet, shows us Pratchett at 36 years old. He cuts an odd figure; wearing a flat cap and a diamond-patterned woollen golfing sweater under an anorak. His beard is already flecked with more than a little grey. The look is finished with a pair of large, tinted spectacles. He looks more like a provincial driving instructor than a successful fantasy author. As his fame grew he would learn to take his appearance more seriously.

Barely a week after meeting Gaiman, Pratchett enjoyed another career landmark – his first dedicated book signing, held at the Andromeda bookshop in Birmingham. Andromeda was a focal point of the Midlands' SF community and was owned by Roger Peyton, the canny former editor of *Vector* who had first encountered Pratchett at Eastercon in 1964. It was Peyton who decided to take a chance on *The Colour of Magic*, despite Pratchett's previous paperbacks selling poorly in store. He takes up the story:

I remember one bright Monday morning, the new Transworld/ Corgi sales rep, Kevin Redmond, called on us at Andromeda – it was his first day with the company and we were his first call. At that time, the decision on how many copies to order was decided by myself and my assistants, Dave Holmes and Ray Gibberd. When Kevin showed us the cover of *The Colour of Magic*, neither Dave nor Ray wanted to order more than five or ten copies because Terry's previous two paperbacks had failed to make an impact. They were totally shocked when I turned to Kevin and said, 'We'll take 100 copies and 200 if we can have Terry for a signing session.' Both Dave and Ray thought I'd lost my mind and tried to argue with me, but I pulled rank – I knew that a book with that wonderful Josh Kirby cover and that superb blurb on the back would just leap off the shelves. Somehow, I knew it would be a bestseller – one of the few times I ever had such a strong gut feeling. Kevin was an excellent salesman – he arranged the signing session and when he went around the other shops in his area, he managed to get them all to put in big orders.

The signing on January 26 was a great success, with us selling all but a handful of copies which were duly signed and sold in the next few days. We also sold several copies of *Strata*, *The Dark Side of the Sun*, first editions of *The Carpet People* and US hardcovers of *The Colour of Magic*. We reordered another fifty paperbacks immediately, and that title remained in our top five bestsellers for three years! After that signing, I knew that Terry was on his way.

It was Terry's very first signing and after taking him for a meal afterwards he made his way back home, calling on the way at a garage for petrol. He'd signed so many books (nearly three-hundred) that his signature on his cheque looked very different to that on his credit card!

Pratchett would hold signings at the tiny store to support every new book he published from 1985 to 2001, when Peyton retired. Book signings would become a huge part of Pratchett's career, to the point his friend David Langford would often joke about finding 'rare, unsigned copies of the latest Terry Pratchett'.

In the spring Terry found himself at a science fiction convention for the first time since the mid-1960s: Eastercon, held in Leeds and dubbed Yorcon III.[3] He attended as a regular convention member, rather than any sort of advertised guest, so was surprised to discover that his reputation had preceded him. Several people brought copies of *The Colour Magic* for him to sign, and he was astonished to find that many attendees knew his name. Plenty of those that *hadn't* yet heard of Terry Pratchett and the Discworld left the event determined to seek out his new book, thanks to a barfly technique Pratchett developed that year and would employ as his standard convention trick. Fantasy author Charles Stross, then a teenage fan hawking his first manuscript around in a carrier bag in the hope of finding an editor, remembered meeting Pratchett at Yorcon and recounts events in a 2015 blog:

There was this thirty-something guy with glasses and a bushy beard propping up the bar. What set him apart from the other guys with beards and glasses was that he had a hat, and he was trying to cadge pints of beer with an interesting chat-up line: 'I'm a fantasy writer,

---

3. The naming of conventions had not come on a great deal in the last twenty years.

you know. My third book just came out – it's called *The Colour of Magic*.'[4] So you'd buy him a drink because I swear, he had some kind of bibulous mind-control thing going, and he'd tell you about the book, and then you'd end up buying the book because it sounded funny, and then you were *trapped in his snare forever*.

The experience would be repeated at Novacon in Birmingham that winter, where Pratchett met SF author and critic David Langford, editor of the long-running genre newsletter *Ansible*. It was the beginning of another long friendship (Langford's main memory of the encounter: '"Ah," I said, fresh from reading *The Colour of Magic*. "Churm Rincewind – one of the twelve red-bearded dwarfs!" "You bastard," said Terry.')[5] At Novacon, Pratchett was invited to sit on his first panel since 1966, though due to some travel delays arrived too late and missed his slot. He also delivered a speech, published as an essay in *Ansible* two years later, called 'Why Gandalf Never Married', a quasi-feminist musing on the way women and men are written differently in fantasy fiction, partly inspired by the portrayal of female magic in Ursula K. Le Guin's novel, *A Wizard of Earthsea*. Pratchett argued that women's magic was usually presented as cheap stuff, concerned with herbs and mind tricks, and often with malevolent intent. Men, meanwhile, practised grand, noble arts, and created works of great power. It's from this intellectual premise that the third Discworld book, *Equal Rites*, would come.

Pratchett would attend several conventions over the next few years, talking up his latest books, sitting on panels and giving readings and Q&As. He came to know a community of fans and writers that would regularly appear at such events including Neil Gaiman, Kim Newman, David Langford, Jo Fletcher and Mary Gentle. He knew how important these weekends were; as a fan himself he understood the profound effect it could have for a reader to meet an author and he resolved to meet as

---

4. Which is, of course, wrong. *The Colour of Magic* is Pratchett's *fourth* book. It's not clear if Stross is misremembering this, or if Pratchett was quietly distancing himself from the more juvenile *Carpet People*.

5. Pratchett lifted his protagonist's name unconsciously from J. B. Morton's 'Beachcomber' column in the *Daily Express*, which he had come across when he was 13. He claimed he'd forgotten all about this, and believed he'd come up with the name Rincewind himself. Langford's near-encyclopaedic knowledge of humour ruined that illusion.

many readers as possible. This was more than simple marketing: it was what Pratchett referred to as 'paying forward'; making himself available to fans and to the SF community at large, in order to help inspire the next generation of writers and play his part in keeping the industry stimulated. He would always consider himself part of that world.

A contract for a sequel to *The Colour of Magic* was signed in 1985, with Colin Smythe once again acting as hardback publisher and a deal already in place for Corgi to take the paperback. The new book dispensed with the short-story format of its predecessor, returning to the chapterless style of *Strata*, with the narrative cutting between scenes and characters in much the same way a film would. Pratchett would use this as his default writing style for the rest of his career, utilised for the majority of his adult-intended novels.[6]

In many ways, *The Light Fantastic*, was an easier book to write, as the heavy lifting needed to build a world had been done by the previous volume. This gave Pratchett the room to sharpen his characters and plot and allowed more freedom for another pinwheeling storm of jokes and references. Once again the gags came at the expense of bad fantasy stereotypes, but that's where the similarities with *The Colour of Magic* stop. *The Light Fantastic* has a solid spine, in the form of a compelling and wholly original story. Rincewind, last seen dropping off the edge of the Disc, has a powerful spell with a consciousness of its own lodged in his head, which is needed to save the world. Meanwhile, a malevolent red star has appeared in the sky, getting bigger as Great A'Tuin, the world turtle, swims towards it, spreading panic across the Discworld as post-apocalyptic 'star cults' rise. Rincewind becomes the McGuffin of the story, as wizards and warriors attempt to recover the spell in his head, while he tries to run as far away as he can, as fast as he can. It's an engrossing tale which, as it gathers pace and hurtles towards a conclusion, feels genuinely exciting.

In this book, Pratchett's characters are better developed. Earlier protagonists Dom Sabalos and Kin Arad may finish their respective stories a little wiser about the universe, but their inner journeys are far

---

6. His children's and young adult (YA) fiction was always written with conventional chapters, breaking the book into manageable chunks and giving parents a get-out clause of 'we can just read to the end of the chapter' when they wanted their child to *finally* go to sleep.

from complex. Rincewind, on the other hand, discovers strength, bravery and compassion in his grubby soul. He finds himself, at the book's climax, the only person who can save the world, and to his own surprise steps up to the task, facing down the hideous monsters of the Dungeon Dimensions. Twoflower also comes a long way. There are cracks in his naivety; we discover that his seemingly unshakeable faith in Rincewind's power is partly a front constructed for his friend's benefit – he knows the cowardly gutter wizard can't do magic. In the book's finale, Twoflower finally stops being the visitor, the observer, and takes up arms to help save the world. It's his bravery that nudges Rincewind into action. By the close of the book the little tourist realises he has seen enough and needs to return home, leaving behind his magical Luggage to pitter-patter through future stories.

The early Discworld novels are all significant in their own way as landmarks in Pratchett's developing career, but that's especially true of *The Light Fantastic*. Pratchett was able to take the silly world of *The Colour of Magic*, hitherto the setting for light, Disc-trotting adventures, and use it as the backdrop for a solid fantasy story. *The Light Fantastic* establishes many of the now-familiar tropes of the series, fleshing out the revolting medieval city of Ankh-Morpork and the culture that surrounds it, and introducing the reader to the stuffy, self-important wizards of Unseen University (though it would be a while before Pratchett established a permanent faculty there). In the first few pages of the story, a throwaway gag sees the university's librarian turned into an orangutan; a side-effect of a powerful spell intended to save the plummeting Rincewind. The reader smiles at the image and thinks no more of it.

Terry Pratchett: Back In Black, the 2017 BBC docudrama, based on Pratchett's own words, maintained that an orangutan librarian was something he had dreamed up in his days as a Saturday boy in Beaconsfield Library, imagining that an ape could swing up to the higher shelves to retrieve hard-to-reach books. However, in a much earlier interview conducted with an Australian TV show called *The 5th Dimension* in 1996, Pratchett admits that the shape of an orangutan only occurred to him during the writing process as a suitably silly animal for a wizard to turn into. As with many Pratchett anecdotes we're left to choose for ourselves which version we'd rather believe.

Whichever we choose, it became clear from the moment Pratchett sends his villain, Trymon, into the library to bribe its custodian with a banana, that a bookish ape had enough comic potential to be given permanent tenure at Unseen University. Like the Luggage, the Librarian would become one of the enduring symbols of the series, much to the surprise of his creator. Neither character was expected to have staying power beyond a few solid laughs.

The second Discworld novel[7] also gives a proper introduction to perhaps the most well-loved of all Pratchett's characters: the 7ft robed skeleton of Death. Death had appeared in *The Colour of Magic*, where he served merely as a plot device and a punchline as Pratchett deftly parodies the old folk tale, *Appointment in Samarra*. The skeletal figure's appearance when Rincewind's life is in peril becomes a running gag across the four stories, though the only personality traits we really see are a tendency to talk in small caps, and mutter the occasional 'SOD YOU THEN'. In *The Light Fantastic* Pratchett puts more flesh on his bones,[8] and Death becomes less of a gag and more of a character in his own right; a slightly vexed figure, just trying to get on with an honest day's reaping of souls. We see him at a party pondering the presence of cheese and pineapple on a stick. Later we visit his home and meet his adopted daughter, setting up the plot for a later novel, *Mort*. Like the Librarian and the Luggage, here was a character that began as the mechanism for a joke and became a fully realised part of the universe. Death would go on to become a favourite among readers, partly because of the ridiculousness of a 7ft skeleton that liked cats and a good curry, and partly because being greeted by a kindly and professional figure at the end of one's life is inherently appealing. In later years Pratchett would receive letters from fans with terminally ill relatives, who had found comfort in the character. It's no surprise that the figure of Death became softened and gentle in the books – Terry Pratchett spent his childhood mortally afraid of skeletons.

The Light Fantastic was completed as word of mouth was pushing *The Colour of Magic* into more and more hands. By Novacon, in the autumn of 1985, Pratchett was already complaining that his publishers were taking

---

7. Okay, *technically* the first – *The Colour of Magic* is a book of short stories so shouldn't strictly be called a novel, but frankly if we go down that road we'll be here all day.
8. Figuratively.

too long in getting the book on to the market, and behind the scenes, was on his way to completing the next Discworld instalment, *Equal Rites.* His fifth book finally saw the light of day in June of 1986, three years after its predecessor. Josh Kirby, whose work had been so instrumental in marketing the Corgi paperback of *The Colour of Magic,* was brought in from the start to provide artwork that could double for the hardback and paperback editions. Once again he excelled himself, painting a scene in which a (still elderly) Rincewind and (still four-eyed) Twoflower ride atop the Luggage, alongside the wizened old warrior, Cohen the Barbarian, and the druidess, Bethany,[9] – the latter wearing substantially less clothing than the text suggests, a Josh Kirby trademark that presumably did sales no harm.

Reactions were positive. Writing in *Space Voyager,* Neil Gaiman describes the book as doing for fantasy 'what Douglas Adams did for science fiction and what pigeons do to Nelson's Column … this is the stuff of which cults are woven.' *Time Out*'s first ever review of a Pratchett book continued with the comparison to Adams, saying, 'If Pratchett had put quill to parchment before Douglas Adams, Ford Prefect would still be stranded somewhere in the Galaxy with his thumb in the air.'[10]

Corgi's paperback followed on 5 September, mere months after Colin Smythe's first edition hardback. Smythe, working this time without the assistance of St Martin's Press, whose fumbling of *The Colour of Magic* wasn't easily forgiven, had printed just 1,034 copies of his edition. The paperback would take up the slack with a mammoth 34,000 copies of *The Light Fantastic* heading for bookshops that autumn. Corgi would need to reprint the book every year until 1994, often twice.

In January 1987 Roger Peyton summarised the success of the first two Discworld books in *Andromeda*'s bimonthly catalogue:

Strangest of all was the sudden burst of interest in Terry Pratchett's *The Colour of Magic* – one of our best-selling books in 1985. *Colour* has sold steadily throughout the year but, due no doubt to the sequel

---

9. With Cohen and Bethany, Pratchett was starting to give characters names that didn't tie the tongue in knots.

10. Of course, Pratchett *had* put 'quill to parchment', or at least fingers to typewriter, before Adams. Ford Prefect still found himself a pretty hoopy frood all the same.

being issued, *Colour* started selling in quantities bigger than most new books, resulting in it being one of our best-sellers for 1986! The third volume is out this month in hardcover and we predict that Terry's books are going to become cult favourites.

Terry Pratchett, the cult fantasy author, had arrived.

Chapter 9

Going Overground

C ult success was all very well but it wasn't paying the bills, and Pratchett was still reporting for duty every day at the CEGB. His books were starting to sell, true enough, but the advances were relatively low and he had yet to see substantial royalties. Book signings and conventions were fun, but food was still needed on the table, and Terry was still needed at his desk. He found himself living a double life; a civil servant dealing with press enquiries by day, and cult fantasy author, bashing out the latest Discworld novel by night. On one occasion he was interviewed twice by the same journalist, who was shocked to find that a CEGB press officer he had grilled about nuclear safety, and the up-and-coming local author with whom he had chatted about his latest novel, were in fact, the same person.[1]

By now Terry was the CEGB's chief press officer in the south west, and was a hugely respected member of the nationwide PR team. Indeed, such was his reputation for efficiency, ruthless competence and occasional snippiness, younger members of the office were known to hold him somewhat in awe. As Barbara Steinberg, a junior member of the organisation's London press office, recalls:

> He was an experienced and competent press officer who could handle anything. His experience of being a journalist meant he knew what sort of questions were likely to be asked and probably thought

---

1. A word of caution here – this claim comes from a Pratchett interview from the mid-1990s. When a Terry Pratchett anecdote throws up such a narratively satisfying tidbit, it's always best to apply the obligatory pinch of salt. That said, it is perfectly possible that this is true: Terry *was* interviewed about his latest book by the *Western Daily Press* in 1987, and after Chernobyl the paper often covered stories about Hinkley Point and other power stations. As *Western Daily* reports don't tend to carry bylines, we can't verify that the same writer covered both stories. Again, it's for the reader to decide in which trouser leg of time they prefer to live.

he could do better than the HQ staff in briefings. I was quite nervous of him; I was just the junior tasked with passing on messages and I remember he was quite sharp, and didn't pull his punches. If he was in the mood he could also be very helpful and explain why he didn't think something was the way to do it or wouldn't work. However, he was so lively, I remember we always looked forward to seeing him.

In April 1986, a few months before *The Light Fantastic* made its way to bookshops, a reactor exploded in a Soviet nuclear power plant. The Chernobyl disaster was the worst accident in the history of atomic power, and deaths as a result of the explosion are estimated at anywhere between 300 and 40,000. The nuclear power industry was, once again, under worldwide scrutiny, and Pratchett's already-intense job at the CEGB became that bit harder. Every minor issue was leapt on by the press, whether it was fragments of radioactive waste accidentally flushed into the sewage system, or a capsized railway carriage. The phone barely stopped ringing, and sleep in the Pratchett household was frequently interrupted. The job wasn't just restricted to phone calls and sitting behind his desk, either. Such was the impact of Chernobyl on the industry and its perception, it required everyone to muck in as best they could to mitigate the damage. At one point Terry found himself at the Slimbridge wildlife reserve, near Gloucester, assisting scientists from the nearby Berkeley Nuclear Laboratories to herd migrating swans into a portable gamma spectrometer. The birds had recently arrived from Russia and it was vitally important that they be tested for radiation (happily they found only safe, background levels present). The point of working for the CEGB had always been to do 'indoor work with no heavy lifting', and as many of his friends suspected, have free time and brain space in which to write. Broken sleep, stressful days and swan-wrangling were presumably not what he had in mind. To cope, Terry took refuge in his other life. After one particularly hard Friday spent fielding calls from newspapers and pumping metaphorical water into the burning reactor of rumour, he came home, sat at his desk and bashed out the final third of his next book, *Equal Rites*, in one long sitting. When the stresses of the job were getting too much, he could always go to Discworld. He resolved to get out of the power industry as soon as possible.

Pratchett's literary career was developing at pace, and it was obvious to Colin Smythe that his operation was too small to properly shepherd his author's growing popularity. He didn't have the resources for large promotional campaigns or the mass distribution required to handle a bestseller, and Great A'Tuin was clearly carrying the Discworld in that direction. The solution was to enter into a co-publishing deal with a bigger company, one whose resources could take Terry's profile to the next level. Word within the industry was already spreading, and the Discworld phenomenon was being discussed in literary circles as the books began to break out of the SF and fantasy bubble. One persistent rumour, which even had Josh Kirby taken in, was that 'Terry Pratchett' was a pseudonym for a substantially more famous author, slumming it in comic fantasy. The theory is, of course, ridiculous, but it does give an indication of how impressed the industry was with this oddball writer who had seemingly come from nowhere.[2]

Smythe turned to his friend David Burnett, a director at publishers Victor Gollancz, suggesting over lunch that the company take a punt on the next Discworld book. The decision to target Gollancz was Pratchett's – he had devoured classic Gollancz SF as a teenager and felt the imprint's existing list would put his work among excellent company. As Gollancz's SF editor, Malcolm Edwards, told *Bookbrunch* in 2015: 'Terry always wanted to be a writer of hard science fiction, and he used to describe what he did as paddling around in the shallow end while watching writers like Greg Bear and Larry Niven do multiple somersaults off the high board.'

Burnett and Edwards had their doubts. The company had very little experience with fantasy, focusing mostly on sci-fi, and they had a full release schedule in place already. Added to this, Edwards – who would be primarily responsible for editing any Pratchett work they published – wasn't a fan of comic fantasy, and didn't feel equipped to judge its viability. In early 1986, Edwards sent typescript copies of the as-yet-unpublished *The Light Fantastic* and the recently completed *Equal Rites* to *Ansible's* David Langford, who was supplementing his income with consultancy work, in an attempt to get a second opinion.

---

2. The 'overnight sensation' label annoyed Pratchett immensely. He felt that since he'd had his first story published twenty years earlier and was on his fifth novel, his success was actually hard won and overdue.

Langford, of course, knew Pratchett from the convention circuit and had thoroughly enjoyed *The Colour of Magic*, giving it an enthusiastic write-up in his column in the fantasy gaming magazine, *White Dwarf*. He was even more impressed with its sequel, thinking it funnier and better plotted, but voiced concern that the formula may have been stretched as far as it could go. With some trepidation he turned to *Equal Rites*, wondering if he'd be proven right. He needn't have worried. 'Equal Rites charmed me with its determination to be more serious,' he told Pratchett fanzine, *The Discworld Chronicle* in 1998. 'Plenty of sparkly surface jokes, but some solid plotting underneath, and a hardening recognition that not everything in Discworld need be funny.' He provided Gollancz with a 1,500-word report recommending they take Pratchett on, though he suggested the opening of the book could be tightened by around 200 words.[3] Reassured, Edwards agreed to a three-book co-publishing deal with Colin Smythe Ltd, beginning with *Equal Rites*, planned for early 1987.

Over dinner, Malcolm Edwards promised to make Pratchett a best-selling author. The company even explored publishing *The Light Fantastic*, though in the end the deal couldn't be done in time and the hardback came out under the Colin Smythe banner alone. It was the last Pratchett novel to do so.

That year, 1987, also saw the first ever piece of Discworld spin-off media – a video game adaptation of *The Colour of Magic*. It was developed by a 17-year-old programming enthusiast, Fergus McNeill, who along with a group of school friends had formed a software company called Delta 4. The team used the newly released ZX Spectrum home computer and an authoring system called The Quill to write text-based adventure games, not unlike Dungeons and Dragons. Players were confronted with a scenario and the computer would ask them what they wanted to do next. There were only a handful of options available, but a player's choices dictated the direction in which the game would go. Their first major success had been with a Tolkien parody called *Bored of the Rings* – not to be confused with the 1969 spoof novel of the same name – advertised in the back of gaming magazines and distributed via mail order, complete

---

3. Since he had to hand the original manuscript back, he has no idea if this ever happened.

with photocopied manuals and hand-dubbed cassettes.[4] It was successful enough to put Delta 4 on the industry's radar, and McNeill received a number of approaches about developing games, including a call from Piranha, the new gaming division of publishing giants, the Macmillan Group. Thirty years later, he said:

> They asked if there were any license properties that might be adapted into a game, and they were particularly interested in book licenses. I'd recently picked up a copy of *The Colour Of Magic*. I'd intended it as a present for someone else, but I accidentally started reading it and found myself unable to stop. When Macmillan broached the subject of suitable licenses, it was the first title I suggested. It's important to remember that this was Olden Times – the 1980s, for goodness sake – so, when I said 'Terry Pratchett', people didn't laugh at my audacity for wanting to work with the great man. They frowned and said 'Who's he?'

Piranha saw the potential in Pratchett's book immediately and McNeill started work:

> Before long I was getting off a train at Bristol Temple Meads Station, and emerging into the daylight to be met by a man with no hat who, just like his writing, turned out to be clever, charming, and funny. I knew straight away that I would enjoy working with Terry. Unlike some other authors, he grasped the challenges of non-linear storytelling for games and we spoke often on the phone about the design. My biggest problem was staying focused – it was very distracting when he started quoting sections of the forthcoming *Wyrd Sisters*,[5] and even worse when he began telling me of another project that would become *Mort*.

Terry was no stranger to the ZX Spectrum or home computing in general, and the enthusiasm he'd had as a boy for tinkering with technology had

---

4. Note for younger readers: before downloads, cartridges, CDs and even floppy discs, games were issued on cassette tapes. If your next question is 'What is a cassette?', cherish your youth, for it will one day fade and the technology you take for granted will become antique.
5. It's likely McNeill is actually referring to *Equal Rites* here.

never dimmed. In 1981 he had bought a Sinclair ZX81, an affordable home computer which he purchased in kit form. He claimed that by adding a series of sensors and other third party add-ons, he was able to get the machine to say 'hello' to him when he walked into his office and, in a voice scrounged from an old video game and later adopted by Stephen Hawking, tell him the date and time, the temperature in his greenhouse and, thanks to a wind sensor, provide a limited weather report. By 1984 he had upgraded to an Amstrad 464 CPC, the first computer he owned that worked as a word processor. He used it to write *The Light Fantastic*, finding the process substantially smoother than typing by hand, since he could edit and redraft as he went along. Before this, a typical Pratchett manuscript was a multi-coloured mess. He would type each revision on a different coloured sheet of A4, with rewritten sections pasted over the original version by hand. He would then retype the whole thing neatly, to create an official first draft he'd submit to his publishers. Word processing enabled him to gallop up and down a living document, making changes as he went. It's a process we take for granted now, but in 1986 very few authors worked this way. A visiting journalist from the *Western Daily Press* left Gayes Cottage reeling in shock after seeing the technological marvel that was Pratchett's spellchecker.

The *Colour of Magic* game was a moderate success, and featured jacket artwork that gave Twoflower the correct number of eyes.[6] Reviews were broadly kind, and the game was praised for its graphics (via Delta 4) and humour (via Terry Pratchett), though most write-ups noted that players unfamiliar with the novel might struggle with the game. One common criticism came as a result of McNeill's team adapting Pratchett's work too faithfully – the usual directions of north, south, east and west being replaced by the Discworld compass points of 'hubwards', 'rimwards', 'turnwise' and 'widdershins', wrongfooting players used to this sort of text-based adventure game. McNeill has fond memories of this time:

Working with Terry on *The Colour Of Magic* game was a huge privilege, and I loved the experience of discussing ideas with someone so creative. My only regret was that it all happened just a

---

6. Teenage computer programmers presumably had the phrase 'four-eyes' thrown at them enough times to pick up the reference.

little too soon – games technology was still very much in its infancy, and I wish those '80s home computers had more capacity so I could have included more of his magic. He was a big inspiration for me and, comedy aside, he talked with great wisdom about the writing process – which helped me as I became an author myself.

Despite Terry's growing fame, life in the Pratchett household in the 1980s was simple, satisfying and rural. Like her father, Rhianna Pratchett remembers her childhood as idyllic. She was often found sitting in an apple tree, reading a book and helping herself to the fruit. Her parents taught her about beekeeping and how to feed chickens and ducks, and milk the goats, which she would also herd back into their pens from the nearby field. It was a responsibility she was proud to be given, though she later learned that her father would watch her from the top of a hill to ensure she got home safely. Terry would take his daughter on long walks and rambles, singing rude folk songs as they went. He taught her which plants were edible and which had health benefits as they gathered mushrooms and berries. They discovered hidden pools and caves, and made water wheels from sticks and twine, feeling that they had slipped into another world in the distant past; something which was reinforced on the occasion a troupe of live-action roleplayers hurtled passed them dressed as Vikings. Like Terry's parents David and Eileen, he and Lyn prioritised quality family time and an interesting life. It wasn't unusual for Rhianna to be woken in the middle of the night and taken outside to see a particularly clear sky full of stars, the passing of a comet or a display of glow worms.

If Rincewind had been a cypher for Pratchett's frustrated bewilderment with the universe, then Eskarina 'Esk' Smith, the young heroine of *Equal Rites*, was a way of preserving Rhianna's childhood. Ten years earlier, when he'd written *Strata*, Pratchett had created a female protagonist from outside of his experience and it was one of the few failings of the novel. His next attempt at a heroine was rooted in a girl he knew intimately, and the level-headed, practical Esk, so like Rhianna in many ways, is *Equal Rites'* greatest asset. He may have been writing fantasy, but his latest book contained much that was uniquely personal.

In the story, Esk inherits a wizard's staff from a careless mage who hadn't realised the 'eighth son of an eighth son' he had been tracking down was actually a daughter. When the staff's magic begins to show itself in strange ways, the young Esk is apprenticed to a local witch, Granny Weatherwax, in the hope that learning witchcraft will tame her powers. Granny would become one of Pratchett's most beloved characters, as she grew in stature, wisdom and rage across many more books. But the Granny of *Equal Rites* is not quite the pillar of strength and power she would become by 1998's *Carpe Jugulum* and the Tiffany Aching stories. Here she is still a hedge witch from a remote mountain village, cunning and clever, but not especially powerful or wise. Granny would later become a barometer of right and wrong, dispensing justice to a whole kingdom. In *Equal Rites,* that kingdom hadn't been given a name, and there is still some distance between author and character. Pratchett would grow into Granny Weatherwax as he grew beyond Rincewind and the Luggage.

Though Terry's sense of righteousness wasn't yet a part of Granny, *Equal Rites* is still a very personal story. Granny's tumbledown, thatched house in the woods is a fictionalised version of his own home, Gayes Cottage, right down to the goats and the beehives. Many of the lessons in herblore and craft taught to Esk by Granny are the same ones Terry had been teaching Rhianna, and much of Esk's plain-speaking curiosity and smart-alec answers came straight from her real-life inspiration. Granny herself was a loose amalgamation of older people Terry had known as a child, filtered through the manner and bearing of his paternal grandmother, Granny Pratchett. He borrowed phrases and habits from all four of his grandparents to bring her to life, such as his grandfather's tendency to dismiss things he didn't understand as 'geometry', which in Granny Weatherwax's mouth becomes the more pleasingly West Country 'jommetry'.

Pratchett utilises his long-standing interest in English folklore as he begins to piece together a Discworld version of witchcraft that is as much about midwifery, doctoring, social work and the symbols and appearance of respect, as it is about actual magic. What magic Granny does do – at least until she gets into a slightly jarring and unexpected duel with a wizard at Unseen University – is subtle and connected to the land and the wildlife around her. Pratchett invents the skill of 'borrowing', where a witch rides in the mind of another creature and sees the world as it does. This leads to his most evocative and terrifying piece of writing yet, as Esk ignores Granny's teaching and takes over the body of an eagle, finding herself trapped and overwhelmed, nearly lost forever in the creature's mind.

Like *The Light Fantastic*, *Equal Rites* uses the Discworld as a backdrop to tell a deeper, darker tale. There are still plenty of jokes, and as Langford observed, they're uniformly excellent, but it's clear Pratchett has something to prove here. *The Light Fantastic*, for all of its galloping plot and character growth, is fundamentally quite a silly tale. It's a romp. A ripping yarn. *Equal Rites* is much more than that. Pratchett realised that turning fantasy on its head could do more than generate a cheap laugh, and from its title onwards, *Equal Rites* is a story with a strong moral centre, focused on a feminist message; that despite every obstacle set in their way, women are capable of (and possibly better at) everything men are. That said, the female characters aren't let off the hook; Granny's naivety and stubborn adherence to tradition are almost as damaging to Esk as the dismissive male world of wizardry.[7] *Equal Rites* is the first Pratchett book that truly has something to *say*. It's also the first Discworld novel with genuine subtext. Esk's journey through magic is also arguably of awakening sexuality, though that particular theme remains deep in the novel's subconscious. In this respect, it has more in common with Barrie's *Peter Pan* than *The Colour of Magic* ever did. The magic finds Esk as she approaches the end of her childhood, and is plagued by troubling dreams in which she feels a hot power growing inside her, and wakes to find it has been discharged. At the end of the novel she joins forces with a troubled young man, Simon, and between them, they create a new kind of magic.

Gollancz – in association with Colin Smythe Ltd – published *Equal Rites* in January 1987, with a still-modest print run just shy of 3,000. Josh Kirby was surprised to be asked to produce jacket art, having assumed Gollancz would use an illustrator they had worked with before. Pratchett,

---

7. Pratchett, very much a product of his time, actually dismissed the 'feminist' label with regards to *Equal Rites*, seeing it as a book about equality for both genders, as the title suggests. His argument was that Granny tries to get Esk into the men-only world of Unseen University not because she believes women should be wizards too, but because she's stubborn and someone told her she couldn't. Despite this, the novel's wholehearted focus lends itself as much to the F-word as any other description, and many feminists have embraced it.

however, had insisted Kirby be retained, recognising that his distinctive style had given the books a visual identity. His artwork for *Equal Rites* is no exception, though once again it plays fast and loose with the text – Granny Weatherwax is depicted as haggard and warty, despite a specific passage in the book in which Granny rues her inability to cultivate warts of any kind. Kirby was nodding to fantasy archetypes just as much as Pratchett – he'd drawn Rincewind as older and white-bearded because fantasy wizards *were* old and white-bearded. Granny had a hooked nose and warts because *that is what witches look like*. A perennial debate in Discworld fandom was between those praising Kirby for the way his art captured the spirit of Pratchett's work, and those who felt his poor attention to detail was somehow disrespectful to the text.[8] Pratchett was delighted with the cover, and was especially pleased with the way Esk's staff gushes magic from its tip while held in a position which is noticeably phallic, seeing it as proof that Kirby saw to the heart of his work.

Gollancz's increased marketing muscle meant that *Equal Rites* was reviewed more widely than any other Pratchett work, with many of the notices coming from outside the comfortable world of SF and fantasy. Broadsheet critics were starting to take notice and a snobbish tone was occasionally creeping in. 'Equal Rites brings to readers another dose of all-too-knowing absurdities,' begins John Clute's review in *The Observer*, 'but High Fantasy, as a form of Romance, is intrinsically unamenable to humour … . Pratchett is deeply hilarious only to those who believe deeply in the worlds depicted, and who secretly think the joke is on the rest of us.' Fortunately, other critics were kinder. Tom Hutchinson in *The Times* declared Granny Weatherwax 'now one of my favourite fantasy heroines', while *Time Out* praised the book as 'a great antidote to all of those sword 'n' sorcery fantasy dramas'.

As with *The Light Fantastic*, Corgi wasted no time in bringing *Equal Rites* out in paperback, and there was nothing modest about their ambitions. In November 1987, the company shipped 61,000 copies of the third Discworld novel out to stores and libraries, doubling the initial print run of its predecessor. It would need to be reprinted before the year was

---

8. However, neither camp would have been satisfied with a later version of the cover produced after both Pratchett and Kirby had died which, in a spectacular example of missing the point, *cropped Granny and Esk out altogether*, leaving only a rather minor character, the male wizard Cutangle.

out. As with *The Colour of Magic,* the book was serialised for broadcast on Radio 4's *Woman's Hour,* read by the actress Sarah Badel. As it had a feminist theme and was written by an author with a unisex name, a fair few listeners mistakenly believed Pratchett was female, and it came as something of a surprise when they were confronted by a small, bearded man at book signings.[9] *Equal Rites* was Pratchett's most successful novel to date. Two years and four Discworld novels later, it was still appearing in *The Telegraph*'s paperback chart.

Following the completion of *Equal Rites,* Pratchett told Neil Gaiman that he planned to put Discworld aside and return to his sci-fi idea about Valienté and the parallel Earths, explaining the concept during one of their numerous late-night phone calls. The pair had formed a strong friendship since their initial meeting in 1985, regularly sending each other their latest work and story ideas. Gaiman is even thanked in the acknowledgements for *Equal Rites,* alongside 'The kids in the H.P. Lovecraft Holiday Fun Club', a reference to the group of authors, including Gaiman, Langford, Mary Gentle, Kim Newman and Jo Fletcher, who were regularly found propping up the bar at conventions across the country. Gaiman loved the parallel Earth concept but voiced a nagging thought about the Discworld. 'Sounds brilliant', he said, 'but I think you should write a book about Death. He's my favourite character.' The next day, Pratchett phoned again, called him a bastard and told him his next novel would be called *Mort.*[10]

Work on *Mort* began as *Equal Rites* was making its way into the hands of Gollancz and Corgi. Pratchett was still working his day job at the CEGB, and at home his writing was taking on a frantic pace. The wait between books became shorter. Five-year gaps had separated *The Carpet People* in 1971, *The Dark Side of the Sun* in 1976, and *Strata* in 1981. Pratchett had no interest in working at such a leisurely pace any longer. He became obsessed with his 400-words-per-day target, hitting it whether it was Christmas Day or the day of his grandfather's funeral. He was determined to have a new book coming down the pipe at all times. If, after 300 words, he found he had finished a book, he would write the first 100 words of the next one. The gap between publishing *The Light Fantastic* and *Equal Rites* was just seven

---

9. Oddly this still happens. When I told a friend I was writing a biography of 'the author, Terry Pratchett', she replied, 'I've not heard of her, what does she write?'

10. This is probably the origin of a persistent fan rumour that Gaiman came up with the plot for a later book, *Reaper Man,* which also focused on Death.

months. *Mort* would follow eleven months after that. From 1987 to 1994 there would be at least two new Terry Pratchett novels every year.[11] In fact, starting with *The Light Fantastic* in 1986 and continuing through to *The Long Cosmos* in 2016, there would never be a year without a new Pratchett novel to look forward to. He even managed to get two novels published in 2015 despite having *actually died* in March of that year.[12]

For many Discworld fans, especially the faction that prefers the earlier books, *Mort* is considered the strongest of the series[13] and is often recommended as a good starting point for newcomers,[14] though curiously when professional critics write overviews of his work it tends to be overlooked. True, it's not as serious a book as *Equal Rites*, a work written by an author desperate to prove he could be more than just funny, but it's substantially more robust than *The Light Fantastic* or *Strata*. Pratchett would often say that it was with *Mort* that he discovered 'the joy of plot', though that does something of a disservice to his previous two novels. One of the factoids Pratchett was fond of littering throughout his interviews concerned the word 'masterpiece', which he had learned was originally used to describe a piece of work created by an apprentice to prove they were now a 'master' of their craft. Neil Gaiman, who knows rather a lot about this sort of thing, thinks *Mort* is Terry's 'masterpiece'.[15]

Like *Equal Rites*, it's the story of a rural adolescent at a crossroads in their life. Mort (short for Mortimer) is seeking an apprenticeship and is surprised when he is hired by Death and is trained in the art of soul reaping. It's one of Pratchett's most straightforward plots, which is probably why it's the Discworld novel most frequently associated with a movie adaptation, though as of the time of writing it remains unfilmed despite numerous false starts. Poor Mort must grapple with the morality of standing aside and letting people die, whether it be from old age or murder. There's intrigue, a mystery to be unravelled, an unrequited romance, which is handled very well, and a blossoming one, which feels a

---

11. He published just one novel in 1995, but he made up for it by producing three in 1996.
12. Pratchett wrote or co-wrote sixty novels before his death in 2015, which is extremely impressive, although it pales in comparison to Barbara Cartland's 722, twenty-six of which were published *in 1977 alone*.
13. It isn't.
14. It is.
15. Pratchett himself disagreed, and thought his actual 'masterpiece' was his 1993 young adult novel, *Johnny and the Dead* (see chapter 11).

little forced. It's a tightly plotted story with plenty of imagination, some beautiful writing (the scene where Mort tries to claim the life of an elderly witch is especially wonderful) and, naturally, the jokes are excellent and the references and homages on point.

The plot mechanics of *Mort,* and even its eponymous hero, are arguably secondary, however. You don't have to be a fluent Francophile to spot the pun in the title: *Mort* is a book about *two* characters, not one, and it's Death's story that really makes the novel sing. Gaiman's instincts, as usual, were good.[16] The Death Pratchett had hinted at in his last three books finally steps into the light, and the character is an utter joy: profound, proud, faintly melancholy, kindly in a severe sort of way, and very funny. There's an innocence about Death, and a good-natured bewilderment at the fundamentals of human nature that remains extremely likeable. Mort's mucking up the nature of reality might be what drives the plot, but it's Death that makes the book work. His fish–out–of–water attempts to join in with humans as he drinks in pubs, dances in a conga line and gets a job in a cafe, drip with humour and pathos. The character would make memorable cameos in almost every Discworld book, but his popularity really begins here.

Mort was published in hardback via the Gollancz/Smythe partnership on 12 November 1987, the day before Corgi sent 61,000 copies of *Equal Rites* out into the world. The breezy, likeable and solidly constructed fourth Discworld novel was, again, Pratchett's most successful to date, and his first to hit the national charts, where it peaked at number two. Every subsequent Pratchett novel would follow it into the bestseller lists. Corgi issued the paperback the following year, establishing a pattern of two new Pratchett hardbacks and two paperbacks per year, one of each published in the spring, and the second set before Christmas. This time Corgi almost doubled its print run to 111,500 copies. Yet again, another printing would be needed before the year was out.

By the middle of 1987, having delivered *Mort* and begun work on *Sourcery,* Pratchett realised, to his immense relief, that with some careful planning, he could finally give up full-time work and make the leap to full-time writer. Lyn was sceptical at first, and the pair combed through the

---

16. Very soon after this, Gaiman would create his own version of Death in *The Sandman* comic series. His was a lot sexier. Pratchett, in turn, would create a Sandman in the Discworld books. Again, Gaiman's is a lot sexier.

numbers until she was satisfied that the family could get by without Terry's regular salary. His main argument was that since the books were becoming the significant part of his income, time away from his writing desk was actually costing them money. Both agreed that it was a risk, but one worth taking. They formed a formal business partnership, and following *Sourcery* all Pratchett novels released within his lifetime would attribute copyright to 'Terry and Lyn Pratchett'. Lyn became Terry's default PA, helping sort his fan mail and manage his diary and finances. Terry resigned from the CEGB, giving three months' notice, and left the organisation in September, following a farewell party held, or so he claimed, on top of a nuclear reactor. Years later he would sign a book for one for his colleagues, Brian Gornall, a former station health physicist at Berkeley, one of the nuclear power stations under Terry's remit. 'To Brian,' it said, 'in memory of many happy days – and a few panicky weekends.'

The nature of Pratchett's relationship with Colin Smythe, his publisher since 1969, was also to change. For years Smythe had been brokering deals for Pratchett that went beyond the usual role of a publisher, and it was agreed that this arrangement should be formalised. Smythe became Pratchett's literary agent, a role he filled for the rest of Terry's career. In order to avoid a conflict of interests, Colin Smythe Ltd ceased publishing new Pratchett novels, and future books were put out by Gollancz or Transworld alone. Smythe's first act as Terry's agent was to secure an open-ended, six-book contract with a £51,000 advance from Gollancz for each book, a whopping £306,000, which Pratchett would tell journalists was the largest in the company's history. Terry Pratchett and the Discworld were now big business. According to *Venue* magazine, fans in 1988 spent £454,279 on *Mort* alone. When you consider that *The Colour of Magic*, *The Light Fantastic* and *Equal Rites* were still selling in their droves, *Strata* and *The Dark Side of the Sun* had been reissued by Corgi and that two new Discworld novels, *Sourcery* and *Wyrd Sisters*, had come out in hardback that same year, the money involved is quite staggering. The first thing Pratchett did with his advance was pay off the £1,400 left on his mortgage and begin building an extension to Gayes Cottage, which he referred to as the '*Mort* wing'. A journey that had started when Terry sold his first story as a 14 year old, had entered a new phase. He was now a full-time, best-selling author.

Chapter 10

When Shall We Three Meet Again?

Writing was now Pratchett's sole professional preoccupation. Where previously he would have a few precious hours in which to squeeze out his daily target of 400 words; he now had the whole day. The downside was that he also had no guaranteed regular income, and was pragmatic enough to know that literary success can be fleeting. If dinner was to continue to arrive on the table, then those vacant hours had to be filled with words. The word processor would be switched on when Rhianna was safely at school and would stay on until the early hours of the morning. Pratchett wrote in hourly chunks, broken up with other tasks in order to give his hindbrain time to work through problems and process ideas.

He had never lost the journalist's instinct to bash copy out quickly and with minimum fuss. His work ethic, learned from his parents, was extraordinary. The five years following the publication of *Mort* were the most prolific of his career, a golden period after he'd shed the distraction of a 'real' job, but before the growing industry around Discworld kept him away from his desk for longer and longer periods. Between 1988 and 1992, Pratchett would publish seventeen novels.

He was usually working on several books at once. In early 1988 he was overseeing the final proofs for the forthcoming Discworld novel, *Sourcery* while polishing the most recent draft of his next book, *Wyrd Sisters*, due in shops at the end of the year. At the same time, he was exploring the idea of expanding one of his old Uncle Jim stories – about gnomes living in a department store – into a new children's book, and updating *The Carpet People* for a new edition. He was also working on the first draft of a new Discworld novel, a parody of ancient Egypt called *Pyramids*, which involved plenty of research. Writing and planning new books was always his favourite part of the job, though he accepted the revisions, approvals and updates as necessary evils. He kept himself interested by dropping what he called 'sherbet lemons' into the text; new jokes, footnotes and even whole scenes which could arrive at any stage of the process between submitting the first draft, and the point when his publishers prised the work from his hands.[1] Were it not for publishing deadlines and the need to actually *sell* the things, Pratchett would happily have tinkered with his stories indefinitely – the first version of *The Carpet People* was published in 1965 and was still gaining sherbet lemons as late as 2014.

As his writing became richer, Pratchett developed several tics and techniques which were to become trademarks of his style. Alongside the sherbet lemons were the 'cigarettes', a word he used to describe the often-jokey extra scenes, character beats and pay-offs which took place after the climax of the main plot. Some were pure gags, others were quite beautiful pieces of writing that underlined the central theme of the book, and some were just clever ways of tying up loose ends. He would tell people that the phrase 'cigarettes' was a reference to old American cop shows, where the hard-boiled detectives and hard-bitten beat cops would smoke at their desks while explaining the plot to each other to make sure the audience at home had caught up. David Langford, writing in his foreword to the academic text *Terry Pratchett – Guilty of Literature*, has a more succinct summary – 'cigarettes after sex'.

The final novel in the Gollancz/Smythe deal, *Sourcery*, was published in hardback in May 1988. *Sourcery* is an odd point in the Pratchett canon in that it's the first novel that is demonstrably inferior to the one that came before. It's not a *bad* book, it's just that after the personal and surprisingly dark *Equal Rites,* and the near-perfect clockwork plotting of *Mort*, the fifth Discworld novel feels something of a throwback. In many ways, it's a direct successor to *The Light Fantastic* and the gag-heavy, parody roots of the series. The approach was entirely intentional. *The Colour of Magic* had been in print for six years and any readers stumbling across the series as it gained popularity would naturally gravitate to the earliest novels as an obvious starting point. Rincewind and the Luggage[2] had

1. The name 'sherbet lemons' was inspired by a sweet shop he remembered from his childhood whose proprietor would always add a few extra sweets to each bag, once the official amount had been measured.
2. He'd tried and failed to write the Luggage into *Equal Rites* and *Mort*. The latter originally had the homicidal suitcase playing a significant role, which was eventually sidelined so much it dropped out of the plot entirely.

become favourites of the burgeoning Discworld fandom, and a common theme in letters and at conventions and signings was 'when is Rincewind coming back?' Pratchett would learn later to trust his own instincts over the clamouring of fans, who as a rule tend to want more of the same. *Sourcery* represents one of the few times he bowed to their wishes. A plot had coalesced around the kind of adventure that suited the two characters.

Sourcery is the closest Pratchett would get to the epic fantasy of, say, David Eddings or Raymond E. Feist, and the only time he would try the classic orphan-child-with-strange-powers-and-a-mythical-destiny trope. It's the story of Coin, the eighth son of an eighth son of an eighth son, born with the limitless powers of a 'sourcerer' (the spelling is Pratchett's – a Discworld 'sourcerer' is a source of magic, rather than the more traditional sorcerer).[3] The little boy is controlled by the spirit of his dead father, the powerful wizard Ipslore the Red, whose essence resides in Coin's staff. Ipslore compels his son to assume command of Unseen University and lead a wizard uprising against the rest of the world. Meanwhile, a beautiful young barbarian woman has stolen a hat worn by generations of Unseen University's archchancellors, which has mysterious powers of its own. The spirit of the hat is determined to find a new wearer and fight back against the sourcerer in a wizard war that will surely destroy the Disc. Somewhere among all of this is Rincewind, trying to run away and once again finding himself in the thick of the action with the responsibility of saving the world. As plots go, it is somewhat more complicated than 'a young girl wants to be a wizard but isn't allowed' or 'Death takes an apprentice'.

Pratchett knew it wasn't his best work. During a 1988 Q&A, held at the Picon Six convention at Imperial College London, he admitted to being slightly embarrassed by *Sourcery*, saying it had been conceived as a gift for those fans who had jumped aboard with the first two books and might have felt short-changed by their less frivolous sequels. He spent far more of the session talking enthusiastically about the work-in-progress *Pyramids* than discussing the book he was supposed to be promoting.

---

3. This is also probably a nod to the tendency of British and American spelling to diverge over the letter 'u', as in 'colour'/'color', 'rumour'/'rumor' etc.

There's plenty to enjoy in *Sourcery* – it's extremely funny, for starters, crammed full of so many references and asides that you'd need to be a very well-read polymath to spot every joke. We get our first introduction to Lord Vetinari, the patrician of Ankh-Morpork; a character who would reappear throughout the series. In several ways, though, *Sourcery* feels like a regression. The world is at risk (again) with the real threat being the creatures from the Dungeon Dimensions (again), and it's all the fault of a youth who can't control their power (again). Pratchett's habit of giving characters complicated fantasy names is back with a vengeance, as we meet Conina, Ipslore, Coin, Spelter, Billias, and the Douglas Adams-ish Virrid Wazygoose, though we can probably let Pratchett have Nijel (a young, skinny nerd whose name is pronounced 'Nigel') and Abrim (whose main role in the story is to wear a hat) because a Discworld novel without puns barely counts as a Discworld novel at all.

After two books that served their female characters well, *Sourcery* struggles to make its sole woman protagonist three dimensional in any way except for her appearance. Conina, the daughter of *The Light Fantastic*'s Cohen the Barbarian, has three roles in the book – to be attractive to the male characters, to beat up and dispatch inconvenient baddies and as a walking gag (she's a deadly assassin who just wants to be a hairdresser). Considering how well rounded Esk, Granny Weatherwax and even *Mort*'s Ysabell were, it's a disappointing turn. She may as well exist with the sole purpose of giving Josh Kirby something to draw (and true to form, a scantily clad, karate-kicking Conina forms the focus of the jacket art). Pratchett was still struggling with the 'Kin Arad problem', finding confident women in their prime too far out of his comfort zone to be relatable. He was excellent at children and the elderly, and very good at awkward and damaged characters, but someone as sure of herself and as consciously sexy as Conina still gave him trouble. The problems, however, aren't with women alone: *Sourcery* draws its male characters just as thinly. Rincewind repeats his arc from *The Light Fantastic*, starting as cowardly and inept and ending as the unwilling saviour of the world, though his self-sacrifice at the story's climax is well-handled. Nijel, the wannabe barbarian, is a one-dimensional Dungeons and Dragons gag, Abrim, the grand Vizier of Klatch, is a pantomime villain, and the various wizards are either pompous and power-mad, or callous bureaucrats.

Only Coin, the unwilling boy sorcerer, and his father, Ipslore, who was banished from Unseen University for falling in love, have the suggestion of unexplored depths, though frustratingly those depths remain just as unexplored at the end of the novel.

If *Sourcery* feels underwhelming with thirty years of hindsight, no-one except Pratchett seemed to notice at the time. The book was another bestseller in both hardback and, the following year, in paperback. It was the first Pratchett book to hit number one in the national bestsellers list and hung around the chart for another three months. Retrospective reviews tend to be dismissive of *Sourcery*, but at the time critics fell over themselves in praise. *The Times'* Tom Hutchinson thought the book was '[Pratchett's] masterpiece',[4] the *Daily Mail* called it his best so far, *The Guardian* praised its style and *Time Out* branded it 'hilarious'. It's telling that almost every notice *Sourcery* received focused on how funny it was – which is absolutely fair, *Sourcery* has a rapid-fire gag rate. It's just a shame that that's *all* it really has. At the time Pratchett was seen first and foremost as a comic writer. Few people were disappointed by *Sourcery* because, in the popular imagination, this is exactly what Pratchett did – high-kicking fantasy romps, with plenty of jokes and a Josh Kirby drawing of a half-naked woman on the cover (true of three of the first five Discworlds). Its success crystalised Pratchett's public image, trapping him into a 'funny fantasy' pigeonhole from which it would take years to wriggle free. After all, of the five Discworld books in print and selling well, three were gag-led parodies.

His success continued throughout 1988, and new fans wanting to increase their collections were spoiled for choice. Demand for Terry's first three novels, *The Carpet People*, *The Dark Side of the Sun* and *Strata* increased with the popularity of Discworld, and since all three were long out of print, copies quickly became scarce.[5] Pratchett was keen to get his two SF books back into print (though he felt the more juvenile *Carpet People* would need to be substantially rewritten if it were to stand alongside

---

4. Whether he means this in the accepted sense of 'his most exceptional work', or the traditional, largely forgotten definition of 'graduation piece' is unclear. Either way, he's wrong.

5. Pratchett reckoned that most first editions of *The Carpet People* floating around were probably stolen from libraries.

his more recent work). Corgi agreed to republish *Dark Side* and *Strata*, commissioning new artwork from Josh Kirby and creating designs which echoed the Discworld books. Both hit shelves on 22 April, capitalising on the pre-release buzz around *Sourcery*, still a month away. By the end of 1988, Pratchett had six paperbacks in print, plus two new hardbacks. He worked hard to promote them, appearing at any convention that would have him, trying, as David Langford wrote in *Ansible*, 'to establish a new record for the most Guest of Honour appearances in a single year (and taking his life in his hands by giving the same speech every time).' He was an old hand at these events by now, even bringing a suitcase containing all the necessary ingredients to keep him in gin and tonic all weekend at conventions he predicted would have poor bar services or small hospitality tabs. He would cheerfully sign anything put in front of him, and happily accept a drink in the bar from anyone. As ever, he knew meeting fans was key to his longevity as an author.

November saw the publication of *Wyrd Sisters*, one of Pratchett's most beloved stories and a contender for the best of the early Discworld novels. If *Sourcery* felt like a backward step, *Wyrd Sisters* was a triple-jump forward. Granny Weatherwax was back, and this time she'd brought friends. The three witches at the heart of *Wyrd Sisters* are some of Pratchett's greatest creations – Granny, the powerful and proud unspoken leader of the coven; Nanny Ogg, who is every amiable, flirty old lady you've ever met in a pub at lunchtime, and Magrat, the textbook new age witch, a wide-eyed idealist hampered by her own naivety. The idea of three witches (or goddesses, or spirits) echoes back through history and literature, and Pratchett pulled from hundreds of different sources to put his trio together, from the old ladies he knew as a child, to the new age spiritualists he frequently encountered as a West Country journalist, to the poems of Robert Graves and the writings of the nineteenth-century occultist Aleister Crowley, via the twentieth century Wiccan idea of 'the maiden, the mother and the crone'.[6] Granny, Nanny and Magrat were birthed from centuries of fairytales and myths and seen through the prism of the three witches in Shakespeare's *Macbeth*.

---

6. Excellently explored in Pratchett's collaboration with Jacqueline Simpson, *The Folklore of Discworld*.

As with many of Pratchett's best ideas, the whole thing began with a joke. In later years he would grow tetchy when the word 'parody' was used to describe his work, seeing it as dismissive. With *Wyrd Sisters* it is an entirely fair description. Terry started the book with a single scene in mind and, so he claimed, no idea of the plot, theme or characters that would follow. All he had was the image of three witches on a wind-blasted moor, in the dead of night:

> As the cauldron bubbled an eldritch voice shrieked: 'When shall we three meet again?' There was a pause. Finally another voice said, in far more ordinary tones: 'Well, I can do next Tuesday.'
>
> – *Wyrd Sisters*

The scene, of course, parodies the opening of *Macbeth*; the 'weird sisters' on the moor, plotting the death of kings. Puncturing the melodrama with the ordinariness of 'I can do next Tuesday' is pure Pratchett, and the theme and character of the entire book really *can* be extrapolated from those five words. *Wyrd Sisters* takes the main beats of its story from *Macbeth*, with a few scenes plundered from other Shakespeare plays, and the occasional fairy story – the King of Lancre has been killed by his visiting cousin, and the land is now ruled by a foul usurper, Duke Felmet, and his wife. Meanwhile, three local witches have intercepted the king's baby son, the true heir to the throne, and decide to hide him among a troop of travelling actors. The plot is pure pantomime, though Pratchett pulls a neat bait-and-switch at the climax; a lesson in the untrustworthiness of stories.[7]

Many of the characters in *Wyrd Sisters* are as thinly sketched as those in *Sourcery*. Duke and Lady Felmet are one-dimensional villains, although that in itself is interesting – most of Pratchett's early novels forego such straightforward baddies, especially in the Discworld series. His favourite trick was to make a petty but ambitious bureaucrat the central antagonist, and make their hubris responsible for summoning terrible, destructive

---

7. Spoiler – the court jester ends up taking the throne, brilliantly foreshadowed earlier in the story with a line about how a new king would have to be a 'fool indeed'. Subsequently Pratchett would work this sort of early stealth spoiler into many books, if you knew where to look.

forces beyond their control. It is surely a coincidence that Pratchett had spent almost a decade working alongside civil servants in the nuclear power industry. Other characters include Nanny Ogg's grown-up children – a collection of bad habits and country bumpkin clichés, – various disposable palace guards, and a crew of actors, each sticking doggedly to one character type, with Hwel the Dwarven playwright an obvious caricature of the Bard himself. Even Tomjon, the hidden heir to the throne of Lancre, is painted with the thinnest of brushes. This too is an interesting creative choice. Every narrative instinct we have, every storybook experience coded into our cultural consciousness, expects Tomjon to be the hero of the piece. He is Prince Charming, charging in to save the day and take his rightful place on the throne. Pratchett has no truck with such expectations, and Tomjon is kept as a peripheral character. In earlier Discworld stories this would be played for a laugh. Here, the technique produces far more interesting results, as characters that would – in a lesser book – be peripheral are drawn into the space vacated by the prince.

This is why *Wyrd Sisters* rests on the shoulders of its central trio, and why the three witches are such an utter joy. Pratchett takes the blueprint of Granny Weatherwax found in *Equal Rites*, with all her stubbornness and skill, and adds greater magical power and, more usefully, a closer understanding of people. He also gives her accomplices. In Nanny Ogg, she has a sidekick who can respect and temper her power and is probably the funniest character Pratchett would ever create. Magrat, the younger witch, is in awe of Granny but also resents the two older women for their dismissive attitude. We never find out Magrat's exact age, but Pratchett's masterstroke here is to make her *slightly* older than her demeanour and naivety suggest, fuelling her resentment even more. The way she is treated by the older witches – Granny especially – reveals *their* flaws in turn. The three characters are impeccably drawn.

Wyrd Sisters is a stake in the ground in Pratchett's writing. He hits upon an idea that becomes fundamental to the series – that our expectations of how something *should* go effect how it *will* go. Later he'd give this a name: 'the theory of narrative causality'. Stories, clichés, myths, legend and folklore becoming self-fulfilling prophecies is a theme he would continue to explore throughout the books. Arguably it becomes the central thesis of Discworld.

It's in *Wyrd Sisters* that Pratchett's fundamental view of humanity starts to dictate his plotting. Much of the story consists of Granny Weatherwax explaining human nature and using it to her advantage. Nanny is an optimist, Magrat is an idealist, but Esme Weatherwax is a realist, and more often than not she's quoting Pratchett's worldview. Granny's realism, which importantly never quite edges into cynicism, is as much a reflection of the author as Rincewind's baffled exasperation with the universe.

There's a confidence in *Wyrd Sisters* that we haven't seen from Pratchett before. The plot gallops along and the gags keep coming, but nothing ever feels frivolous or out of place. It's the first time he feels comfortable enough to set a story in one location.[8] All of his other books had seen characters zip around their respective universes, and the five previous Discworld novels could all be considered grand tours. In *Wyrd Sisters*, the land of Lancre is almost a character in its own right. It grounds the narrative. It's also the first Discworld story that doesn't feel the need to put the whole world in jeopardy. This is a story of one tiny country, which makes it first and foremost a story about people.

It's not perfect by any means. The section where the witches move the whole kingdom forward fifteen years in order to allow Tomjon to come of age makes, frankly, no sense whatsoever if given more than a moment's thought[9], and the plotting relies on parody a little too often to feel truly inventive. Shakespeare himself does a lot of the narrative heavy lifting. It says everything about the characters, the atmosphere and the jokes that these issues feel totally inconsequential. *Wyrd Sisters* is a delight.

Critics, especially in the canny SF press, were starting to catch on to the fact that there was more to Pratchett's work than groan-inducing puns and well-aimed jabs at fantasy tropes. The suspicion that Discworld might have some literary merit of its own was starting to spread. Broadsheets

---

8. Alright, yes, the action does briefly move to Ankh-Morpork, but it's more of a cutaway. You could take those scenes out without causing much of an issue.

9. In Discworld fandom this became known as the 'Lancre time shift' and caused endless headaches for fans trying to plot the chronology of the books. Pratchett had said that the stories were in chronological order, and inserting fifteen years into book six has led to some very creative thinking among those trying to make the timeline work.

could still be sniffy, often seeing Pratchett as the concern of spotty 14 year olds that spoke Klingon (*The Sunday Times* and *Observer* were particularly guilty of this), but the genre press recognised his brilliance. A review in *White Dwarf* was one of the first to stop namechecking Douglas Adams and start referencing P. G. Wodehouse, while *Dragon Magazine* spotted that his 'lunacy is checked by wisdom'. The public was clearly in agreement. *Wyrd Sisters* entered *The Sunday Times*' hardback bestseller list at number one, a feat that would be repeated by every subsequent Pratchett novel.

In 1989, Pratchett published three novels, four short stories and a lightweight, illustrated book about cats.[10] Summer brought with it *Pyramids*, the seventh Discworld novel and a continuation of Pratchett's good form. It opens with a superb piece of writing, in which novice assassin Teppic (short for Pteppicymon) completes the harrowing final examination of the Assassin's Guild; a breathless run across the rooftops of Ankh-Morpork, scaling walls and avoiding traps. Pratchett would later say that this section was written in a trance-like state and that he had no idea where it was going. It was one of his favourite passages. He weaves the exam skilfully between flashbacks of Teppic arriving at the school as a young boy, an on-the-nose parody of the classic Victorian boarding school story *Tom Brown's School Days*. *Pyramids* set the template for future broad-brush Discworld parodies, in which Pratchett would take one topic – in this case, ancient Egypt (later, movies, rock music, Australia, newspapers and so on) – and wring as many jokes as possible from it, relying on the reader to know just enough about the subject to keep up with the gags. Sadly the book suffers due to Pratchett's occasional struggle to write realistic young people, and the hero, Teppic, feels rather flat; as does the heroine, PTraci, who like *Sourcery*'s Conina, is essentially there to give Josh Kirby someone curvy to put on the cover. The book does

---

10. As much as it pains me to say it, we really don't have room to talk about *The Unadulterated Cat*. We've got a hell of a lot to get through. Here's a summary: it's written as a guide to 'real' cats (as opposed to the pampered, pedigree sort), it's illustrated by Gray Joliffe, who created the *Wicked Willie* comic strips, it's pretty short and is quite funny in a leave-it-in-the-bathroom-to-read-on-the-loo kind of way. It's worth a look, especially if you like cats, but if you never get around to it, you'll probably be alright. It was the bestselling book in the UK in 1989, at least according to an article published by *The Wolverhampton Express and Star* in 1997. You'd think that would be mentioned more often.

have a cracking villain in Dios the high priest, however, and closes with a 'cigarette'[11] giving him an ouroboros-style fate that verges on genius. The habit of the citizens of the kingdom of Djelibeybi[12] of adding a silent 'P' to the beginning of names beginning with 'T' also gave Pratchett an online username, 'Pterry', still used by many fans today.

Pyramids was followed later that year by *Guards! Guards!*, a book which sits alongside *Wyrd Sisters* as one of the strongest of the era, and another excellent starting point. *Guards! Guards!* and *Wyrd Sisters* can be considered to be companion novels. Both take place in a single location, respectively the rural kingdom of Lancre and the sprawling, smelly metropolis of Ankh-Morpork, and both quietly subvert the reader's expectations by pulling bit players into the spotlight. *Guards! Guards!* is more explicit about this, and is dedicated to the faceless cronies whose sole job is to be killed by the hero of any given book or movie as he tries to reach the villain. However, there's a subtler twist on our assumptions at play here – and one that even Pratchett didn't see coming. The story is set up to follow Carrot, a young man of Adonis-like proportions, raised by Dwarves in the mountains, who comes to the city to seek his fortune, sporting a sword that never needs sharpening and charisma that could illuminate the sky. He may as well have 'true heir to the throne' written across his face in thick, black ink. Pratchett had intended Carrot to be the hero of the piece – his megawatt allure is so bright, even his own creator is taken in. The author put an inconvenient upturned rake in the road, though. He created Sam Vimes.

Vimes, like Granny and Rincewind, is a character that grew out of Pratchett's need to put his personality on the page. Vimes is a deposit for the author's burning anger, and is fuelled by a deep sense of injustice that Pratchett had so far managed to keep a lid on. The character is utterly flawed. He's a drunk, he spends his life miserable and despite a keen intelligence, has a habit of speaking truth to power that has kept him from rising further than the city's least-desirable command – captain of the night watch. Vimes would grow, becoming more complex and, if anything, angrier as the decades past, graduating to become comfortably

---

11. Additional material after the climax of the plot. Do keep up.
12. Say it out loud. Good, eh?

Pratchett's favourite character, and the one he returned to most often. In *Guards! Guards!* that anger has yet to be fully honed, but even so, Vimes is a formidable creation from the off, and as the story develops it becomes clear who the real focus of the piece is.

Guards! Guards! is also the book where the squalid city of Ankh-Morpork, like Lancre, becomes a character in itself. The revolting tumble of medieval streets and thatched roofs that Pratchett had created for *The Colour of Magic* had been a stand-in for pretty much any fantasy city. By *Guards! Guards!* it was beginning to feel like a real place, dragged forward from the Dark Ages to resemble renaissance London or Bucharest, mixed with a lawless, nineteenth-century New York. It has an internal logic to its guilds, temples, wizards and factions that gives the sense of a real working city, the perfect setting for a plot which is part dragon-slaying parody and part hardboiled crime thriller.

The book also introduced another of Pratchett's greatest comic creations – the everyman duo of Sergeant Colon and Corporal 'Nobby' Nobbs, the two reluctant, salt-of-the-earth guards usually found hiding out of the wind, having a quick smoke and discussing any passing plot. The homage is probably to Akira Kurosawa's 1958 film *The Hidden Fortress*, in which the focus stays on two bumbling idiots as an epic story unfolds around them.[13] Nobby and Colon act as a Greek chorus, though they never address the audience directly. They are the man on the street and the bloke in the pub and are usually the source of the book's best jokes.

Finally, *Guards! Guards!* adds a third patented Pratchett technique to the sherbet lemons and the cigarettes – 'figgins'. This was Terry's word for a running gag that resurfaces several times throughout the book, and is based on a joke in *Guards! Guards!* where a character threatens someone with having their figgin toasted. We later learn that a figgin is a type of bun. The phrase comes back several times to terrify people at cross purposes. The figgin technique would be used in almost every Discworld story.

The Discworld series was now seven years – and as many books – old, and had turned Pratchett into one of the country's most popular

---

13. George Lucas famously borrowed this technique for the opening third of *Star Wars*, with the peasants replaced by R2D2 and C-3PO.

writers. For many literary franchises that would be considered plenty but Pratchett was just getting started. There were thirty-four Discworld novels to come. It had taken seven books for Pratchett to develop the series past fantasy parody into something earthier and more interesting. Each of those first novels, with the possible exception of *Sourcery*, brings another building block to the structure, another colour to the palette, as Discworld becomes a mirror of our own world. Pratchett still had some growing to do as a writer, and it would be a while before he really cracked younger adults and, especially, young women, but the version of Discworld in which we find ourselves by *Guards! Guards!* is the template for the next decade of the series. The pieces are all in place, allowing Pratchett to revisit Rincewind, the Witches, Death, and the City Watch through subsequent novels, with the occasional new character thrown in. Somewhere, far below the streets of Ankh-Morpork and Lancre, the turtle still swam, but for characters and fans alike it was becoming less and less important. The Discworld was no longer just a platform for parody; it had become a place that actually *worked*.

Not everybody was pleased by this. Pratchett always said he would rather kill himself than continuously write new versions of *The Light Fantastic*, but that didn't appease a vocal part of Discworld fandom who preferred the knockabout traditional fantasy stories. Even some critics in the SF world were voicing concerns, with *Interzone*'s John Clute (who had warmed to Pratchett since making digs at Discworld readers in the *Observer*'s *Equal Rites* review) worrying that a speech about the inherent darkness of man delivered by Lord Vetinari in *Guards! Guards!* was the type of thing that 'comes close to shattering the comic pulse of the Discworld', and suggested the series needed resting before it became too serious for its own good. It's an interesting passage to single out, since it's one of the most powerful in the book, and probably the most revealing of Pratchett's personal philosophy. Clute was worrying about the wrong thing. For Discworld to survive, it *had* to grow up and echo more of its author. If Pratchett had continued to churn out books like *Sourcery*, it is doubtful he would have enjoyed the longevity he did.

The greater public didn't seem to mind the evolving tone, and sales of each book regularly surpassed the last. Publishers also realised that the words 'Terry Pratchett' on the jacket meant a book would likely sell by the truckload. In 1989, both Corgi's paperback of *Sourcery* and Gollancz's hardback of *Guards! Guards!* made the author's name bigger than the title of the book on the cover. All subsequent reprints of the first six Discworld paperbacks would switch the position of the title and author to emphasise Pratchett's name and growing brand. Even so, his next move would be risky – showing the world that he didn't need a giant turtle and a flat planet to succeed.

Chapter 11

The Children's Writer

The Discworld series was making Pratchett a household name, but he knew instinctively that there was more to life than turtles and elephants. As early as 1988, Colin Smythe had approached Corgi's children's editor, Philippa Dickinson, at Terry's request about publishing fiction aimed at younger readers which took place away from the Discworld. Pratchett had two projects in mind, both based on ideas he'd had early in his career. One was to expand a story he'd written for the *Bucks Free Press* into a trilogy, and the other was to update *The Carpet People*. By now there was growing interest in his pre-Discworld work, and while he was happy for *The Dark Side of the Sun* and *Strata* to be reprinted in their original forms, he felt that his debut novel would need substantial rewriting before it could sit alongside his more recent output. Both projects would emerge on hardcover via Transworld's Doubleday imprint, as Gollancz had no history with children's fiction. They would be his first children's novels in eighteen years.

First out of the traps was *Truckers*. It's the story of tiny 'nomes', 4-inch-high creatures that live their lives at ten times the speed of humans. The book's hero is Masklin, the hunter/gatherer of a dwindling nome tribe residing in a motorway layby, believing they are the last of their kind. The nomes are stunned when they discover that hundreds of their species have built an insular nome society beneath the floorboards of an old department store, no longer believing that the world outside of its walls exists. The story has its roots in the trip to Gamages department store Terry took with his mother as a 5 year old. His imagination had peopled the floors with tiny figures, hiding from the humans and coming out at night to wreak havoc. Perhaps more importantly, young Terry had *been* a tiny person in a giant department store and was dazzled by the scale of the place. Whenever he needed to tap into a sense of genuine awe, that memory was always waiting for him.

His first published attempt to capture that experience was in 1973. Pratchett had written a story called *Rincemangle, The Gnome of Even Moor*, which ran in the *Bucks Free Press* for eleven issues. It's a simpler, shorter version of *Truckers* aimed at a younger audience, with a smaller[1] cast and a less substantial threat. It was a charming enough tale, full of child-friendly wish-fulfilment. The gnomes use toy trains to create an underfloor rail network, race around in toy cars and play gnome-sized football with a Subbuteo set. Rincemangle, the outsider, encourages the gnomes to steal a lorry and escape back to his old home of Even Moor, just outside of Pratchett's go-to fictional market town of Blackbury.

As Colin Smythe says, Pratchett was 'not a person who would let good ideas go to waste', and fifteen years later, the story of Rincemangle was still playing on his mind. By now, of course, he'd recycled his main character's name in the Discworld series, but the plot was still there for the taking, and the idea – with its memorable image of hundreds of tiny creatures driving a truck by committee – was too good to leave in the forgotten pages of a local newspaper. The new version, retitled *Truckers*, emerged as a children's novel in 1989. The skeleton of the story remains largely the same, though once the nomes[2] reach the store there's less racing cars and playing football and more religion and politics. When Terry wrote for children he heightened the emotions just as he shortened the words, and spelled out his theme in great big letters. *Rincemangle* is a story about tiny people having fun, and working together to resolve their differences. *Truckers* is a book about the nature of faith and our perception of reality.

It's worth stopping here to nail down the difference between Pratchett's 'adult' and 'children's' books. Older children are quite capable of enjoying the Discworld series, though they might not get all the jokes.[3] Any adult can pick up the nomes' books and find them just as engaging as their grown-up cousins – and a more straightforward reading experience since Pratchett doesn't need to hide two dozen gags on every page. If you're 12 years old, with a foot in each camp, there's basically no difference at all. *Truckers* was written for the children's market, published by a children's

---

1. Relatively speaking.
2. Possibly the 'g' was traded in for the extra 'u' in 'Sourcery'.
3. Or at least you hope they don't.

imprint and given one of Josh Kirby's most cartoonish covers, but Pratchett always maintained that, with a more grown-up presentation, no-one would really have known the difference. As if to prove the point, *Truckers*, advertised as 'for readers of all sizes', not only topped the children's bestseller list, it appeared in the adult hardcover chart as well, prompting a livid letter in industry magazine *The Bookseller* from the director of rival publishers Penguin Children, who claimed Pratchett was getting preferential treatment.[4]

Pratchett used the simple plot of *Rincemangle, The Gnome of Even Moor* to ask complicated questions. To the nomes, the store is the entire universe, with Arnold Bros (est. 1905) – the name of the store – as a god figure at the centre of a detailed religion. Nothing can exist outside of the store, because nothing can exist outside of the universe. Signs like 'Everything under one roof'; 'If you do not see what you require, please ask' and 'Everything must go!' become religious commandments. Ultimately *Truckers* is not a story about mythical little people, department stores or lorries. It's a story about a world that is so much bigger than you could ever have expected, which also makes it a story about leaving childhood. This theme is underlined in *Diggers*, his second book of the series, published in 1990. Grimma, the female protagonist and the cleverest and most capable of the nomes, rants at a bewildered Masklin when he suggests they get married, quoting from a book she'd found in the store. The speech is one of Pratchett's most famous pieces of writing:

> Right in the top branches of the trees there are these, like, great big flowers called bromeliads and water gets into the flowers and makes little pools ... these little frogs live their whole lives in the flowers ... and don't even know about the ground.

Discovering that the world is so much bigger than you'd ever dreamed, and that you may never get to see all that is to be seen, can be heartbreaking. Pratchett understood this feeling. It's one he had experienced himself, as he worked his way along the shelves of Beaconsfield Library as a

---

4. Colin Smythe claims that *Truckers* was the first book ever to feature in both lists, though *The Bookseller* points out that works by Salman Rushdie and Sue Townsend had also done 'the double'.

boy, feeling the universe opening like a flower. It crops up continually in his work. It's there in Twoflower, devastated because he can't visit every planet in the sky in *The Colour of Magic*. It's there in Cohen the Barbarian, sulking because there are no more worlds left to conquer in *The Last Hero*.

The passage lends the series a perfect collective name: *The Bromeliad*.[5] The final novel in the series, *Wings*, ends perfectly with Masklin delivering a bromeliad flower to Grimma, showing her that, finally, he understands.

The *Bromeliad* novels were fantastically successful and played a large part in establishing the longevity of Pratchett's fanbase. *Truckers* was shortlisted for the prestigious Smarties Prize, Pratchett's first major award nomination outside of the SF scene. An unofficial panel of children declared it the overall winner, though sadly the official judges didn't agree.[6] The snub didn't hurt the commercial success of the series. By the time *Wings* was published in paperback in 1991, the three books sat together at the top of the children's bestseller list. The success of *The Bromeliad* was a vital step in Pratchett's career, and its influence rippled forward in time. Many an adult Pratchett fanatic, buying every new novel on the day of publication, started their career as a 10 year old reading *Truckers*.

Truckers was also the first Terry Pratchett novel adapted for the screen. An animated series based on the book debuted on ITV in 1992, made by the British studio Cosgrove Hall Films, responsible for classic cartoons such as *Danger Mouse*, *Count Duckula*, *Chorlton and the Wheelies* and *Jamie and The Magic Torch*. Co-founder Mark Hall had pitched a stop-motion animation of *Truckers*, to be made by the same team behind the BAFTA and Emmy-nominated adaptation of *The Wind in the Willows*, and Pratchett was impressed enough to commission the studio over a handshake. Four other companies, including big American players, had pitched for the rights, but Pratchett remained convinced that Cosgrove Hall would do the best job, and Hall was impressed by Pratchett's loyalty.

---

5. The name could be a play on David Eddings' hugely successful series *The Belgariad*, though it's more likely that both were a nod back to Greek myth and *The Iliad*.

6. One of the reasons judges marked the book down was because, absurdly, it promised a sequel. This prompted a livid Phillipa Dickinson, Pratchett's editor at Doubleday, to write a sharp letter to *The Bookseller* listing children's classics that had been part of a series.

The series is exquisite, and comfortably the studio's most accomplished piece of filmmaking. The stop-motion puppets are flawless, and the writing captures the heart of Pratchett's work. The animators felt they'd created something nuanced and quite grown-up and were surprised and disappointed when Thames TV chopped it into ten-minute chunks and gave it a late-afternoon slot, usually reserved for shows aimed at younger children. It's an odd decision considering the weighty themes and dark tone of the show ... and the fact that a character is eaten by a fox in the first five minutes. Despite going out at a time more befitting of *Postman Pat*, *Truckers* was still popular and received generous write-ups in the press. A full-length cut was even submitted to the 1993 Chicago International Film Festival, where it claimed the prize for Best Animated Picture. Unfortunately, a planned second series, which would have covered *Diggers* and *Wings*, was scrapped after Thames Television lost its ITV franchise.[7]

The Bromeliad, alongside *Mort* and *Good Omens*, is also one of the few Pratchett properties continually associated with a movie adaptation. Steven Spielberg's Dreamworks studio obtained the rights to the books in 2001 for a reported $1 million, with producer Jeffrey Katzenberg taking a private jet from Hollywood to Somerset to close the deal. Dozens of big names were attached over the years, though the movie never escaped that most Hollywood of traditions, development hell. The excitement around the project ebbed away soon after the deal was done, and Pratchett believed that the unexpectedly huge success of 2001's *Shrek* meant the studio cleared the decks to make Shrek 2, 3 and 4. The *Truckers* movie came to life again in 2008 with Oscar winner Danny Boyle set to direct from a script by Frank Cottrell Boyce. A year later, Boyle's *Slumdog Millionaire* collaborator Simon Beaufort took over scriptwriting duties, though by this point Boyle was off the project: 'That fell apart,' he told *Empire* magazine that year. 'It's sad – wonderful books.' Dreamworks was still looking for a director in 2010, by which time a writer called Craig Fernandez had rewritten Beaufort's script, which he retitled *Everything*

---

7. Until very recently ITV comprised dozens of local broadcasters, sometimes all showing the same programme, and sometimes showing regional variations. Thames Television had owned a stake in Cosgrove Hall Films, so when it lost its ITV franchise, Cosgrove Hall lost a lot of funding.

Must Go. The last concrete news on a *Truckers* movie came in 2011. TV director Anand Tucker was attached to direct, with a script by John Orloff, who had recently written the children's fantasy *Legends of the Guardians: The Owls of Ga'Hoole*. Eventually, the whole concept was deemed too similar to that year's hit *Gnomeo & Juliet* and the project was quietly dropped, though not before an attempt was made to merge Pratchett's nomes with the big-haired classic Danish Troll dolls, as Dreamworks had recently acquired the movie rights to the toys. The idea of Masklin, Angelo and Grimma rendered as pudgy, naked figures with huge eyes, faint smiles and giant, coloured tufts of hair is an uncomfortable one.[8]

In 1992 Doubleday published a substantially rewritten version of *The Carpet People*, with an author's note informing the reader that this was a collaboration between two writers. One was a 43-year-old bestseller called Terry Pratchett, and the other was a wet-behind-the-ears 17 year old, also called Terry Pratchett. As ever, Pratchett had simplified reality somewhat. It seems particularly unfair on the 22 year-old Terry Pratchett that he doesn't get credit for the rewrite he did around 1970.

The Carpet People had already received a few significant overhauls since Terry first dreamed up the idea at school. Each revision tells us something about the writer he'd become. The story printed in the *Bucks Free Press* in 1965 was imaginative but naive, while the novel published by Colin Smythe in 1971 was beautifully written, but derivative and comprised of stock parts. The 1992 revision shows us how far Pratchett had come. Just as the simple, rather silly story *Rincemangle, The Gnome of Even Moor* had been used as the base stock for the more sophisticated *Truckers*, the *Lord of the Rings*-lite adventure of *The Carpet People* became darker, more nuanced, and funnier. The description of Glurk as 'a man of few words, but words worth waiting for' becomes, 'He's a man of few words, and he doesn't know what either of them mean.' The world of the carpet now felt more tangible, and its society more complicated. Pratchett was letting his themes, rather than the plot lead his writing. As a young man, he'd thought fantasy was about 'battles and kings', as he says in his

---

8. Dreamworks, of course, went on to make a Trolls movie anyway. Quite predictably, it was a massive success.

author's note. As an older man, he knew the most interesting questions were about how desperately both should be avoided.

He added an abstract inner world to the characters, and deepened the mysticism that underpins any fantasy story worth its salt. In the updated version, Snibril can sense when the mysterious Fray is going to attack, suffering an intense pressure inside his head. The evil Mouls can sense it, too; creating a connection between characters that was never there before. The mysterious Wights are stripped of their more obvious Elvish tendencies and instead are given the very Pratchettian ability to 'remember' the future, a gift that would also be given to Death in the Discworld series. It's a more distinctive and narratively exciting idea than the Elder mystics of the original novel.

Lastly, the writing here is simply better. Pratchett had learned to show, rather than tell. Lumps of exposition previously revealed in dialogue are now buried in the action, or even hinted in the subtext. He skips through the book pruning excitable adjectives, unnecessary exclamation points and generic fantasy clichés from the dialogue. Occasionally the voice of Pismire, reinvented here as drier and more scatterbrained than 1971's budget-Gandalf, passes comment on the emotional language used by any character that sticks to their 1971 script. It's a level of self-awareness the younger Pratchett was simply not capable of. Ed James, writing in the 2004 edition of *Terry Pratchett: Guilty of Literature*, believes that the updated Pismire became a cypher for Pratchett himself, quietly judging the writer he'd been in the very pages of his own book.

The battle scenes are reworked substantially, and a great deal of elbow grease has gone into rebuilding the end of the book. There are entire sweetshops of sherbet lemons added here, and whole tobacconists' worth of cigarettes. Our heroes don't just defeat their foes; they realise the need to make their world fairer and more equal. It's telling that all the best lines, many of the memorable images and most of the central themes in the 1992 version aren't present at all in 1971.

By polishing and improving the work of his younger self, rather than scrapping it entirely and starting again, we're left with something of a curio. It's not quite the historical document of the original – which is now almost impossible to track down and changes hands for enormous amounts of money – and it's not quite the tightly plotted adventure the

Terry Pratchett of *Truckers* and the Discworld would have written. Still, the book did well among audiences and critics. *The Bromeliad* had proven that Pratchett could write serious children's fiction, and *The Carpet People* was received in the same spirit. Like *Truckers*, it appeared on both the adult and children's bestseller lists.

The 1992 *Carpet People* finally gave Pratchett's debut novel – a story that meant a great deal to him – the readers it deserved. It was only a modest success by the standards of his 1990s output but still reached an audience Pratchett and Smythe could scarcely have imagined twenty years earlier. The original hardback had a print run of just 3,000, and copies were still available when Corgi published *The Colour of Magic* over a decade later (Roger Peyton still had it in stock at *Andromeda*, in 1985*)*, though they sold out pretty quickly after that. The new version had a hardcover run of 18,000 and an initial paperback printing of 115,000. It has been reprinted numerous times, including, finally, a proper US edition in 2013, which used Pratchett's original artwork for the first time since 1971.[9]

Despite its origins, the 1992 version of *The Carpet People* could be considered a fairly typical 'Terry Pratchett', with its fantastical concept and Josh Kirby cover. The same cannot be said of *Only You Can Save Mankind*, published three months later. *Only You* was one of two stories Pratchett had been working on about an introspective 12 year old called Johnny Maxwell. The second idea became *Johnny and the Dead*, and emerged the following year, while a third Johnny Maxwell story, *Johnny and the Bomb*, was published in 1996. *Johnny and the Dead* was intended as the first book in the series, but was pushed back in favour of *Only You Can Save Mankind*, as the outbreak of the Gulf War made its story topical, and Pratchett worried someone else might sieze on the same idea: that the ubiquity of war footage desensitised the viewer until it became as real to them as a video game.

The Johnny Maxwell books, like the three novels of *The Bromeliad*, are among Pratchett's most poignant and most pointed, and their messages are writ large so as not to be missed by an adolescent reader. The three books have a contemporary setting, and the action takes place more or

---

9. The 1992 edition and subsequent printings used covers by regular Discworld artists Josh Kirby and Paul Kidby because Transworld know brand recognition when they see it.

less in the year each book was published, hence the specific mid-Gulf War setting of *Only You* and references to *The X-Files* and a barrage of sci-fi movies in *Johnny and the Bomb*. While the setting made the stories relevant, it dated the books quickly. The video games in *Only You Can Save Mankind* might baffle a twenty-first century teenager. (Joysticks? Discs? Manuals? Even the notion of buying games in a shop is becoming archaic in the age of downloads and micropayments.) As would the pop culture references, such as Kirsty's *Alien 3* poster, nickname of Sigourney, or mentions of Stormin' Norman.[10] Even more dated is the slang used by the kids; 'yo', 'rad' and 'well wicked' all sounded hopelessly naff after just a few years, though the idea of teenagers frantically trying to keep their buzzwords up to date will presumably always be relevant.

What hasn't dated are the book's themes and the way they capture the difficulties of adolescent life. Johnny, the introverted dreamer, less a hero and more someone things just happen to, will resonate with many. Here Pratchett is channelling his younger self, a compulsive worrier with a fertile inner imagination. The three books quietly, and with minimum fuss, nod to racism, sexism, mental health, suicide, grief, cultural guilt, desensitisation and the pressures put on young, working-class men while still being proudly about aliens, ghosts and time travel. Some readers assume the supernatural elements of the stories are intended to be read as daydreams or hallucinations and that the books are about a boy who processes his pain by creating imaginary worlds. This theory is supported by a line in *Johnny and the Bomb* when the character of Yo-less speculates that his friend is reacting to the depression and stress he suffers due to the 'troubled times' of his parents' divorce. Pratchett poured cold water onto this theory when asked about it online. To him, Johnny really did fight alongside aliens, talk to dead people and travel in time.[11] The books might be set mostly in the 'real' world, but at heart, Terry would always be a sci-fi and fantasy writer.

---

10. The nickname given to General Norman Schwarzkopf, the commander of the allied forces in the first Gulf war. Presumably, he was one to enter rooms with unexpected enthusiasm.

11. It's pretty clear actually – in *Johnny and the Dead* the 'dead' use a phone to call a local radio show, and Johnny's friends see them levitating a newspaper. At the end of *Johnny and the Bomb* most of the boys instantly forget the adventure, but Kirsty remembers again, while the time-travelling Mrs Tachyon eats chips in 1996 wrapped in paper from 1941.

ligh Wycombe Technical School, 1961, hotographer unknown. Terry is bottom row in he middle (making a face). (*Ivan Sparrow*)

Terry and Lyn on their wedding day in 1968, as it appeared in the *Bucks Free Press*. It is one of the last times Terry was seen without a beard. (*Photographer unknown*)

'he subs' room at the *Bath Evening Chronicle*, circa 1975. Gerald Walker is on the right. Terry (who ; not in the photo) would sit at the desk on the left. The tall journalist with the bow tie in the back is rmer BBC royal correspondent, and later Harrods spokesman, Michael Cole. (*Provided by Gerald Walker; photographer unknown*)

The staff of the *Bath and West Evening Chronicle*, taken from the centenary editon of the paper i 1977.

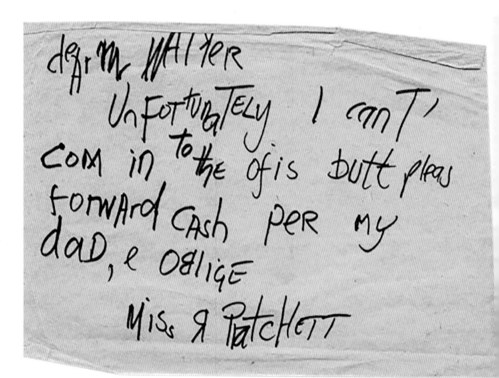

A note to Gerald Walker from a young Rhianna Pratchett declining the offer of an ice cream, sometim in the late 1970s. (*Gerald Walker*)

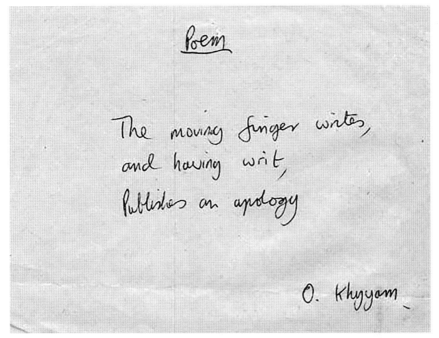

Poem

The moving finger writes,
and having writ,
Publishes an apology

O. Khyyam

A handwritten note passed from Terry to Gerald Walker at the *Western Daily Press*, featuring a quote from the eleventh-century poet Omar Khayyam, some time in the late 1970s. (*Gerald Walker*)

Terry at the first ever Discworld Convention in 1996, with The Guild of Fans and Disciples' Elizabeth Alway dressed in costume as Magrat Garlick. (*Elizabeth Alway*)

Josh Kirby working on the jacket art for *The Last Continent*, circa 1997. (*The Josh Kirby Estate*)

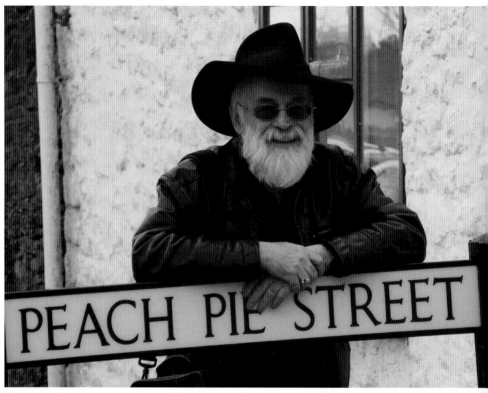

Terry attending a street naming in Wincanton, the Somerset town that is twinned with his fictional cit of Ankh-Morpork, the location of the original Peach Pie Street, April 2002. (*Discworld Monthly*)

Terry with a fan cosplaying Tiffany Aching at the 2003 Clarecraft Event in Woolpit, Suffolk. (*Ian Oldroyd*)

At the 2005 Clarecraft Event in Woolpit, Suffolk, with a fan-made prop themed around *Monstrous Regiment*. (*Ian Oldroyd*)

Terry with Bernard Pearson, aka 'The Cunning Artificer', at a Hogswatch Christmas party, December 2004 in Wincanton, Somerset. (*Ian Oldroyd*)

Terry at an event to celebrate twenty-one years of Discworld, held at the Royal Society of Arts, London, September 2004. He is pictured with a model of The Octavo, the spellbook that appears in the first two Discworld novels. Created by Bernard Pearson, it would later reside in Terry's study. (*Ian Oldroyd*)

At the 'Sweet FA Cup', a football match organised to promote *Unseen Academicals*, Wincanton, Somerset, 2005. (*Discworld Monthly*)

Terry at the 2005 Worldcon, held in Glasgow. (*Szymon Sokół, Wikimedia Commons*)

Terry with Discworld fan Davina, at an event in Wincanton, Somerset, April 2005. (*Discworld Monthly*)

Terry with fans at an event in Wincanton, Somerset, April 2005. (*Discworld Monthly*)

Terry at the Discworld Emporium, with Bernard Pearson looking on, April 2006. (*Discworld Monthly*)

Artwork created by Josh Kirby for the Discworld video game, 1995. (*The Josh Kirby Estate*)

On stage at the 2008 Discworld Convention in Birmingham, not long after announcing his Alzheimer's diagnosis. (*Ian Oldroyd*)

Terry enjoying a Guinness after receiving his honorary degree from Trinity College Dublin, 2008. (*Patrick Theiner, Wikimedia Commons*)

At the 2010 Discworld Convention gala dinner in Birmingham. (*Ian Oldroyd*)

Terry with a fan at the 2010 Discworld Convention. (*Ian Oldroyd*)

Team Terry at the 2010 Discworld Convention gala dinner. L-R: Terry, Professor Ian Stewart (co-author of *The Science of Discworld* series), Stephen Baxter (co-author of *The Long Earth*), Colin Smythe, Professor Jack Cohen (the other co-author of *The Science of Discworld* series). (*Ian Oldroyd*)

Terry gives a speech following a performance of *Maškaráda čili Fantom opery*, an adaptation of *Maskerade*, Prague, March 2011. (*Wikimedia Commons*)

The midnight launch event for *The Shepherd's Crown*, Waterstones Piccadilly, London, featuring *Discworld Monthy*'s Rachel Anthony-Rowlands in costume as Tiffany Aching, August 2015. (*Discworld Monthly*)

A knight based on Terry, created by Paul Kidby as part of the Barons Charter project, sighted in Salisbury, England, as part of the celebrations around the 800th centenary of the sealing of Magna Carta. (*Richard Avery, Wikimedia Commons*)

Rhianna Pratchett, appearing with colleagues to discuss her work on *Rise of the Tomb Raider* at the Game Developers Conference, March 2016. (*Official GDC*)

ob Wilkins and Paul Kidby answer questions at the Chalke Valley History Festival, June 2016. (*Discworld Monthly*)

ob Wilkins with *Discworld Monthly*'s Rachel and Jason Rincewind Anthony-Rowlands at the Chalke alley History Festival. (*awdphotography.co.uk*)

Discworld Monthly's Jason Rincewind Anthony-Rowlands with Stephen Briggs and … Stephen Briggs, at the 2016 Discworld Conventi[on] in Birmingham. (*Le[e] Brook*)

The plaque outside Beaconsfield Library, where Terry worked as a Saturday boy in his youth. (*Author's own*)

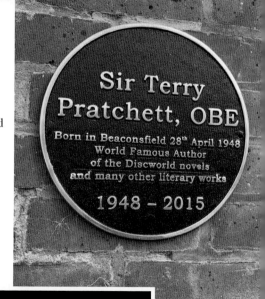

Sir Terry
Pratchett, OBE
Born in Beaconsfield 28th April 1948
World Famous Author
of the Discworld novels
and many other literary works

1948 – 2015

Lowri Belson as the Librarian in a costume by Lizzie Mulhall, taken from a performance of *Guards! Guards!* by Monstrous Productions, directe[d] by Amy Davies. (*Photo by Craig Harper, provided by Nick Dunn*)

eil Gaiman and the cast of the Good Omens TV show (Miranda Richardson, Michael Sheen, Jon Iamm and director Douglas Mackinnon) discuss the show at New York Comic Con, October 2018. *Rhododendrites, Wikimedia Commons*)

ast and crew of the *Good Omens* TV show, at the premiere in London, 2019. (*Discworld Monthly*)

Terry Pratchett on day two of the 2012 New York Comic Con, Friday, 12 October 2012, at the Jaco K. Javits Convention Center in Manhattan. (*Luigi Novi, Wikimedia Commons*)

The trilogy is full of stunning moments and beautiful writing. Bigmac's discovery of his mate's dead body in *Only You Can Save Mankind* saw Pratchett reflecting on his own experience of death as a trainee reporter. It's an effective piece of writing, leaving a young man shaken as he's confronted by grim reality for the first time. There are emotional subplots for each of Johnny's friends across the three books, ticking away behind the main story. Bigmac shrugs himself free of his bullying family; Kirsty learns that her feminist outlook and hyper-intelligent views on welfare and society mean she occasionally ignores the humanity in others; while the character of Yo-less explores blunt racism, and a subtler stereotyping that can't accept a young, black kid as thoughtful, academic and uncool. In *Johnny and the Bomb* Pratchett deploys, for the only time in his published career, the word 'nigger', detonating it like a landmine in the middle of the text in a way that makes the reader question its use and the effect on those who have the word thrown at them on a daily basis. It created some friction between Pratchett and his editor, Philippa Dickinson, who wanted it removed. Pratchett planned to use the word as a bargaining chip to get other provocative or contentious ideas into the novel instead. Dickinson yielded, however, and the expletive made it into the final book.

Pratchett told BBC's *Blue Peter* in 2006 that the Johnny books had been his favourite to write, though since he was promoting a TV adaptation of *Johnny and the Bomb*, he may have just been playing up to the theme of the day. It would be entirely in character. He was certainly proud of the trilogy and considered the poignant *Johnny and the Dead* to be his 'masterpiece', in the sense that it was the book that marked the end of his apprenticeship as an author. *Vector*'s Martin Taylor agreed, calling it 'the best he has ever written, one that would shift him – if there was any justice – from the ranks of "mere" bestsellerdom and into the realm of literature.' The three books are full of personal references, far more than most of his other work. *Only You Can Save Mankind* channels his love of video games – especially space adventures such as *Wing Commander* – set against his natural distaste for jingoism and war. *Johnny and the Dead* is peopled with characters from his past, not least the avowed socialist William Stickers, based on his old *Bucks Free Press* colleague George Topley. Here he touches on an evergreen Pratchett bugbear – grey-faced bureaucrats advancing an agenda at the expense of ordinary people – and the fascinating lives to be found behind every curtain, and in every head. Finally, *Johnny and the Bomb* takes its inspiration from *The Bath Blitz*, a book about the bombing of the city of Bath during the Second World War, written by Pratchett's old *Bath Chronicle* colleague, Martin Wainwright. Terry had given the book an enthusiastic review back in 1975. A theme from *Johnny and the Bomb* – that time can also be a place – would reappear in another of Pratchett's very best works, 2002's *Night Watch*.

The *Johnny* books, with their dated contemporary setting, tend to be discussed less often and less fondly than the *Bromeliad* trilogy, though they made a significant impact on publication. *Johnny and the Dead* was the first Pratchett novel to receive almost unanimous praise from the literary establishment, which seemed to have an easier time accepting a fantasy author if his work was aimed at children. It was named Best Children's Book by the Writers' Guild of Great Britain, and was nominated for the Carnegie Medal, comfortably the most prestigious prize for children's literature in the UK, (it missed out on the prize due to having 'too many big words', according to one judge, who complained that 'my nephew didn't understand it'), and earned Pratchett a place on the shortlist for Children's Author of the Year. *Johnny and the Bomb*, meanwhile, avenged the snubbed *Truckers* by taking the silver award in the 'ages 9–11' category of the 1997 Smarties Prize, received another Carnegie Medal nomination and, along with *Only You Can Save Mankind*, made the shortlist for *The Guardian*'s Children's Fiction Prize. Both *Johnny and the Dead* and *Johnny and the Bomb* were adapted into well-received TV dramas, though they were filmed nearly a decade apart and broadcast on different channels. Both featured a high-profile cast of venerable British actors, and Brian Blessed's performance as William Stickers is especially memorable. Less predictably, *Only You Can Save Mankind* was turned into a stage musical in 2004. Pratchett sold the rights to producer Sarah Broadhurst for an old-fashioned sixpence, reasoning that anyone mad enough to attempt that particular story as a musical needed all the encouragement they could get. The show ran at the Edinburgh Fringe to decent reviews, and a soundtrack album was released, though a hoped-for transfer to the West End never materialised.

The seven[12] children's novels written by Pratchett between 1988 and 1996 were a crucial part of his development as a writer and literary figure. The popularity of the *Truckers* books essentially future-proofed his audience, and the Johnny Maxwell stories won fans in the burgeoning 'young adult' market. The two trilogies, and to a lesser extent *The Carpet People*, also proved that there was more to Pratchett than the Discworld. He was far from a one-trick turtle; he could tackle the biggest of issues and make them work for the smallest of readers. His journey from oddball cultist to 'Professor Sir Terry Pratchett, OBE, national treasure and accepted literary genius' would have been a lot less likely had he kept churning out Discworld stories at the expense of all else. It's something a lesser publisher than Transworld and a lesser agent than Smythe might have encouraged a lesser writer than Pratchett to do. The Discworld, after all, was a cash cow. Children's books carried smaller advances, generally sold fewer copies for less money, and without the brand recognition of the Discworld presented a far greater risk.

After the publication of *Johnny and the Bomb* in 1996, Pratchett put children's fiction aside, dedicating his time to the Discworld and the growing cottage industry that surrounded it. It would be another five years before he returned to his younger readers.

---

12. Alright, six and a half.

Chapter 12

The Satanic Verses:
The Making of A Cult Classic

S omewhere in 1985, shortly after he had interviewed a part-time fantasy author (and full-time press officer) in a Chinese restaurant in Soho, Neil Gaiman had an idea for a story. Like all the best story ideas it hinged on a simple, brilliant concept: retell the plot of the classic horror movie *The Omen* in the style of Richmal Crompton's *Just William* books. He envisioned a mix up at a hospital that meant the son of Satan, intended to be raised by a powerful American diplomat, grows up in a sleepy English village, away from the influence of Satanic powers. At the same time an inept demon and a prissy angel, whose rivalry down the centuries has developed into a comfortable familiarity, are less than thrilled at the prospect of impending Armageddon and attempt to put a spanner in the works. Gaiman worked on the first 5,000 words of the story, which he titled *William The Antichrist*, bringing the tale up to the point where incompetent Satanic nurses mixed up two babies. And there he stopped, because he didn't really know what happened next.

At the same time he was working on an official companion book to Douglas Adams' *The Hitchhiker's Guide To The Galaxy*, which meant interviewing Adams extensively at his home in Islington, north London, and discussing the development of his famous work. Inevitably something of Adams' tone seeped into *William the Antichrist*, and melded with the intentional nods to Crompton, and the strata of Englishness Gaiman wanted to layer into the story. The result was a wry, oddball and humorous style, not dissimilar to another book Gaiman had read recently – set on the back of a giant turtle, written by a full-time PR man who dressed like a driving instructor, whom Gaiman now counted as a good friend. He sent copies of the story to several people whose opinions he respected, and because he had a vague idea that he could do for horror what *The Colour of Magic* had done for fantasy, one of those people was

Terry Pratchett, who read it, was intrigued, and then metaphorically, and indeed literally, popped it in a drawer for later.

On the surface, Neil Gaiman and Terry Pratchett were not obvious friends. Pratchett was twelve years older, for starters. The son of a mechanic and secretary, his work ethic was shaped entirely by his working-class background and a post-war culture of 'making the best of it'. After leaving school he trained diligently in his chosen profession, spending his twenties and most of his thirties, creating a settled and solid life in the country, based around work, nature and family. Gaiman, meanwhile, was the son of a property broker who became head of the Church of Scientology in the UK. He was a product of the 1960s and 1970s, an era in which creativity, art and rebellion seeped into the youth culture of the country.

At the age Pratchett discovered full-time work, Gaiman was discovering punk rock, fronting a Lou Reed-influenced DIY punk band called the Ex-Execs, who played around the London scene knocking out covers of Bowie, The Stranglers and the New York Dolls, as well as a handful of Gaiman-penned originals. Unlike Pratchett, who could charitably be called eccentric with his hooped sweaters and scraggly beard, Gaiman was *cool*. He was good looking and tall, wore a leather jacket and had unruly black hair.[1] When the pair met, Pratchett was a company man who had worked for just two employers for the best part of a decade, while Gaiman was an odd-job writer, taking on any work he could. He reviewed films and books and wrote features for top-shelf magazines including *Penthouse* and *Knave*, the latter of which he helped evolve (albeit briefly) into a classier 'read'. His career was an opportunity to write thousands of words about the pop culture he loved, with the added bonus of getting into gigs and movies for free, getting sent records and books to review and interviewing his heroes, while (as Pratchett frequently noted in later interviews) living off the free food laid on at press events. By 1985 Pratchett, supported by his steady journalism and PR jobs, had published four books for the sheer pleasure of writing them. Gaiman had managed just one – a biography of 1980s pop giants Duran Duran, which

---

1. Occasionally covered by the aforementioned grey homburg hat, which he eventually left in a restaurant.

he claims is the only thing he ever wrote for the pay cheque alone (he has never allowed it to be reprinted).

However, the pair soon found they shared common ground. Both had grown up in small towns in the south east of England – Beaconsfield and East Grinstead respectively – and both had their lives changed when they discovered the local library as children, uncovering a thirst for knowledge of all kinds, especially mythology, history and science. Both had fallen deeply in love with *The Lord of the Rings* at a similarly impressionable age and found it a gateway to new worlds of the fantastic, where they discovered a universe of science fiction classics, and joined the convention-dwelling, fanzine-writing scene that dangled from its misshapen underbelly. Both had made their living from words, though Pratchett's route was structured and Gaiman's rather haphazard, and both had written a children's book as their first attempt at a novel (Gaiman's *My Great Aunt Ermintrude* remains, alas, unpublished). They also shared a worldview and sense of humour, both being huge fans of the eminently quotable G. K. Chesterton and P. G. Wodehouse. They made each other laugh, and they could make each other excited.

The pair would meet regularly on the convention circuit, and fell into the habit of long, late-night phone conversations in which they'd read each other their latest work, which was invaluable for Gaiman as he began to move from journalism into fiction, even turning down an offer to be the full-time features editor at *Penthouse* in order to cultivate his growing reputation as a comic book author.

By 1988, his work for *Total Eclipse, 2000AD* and especially his graphic novel *Violent Cases* had gained the attention of DC Comics, the giant American publishers of hundreds of legendary comic titles, including *Batman, Superman* and *The Justice League*. They were hoping to import back to the US some of the grit and verve that was generating a renaissance in British comics. Gaiman had pitched a revival of a long-neglected DC title, *The Sandman*, reinvented as a dark, modern fantasy. He was hip deep in the story, having been working hard for almost a year, when Terry Pratchett called.

Pratchett, now a full-time author, had stumbled across his forgotten copy of *William the Antichrist* and re-read it, realising that he knew what should happen next, and that he wanted to be the one to write it. He called Gaiman, offering to co-author the story or, if he wasn't interested in pursuing it any more, buy the idea from him and write it himself. Gaiman agreed to collaborate almost on the spot. Later he would often say that their collaboration was between two men yet to reach their potential as writers. 'In those days Neil Gaiman was barely Neil Gaiman and Terry Pratchett was only just Terry Pratchett' say the notes in the 2019 edition of *Good Omens*, although by 1988 Pratchett was a bestseller with a growing audience and a ferocious work rate. Gaiman, who had yet to publish a novel, recognised that working alongside the older man would be a tremendous learning opportunity that would do no harm to his profile. Besides which, it would be fun. The pair began the process of long phone calls, mailed computer disks and, on one occasion, utilising a primitive computer network[2] that would result in a rough first draft.

Pratchett got the ball rolling, taking Gaiman's initial 5,000 words and turning it into 10,000, including a redraft of the existing text, making major and minor tweaks. The Satanic nurses became a coven of Satanic nuns,[3] and a character called Crawleigh, a somewhat ineffective demon who drove a Citroen 2CV and was looked down on by his demonic brethren, was given a makeover. Pratchett changed his name to Crowley, gave him a sneaky intelligence, a lot of swagger, and several character traits borrowed from Gaiman himself, including a tendency to wear sunglasses indoors and a black leather jacket. He also introduced the story's McGuffin; a book of prophecies by a seventeenth-century witch called Agnes Nutter, who had been burned by witchfinders, and – due to some carefully placed barrels of gunpowder – took her captors down with her. The character had been intended for a Discworld novel, but slotted neatly into the mythology of *William The Antichrist*. The ball was then batted back to Gaiman who, since this was a book about the end of the world, added the four 'horsepersons' of the apocalypse.

The pair would spend hours on the phone, talking at least once a day to work on the plot and the characters, before splitting off to write. Since they were working on a novel – Pratchett's territory – it was decided that he should be responsible for maintaining the continuity of the emerging

---

2. The operation involved two basic modems and took the best part of a day. Pratchett joked that it would have been quicker to hand deliver the manuscript.
3. Nuns are always funnier. Always.

story, dubbing himself 'the keeper of the disks', and making sure there was always a master draft to work from (he always maintained that, had they been writing a comic, it would have been the other way round). By necessity it was Terry that did the bulk of the actual typing – he estimated perhaps two thirds while Gaiman puts the split at 65,000/45,000 words – as Gaiman (who writes longhand) had the relentless pace of *The Sandman* and other comic projects to keep on top of. Gaiman watched how Pratchett would weave and sew the narrative together. The plot, characters and ideas, however, were a fifty-fifty split.

However busy Gaiman was with *The Sandman* he would always, regardless of the time, write 500 words of *William* before he went to bed, sometimes mailing a disk to Pratchett to be sewn into the master draft, sometimes talking it through the next day. Pratchett was an habitual early riser, as country people often are, and did much of his work in the morning. Gaiman would emerge from bed, bleary-eyed, much later in the day to find his answerphone blinking.[4] He would call Pratchett back and they would talk each other through their work that morning and the previous night. Much like Beatles fans who try to spot a Lennon song from a McCartney one, fans of Pratchett and Gaiman have spent thirty years debating which author was responsible for which idea, and which piece of writing. Pratchett initially wrote the sections featuring 'The Them', the gang of scabby-kneed kids led by the eponymous juvenile antichrist. On the surface the gang are clearly nodding to Crompton's *Just William* books, but scratch a little and you'll find Pratchett's own childhood in Forty Green, right down to the local American airbase and the copse of trees that formed a den for the gang to play in. It was Pratchett that added another important 'what if?' to the original plan: what if in *The Omen* sequels Damian had free will to do with his power as he pleased?

Gaiman was responsible for the four horsemen, the motorcycle gang that follow them along for the ride, and much of the story involving Crowley and his angel counterpart, Aziraphale. The beginning of the book was Gaiman's, the end was Pratchett's. However, each wrote and

---

4. Probably the reason answerphones containing nagging messages feature quite heavily in the book.

rewrote the other's sections to the point that the lines become blurred beyond recognition, especially as each was basing their work on ideas that came out of their joint conversations. Both worked on the major characters, and as the finale of the book approached, Gaiman took over the writing of The Them while Pratchett inherited the horsemen. It's interesting to note that, while the skeletal figure of Death bears a close resemblance to the benevolent reaper of the Discworld (right down to his MANNER OF SPEAKING), this Death was written predominantly by Gaiman, and is a far darker, less kindly character than Pratchett's.[5]

There's an assumption that Gaiman wrote the nastier sections of the book and Pratchett the nicer bits, and to an extent that's true. The broad strokes of the plot are Gaiman's as are some of the grizzlier ideas, such as the demon Hastur manifesting out of a phone receiver in the form of thousands of maggots, but the tone at the end of the story is Pratchett's. He insisted that any damage done in the story would have to be undone – there could be no blood on their child protagonist's hands, and it would be the boy's free will that ultimately saves the world. It wasn't as black and white as this, though. Both could write with warmth and humanity, or with a sneaking nastiness. Later Gaiman would say it was a gross oversimplification to view the book as a meeting of his tendency towards the macabre and Pratchett's sweetness and light. The two friends approached their work from exactly the same mindset, and knew the tone they wanted to achieve, which was somewhere between Crompton, Adams, Wodehouse and Chesterton, with a modern horror twist. They would rewrite each other, throwing in jokes and footnotes (those sherbet lemons again) until often they were unsure who had written which bit, joking that there were whole sections of the book neither of them remembered writing at all. Mostly it became a game of each making the other laugh, and then, as Gaiman's biographer Hayley Campbell put it in her 2016 book *The Art of Neil Gaiman*, 'racing each other to write the good bits.'

The first draft was completed in nine weeks, with the pair working separately. The second draft took another four months as the authors

---

5. Though nothing like Gaiman's *other* Death, the elder sister of Dream in *The Sandman* comics, and one of the series' most popular characters.

tamed their wild, partially structured ideas into a coherent whole; gender swapping the characters of Pepper and War and further refining the plot. Gaiman travelled to Somerset to stay at Gayes Cottage so the two could nudge their opus over the finishing line. He remembers one morning finding two doves that had escaped Terry and Lyn's dovecote, wheeling around his room in a state of panic, and assumed this sort of thing happened all the time (according to Pratchett this never happened to any other visitor).

One of their final jobs was to come up with a new title. As the book evolved, the character of William had been renamed Adam, therefore *William The Antichrist*, with its double nods to *Just William* and William the Conqueror had to be changed, and *Adam The Antichrist* would have none of the associations they wanted. More to the point, it was clear this wasn't just Adam's story – a full cast list included at the start of the book made that obvious. If anything, Crowley and Aziraphale had become the heroes of the piece. It was Gaiman who thought of calling the book *Good Omens*, punning on *The Omen*, while Pratchett favoured *The Nice and Accurate Prophecies of Agnes Nutter, Witch*. A compromise was reached by making Pratchett's suggestion the subtitle and putting Gaiman's snappier suggestion at the top: *Good Omens: The Nice and Accurate Prophecies of Agnes Nutter, Witch.*

Uniquely in Pratchett's career as a professional author, *Good Omens* had been written on spec. Since *The Carpet People* he'd been operating on commission, with fees and deals organised before the real work began, and a publisher lined up. *Good Omens* was different. Pratchett and Gaiman had written it off their own backs, fitting it in alongside other work. Later Pratchett would describe it as a 'summer job'. The book was done, but the job wasn't finished – Terry often said a piece of writing wasn't complete until it had been read by its intended audience, an instinct he'd learned as a journalist. The circle had to be closed. It was time to find a publisher.

To their delight, *Good Omens* prompted that most exciting of publishing traditions – the bidding war. The rights were auctioned publicly by Gaiman's American agents, Writers House, and were ultimately won in the UK by Gollancz, with Transworld/Corgi handling the paperback. Neither company was about to let one of its most successful talents drift into the path of a rival. Interest from other publishers ensured a much higher advance than Pratchett was accustomed to – a numerically satisfying £150,150, which the authors split evenly. Pratchett was ecstatic, while Gaiman, naturally, played the whole thing down, though it's hard to believe a writer selling their first novel for a £75,000 share wasn't dancing a jig inside. An additional deal was done with a US publisher, Workman, for American hardback rights. Pratchett was, at best, an underground name in the States, while the roaring success of *The Sandman* had made Gaiman a force to be reckoned with. Thus in America the book is credited to 'Neil Gaiman & Terry Pratchett', while back in the UK the reliable bestseller Pratchett was treated as the headline act.

Good Omens, advertised with the strapline, 'Funnier than Stephen King, scarier than Tom Sharpe', was an immediate success and well received on both sides of the Atlantic. 'Wickedly funny … . The theological debates top even *Life of Brian. Good Omens* is heaven to read and you'll laugh like hell,' wrote a breathless *Time Out*. For the first time Pratchett found his work under the gaze of American broadsheet critics. Though *The New York Times'* Joe Queenan absolutely *hated* the book's 'reams and reams of undergraduate dreck and recycled science-fiction clichés',[6] *The Washington Post* delivered a glowing write-up: 'It's a wow!', and *The San Diego Tribune*'s review positively vibrated with joy: 'A steamroller of silliness that made me giggle out loud.' As Pratchett and Gaiman embarked on a promotional tour that took in the US and UK, they started to realise they had written something that resonated deeply with readers. Over the years they were rarely asked to sign a pristine copy of *Good Omens*, unless it was being bought as a gift or as a replacement for a lost or worn-out book. Instead they were handed paperbacks with crinkled and folded pages and creased covers, sometimes held together with tape and, not infrequently, swollen and deformed where they had been dropped in the bath or a hotel swimming pool. *Good Omens* was a book people truly loved, and read over and over again. They lent it to their friends and bought copies to give as gifts. Word of mouth spread quickly, and a wave of affection hurried after it. For the rest of their careers it was rare that either writer could get through an interview, signing or Q&A

---

6. His review also takes pot shots at Benny Hill, East End pubs and people from Liverpool, so he was clearly in a bit of a mood that day.

session without being asked about the collaboration. The icing on the cake came with two award nominations; Best Novel at the World Fantasy Awards and Best Fantasy Novel at the respected Locus Awards.

Touring *Good Omens* helped solidify the pair's friendship. Working together on a book is one thing but to spend several weeks sharing hotel rooms is to truly know someone. The pair developed an odd-couple double act, entertaining panel audiences by one-upping each other for the best laughs, putting Terry's hat and Neil's jacket on chairs to illustrate the real writer of the book – a composite entity called 'Neilandterry'. In a hotel room at the World Fantasy Con in Seattle, months before the book's release, Pratchett chastised Gaiman for getting in late ('your mother and I have been very worried') and the pair lay on their twin beds in the dark, planning out a sequel, provisionally – and brilliantly – titled *668, The Neighbour of the Beast*. The tour was full of adventures that both remembered fondly; the time they had to keep a straight face during a radio interview in New York because the DJ had assumed the book was the factual account of a real, historical old witch whose prophecies all turned out to be true. There was the hotel where Gaiman's TV could only tune into porn and Pratchett's would only show *Mr Ed*, and the adventure Pratchett mysteriously referred to as the time they met the 'spider woman'. In San Francisco they decided to walk to a radio interview and turned up forty minutes late, livid with themselves for misjudging the distance. Gaiman wrote about it in his foreword to *A Slip of the Keyboard*, saying it was the first time he'd detected the simmering anger that lay just below the surface of his friend's jolly demeanour and fuelled his best writing.

Discussions about a *Good Omens* movie began before the book was even in the shops. It was such an obviously filmic story, full of appealing visuals and compelling characters, that Hollywood took notice almost immediately, helped by *The Washington Post* saying it would 'make one hell of a movie'. The publishers had sent a copy to Monty Python star and cult filmmaker Terry Gilliam, hoping he could provide a quote for the cover to sit alongside those from Clive Barker and James Herbert.[7]

---

7. Comics legend Robert Crumb was also approached for a quote. His response on reading the book was to send the publishers a lengthy letter detailing how much he hated the story, and begging them not to publish it.

Somehow, the accompanying note was lost and Gilliam assumed he'd been sent the book for consideration as a movie. He began negotiating for the rights straight away, although ultimately, for whatever reason, discussions went nowhere. The rights ended up with Sovereign Pictures, a film-financing firm which had had success with the Oscar winning *My Left Foot* and a version of *Hamlet* starring Mel Gibson. Sovereign, like much of Hollywood, was money-focused and not driven by creative ambition. Its involvement marks the point when *Good Omens* began its journey – appropriately enough given the story – to development hell.

There was always a sense that Hollywood didn't really 'get' *Good Omens*. Pratchett and Gaiman travelled to LA and endured meeting after meeting with producers, most of whom insisted that the original authors should write the screenplay, but wanted to impress upon them how much of the book would need to be changed. Gaiman remembers one meeting where a studio exec – he remains tight-lipped on who – outlined a vision that would see the awkward Newton Pulsifer played by a 'Tom Cruise-type', with Julia Roberts starring as 'Ananthamawhatever'. A scene involving a Japanese whaling ship also caused problems, since Sovereign was hoping to tempt a Japanese firm to invest in the picture. 'Would it be okay,' they asked, 'if the whaling ship were to be made Dutch instead?' The authors would sit through meetings and then head back to their hotel to work on a new story outline, based on the studio's notes, only to find no-one was bothering to read them anyway. The plot twisted and turned, this way and that. As Pratchett and Gaiman pillaged their planned sequel for new characters that could expand the world of the book, they eventually delivered a script that departed from the original novel quite a bit, adding new action sequences, including one where angels in the British Museum use their halos as killer frisbees.[8] Sovereign were still unhappy, and asked for another draft that would move even further away from the original novel.

At this point, Pratchett threw his hands up and walked away from the project, urging Gaiman to do the same. Sadly matters weren't that simple – the contract they had signed meant that Sovereign had every right

---

8. This particular image turns up in a 2007 episode of *Doctor Who*, 'Voyage of the Damned', written by Russell T. Davies. It's almost certainly a coincidence. Meanwhile, Gaiman would revisit the idea of angels in the British Museum in his TV series and novel, *Neverwhere*.

to demand a second draft of the script, and could potentially sue were one not forthcoming. Gaiman stayed on to try again, this time setting the story in America, much to Pratchett's dismay, and abandoning key characters such as the four horsemen. This version was also rejected, this time – maddeningly – for departing *too far* from the source material. Thankfully Sovereign Pictures went bankrupt before much more work could be done, and the rights reverted back to the authors, though the pair now found their enthusiasm for a *Good Omens* movie had all but evaporated. Working on the screenplay had also put a dent in their relationship. Gaiman admits to some friction, but says it was short-lived, telling *The Times* in 2015, '[Terry] was grumpy with me for a couple of years but we went back to being friends because it was easier. He missed me and I missed him.'

Nevertheless, the *Good Omens* movie was not dead. In 1999, British film producers Peter and Marc Samuelson, approached Pratchett and Gaiman about the rights. Pratchett was sceptical but Gaiman felt the Samuelson brothers understood the fundamentals of the story, especially when they approached a delighted Terry Gilliam to write and direct. Things were, at last, moving forward. Details of Gilliam's script, written with regular collaborator Tony Grisoni, are thin on the ground, though he has said the ending of the story would have been substantially different from the novel as 'with each pass it becomes even more loosely based on the book'. Gilliam told the movie website *Dreams*: 'Perhaps the fans will never speak to us again.' Together Gilliam and the Samuelsons had secured $50 million in funding from Renaissance Pictures and had provisionally lined up megastars Johnny Depp and Robin Williams to play Crowley and Aziraphale, with Kirsten Dunst in line to play Anathema. Gaiman and Pratchett were happy to stay clear of the project and let the director get on with it. Both were huge Gilliam fans, and Pratchett considered his 1981 classic *Time Bandits* to be one of his favourite films. He was, however, a realist, and continually stated in interviews that he doubted the film would ever get made. He was right. It needed an American distributor to guarantee transatlantic success and to make up the rest of its predicted $60 million budget. Sadly, in the paranoid and cautious period that followed the 11 September attacks in New York, no-one in Hollywood was looking to invest in a movie about the end of the world. With only eighty per cent of the budget raised and no American distributor in place, support began to slip away. Gilliam was still hoping to get *Good Omens* off the ground as late as 2006, but it wasn't meant to be. The rights eventually reverted back to Pratchett and Gaiman, and it would be several years yet before 'the old girl', as Terry had taken to calling the project, eventually made it to screens, this time re-envisioned as a prestige television show.

Pratchett wouldn't live to see the lavish production of his 'old girl' that debuted on Amazon Prime in 2019, though he and Gaiman did provide cameos as traffic policemen for a 2014 radio adaptation that aired on the BBC just before Christmas. The 2019 TV show (more of which later) was written by Gaiman, who took on the role of 'showrunner' as a labour of love, with complete control over the project. It was rapturously received, and thanks to Amazon's heavy marketing found a whole new audience, much of which now wanted to read the book that had inspired their new favourite show. In the spring of 2019, almost thirty years after it was first published, *Good Omens: The Nice And Accurate Prophecies of Agnes Nutter, Witch* entered *The New York Times* bestseller list for the first time.

Chapter 13

We Need To Talk About Kevins

In 1990, Terry Pratchett's publishers outlined their plans for the coming decade in a marketing document entitled 'Into the Nineties With Gollancz and Corgi'. It summarised Pratchett's current position as a bestselling, but still cult author:

> The growth of Terry Pratchett's sales over the past six years has been one of the great success stories of the 'eighties. Each new Terry Pratchett hardback and paperback is billed as a major event to the trade and promoted heavily to the public ... Terry's celebrity is growing all the time. His books now regularly appear on bestseller lists, the last two Discworld paperbacks at number one in *The Sunday Times*.

The document goes on to point out how Pratchett's signing sessions had graduated from specialist bookshops to larger, more general stores, and how his backlist remained in print and selling well. The two publishers outlined a plan to push Terry out of the niche fantasy market and into the mainstream: 'Our efforts over the next few years will be particularly concentrated on selling Terry Pratchett to the general reader ... i.e. by positioning Terry as a humorous writer who anyone can enjoy, rather than as a writer of "funny fantasy".' The marketing plan involved a press blitz via the broadsheets, targeting *The Times*, *The Sunday Times* and *The Daily Telegraph* for profile interviews that would see Pratchett recognised as 'an influential and important writer'. Terry had entered the new decade as a bestselling author but it's clear the team around him saw even greater success[1] to come.

In 1990 Pratchett's profile arguably outpaced his cult appeal, and all sorts of people – from every facet of life – declared themselves to be

---

1. And, yes, more money.

fans. His publicity team worked hard at their plan, and Pratchett did indeed find himself profiled by *The Times*, *The Sunday Times* and *The Daily Telegraph*, among the usual merry-go-round of niche magazines. Bestselling books are all very well, but you know things are really moving when you're in the Sunday supplements. Early in the year, a woman called Mrs Dougal wrote to *The Sunday Times* asking for recommendations for humorous novels her children could read on an upcoming holiday. The paper was inundated with readers recommending Terry Pratchett novels, with two thirds of the printed replies dedicated to *Truckers* or the Discworld.

The years following Pratchett's move to full-time writer had been productive to an almost ludicrous degree, and many of those projects came to fruition as the new decade dawned. In 1990, Gollancz and Doubleday published *five* new Terry Pratchett novels between them – the most that would be published in a single year. *Diggers*, the sequel to *Truckers*, got the ball rolling in April, followed by *Good Omens* in May, *Eric*, a short Discworld novella, was published in August, while September saw the release of the final book in the 'nomes' trilogy, *Wings*. Just for good measure a full Discworld novel, *Moving Pictures*, hit stores in time for the Christmas market. Terry also contributed three short stories to various publications and anthologies, and a book review to *The New Scientist*. This might seem like overexposure, but the appetite for new Pratchett products kept growing.

This was a period of escalating fame for Pratchett, a decade where he graduated step-by-step from weirdo fantasy author to national treasure. Each book sold better than the last, and each in turn led to more interviews, more mentions in the press, more word-of-mouth recommendations and a higher profile, which guaranteed the next book would do even better. This upward curve would, to a greater and lesser extent, continue for the rest of his life. He was also getting better at handling himself publicly. He was learning to sidestep awkward, personal questions in interviews and not say anything controversial or that could be taken out of context. As a former journalist, he knew how to give good copy and made sure every interview was peppered with oneliners and pull quotes. His interviews were often as quotable as his novels. Such lines would be worked out well in advance – more sherbet lemons to be tossed liberally into conversation. The downside was that any Pratchett press campaign inevitably included interchangeable interviews, and it took a skilled reporter to crack his carefully calculated facade and pull out something new.

As his fame grew, his work began to polarise opinions in the press. On the one hand were the Pratchett fans, the ones who could read past the elephants and the turtle, and even between the jokes. They saw instinctively that Terry was building a complex and relatable world of human values and warmth. His books were often reviewed in the broadsheets just as enthusiastically as they were in genre magazines such as *SFX* and *Locus*, with reviewers making comparisons to Dickens and Wodehouse rather than Tolkien or even Douglas Adams.

On the other hand were those critics consistently baffled by Pratchett's success, dismissing him as an amateurish spinner of potboilers with a spoddy, troglodyte following they simply couldn't understand. Even the critics who enjoyed his work often felt the need to couch their praise in sneery broadsides at what they perceived to be Pratchett's typical audience. 'Terry Pratchett is an annoying author' began a 1994 piece in *The Times*. It continued: 'Once upon a time, everyone knew that dragons and wizards and mythical quests were as ineffably naff as a heavy-metal record collection and a taste for snakebite. But now Pratchett's tales … sit comfortably on the shelves of dons and deacons.' On an episode of BBC 2's *Late Review*, the poet Tom Paulin gave a withering summation of 1994's *Interesting Times*, pronouncing Pratchett to be an 'absolute amateur' who 'doesn't even write in chapters'. The *Nottingham Evening Post* dismissed his world as 'Middle England with spells'. A sniffy review of 1991's *Reaper Man* in *The Guardian* issued its praise through gritted teeth: 'Its sole raison d'etre is the laugh', wrote critic Jonathan Coe. 'Pratchett has no axe to grind, no political point to make, no intention of imagining a consistent, Tolkien-like world, just a babyish glee in keeping the gags firing off the page … the effects will soon wear thin.' It's a baffling response to a book that has an entire secondary plot about mass consumerism and literally portrays shopping malls as parasites that suck the life out of cities. Pratchett wasn't just grinding an axe, he was wielding one. It's especially galling to see one of mid-period Discworld's most achingly human stories dismissed as a mere gag book. More damning still was a *Sunday Times* review of *Witches Abroad* which concluded: 'Pratchett gamely jests that "occasionally he gets accused of literature". I cannot for the supernatural life of me imagine by whom.' Every new work, without fail, would attract a handful of such reviews. When *Only You Can Save Mankind* made the shortlist for *The Guardian*'s Children's Literature Award, one judge was heard to ponder: 'It's a good read but is it good literature?'

Publicly, Pratchett took such criticisms in his stride, usually pointing out that he was making quite large amounts of money, which was more than adequate compensation for not winning over London's snobby literati. Privately, they stung. His bitterness was occasionally betrayed in interviews, where he could be pushed into waspishness on the subject, snapping that he'd rather be down the pub than at a posh literary dinner, and saying that if he'd described his books as 'magical realism' rather than 'fantasy', the Booker Prize judges might be knocking at his door. He'd often cite Salman Rushdie's *Midnight's Children* and Martin Amis's *Time's Arrow* as examples of fantasy deemed 'acceptable' by the establishment.

Though he was capable of laughing off bad reviews, at least in public, Pratchett would come out fighting if he suspected genre fiction and fandom were being belittled. He regarded fantasy as an 'ur literature' (meaning an original form of literature), pointing out that the oldest stories were really fantasy stories, often quoting his beloved G. K. Chesterton;[2] echoing the belief that fantasy showed us the world from another angle, meaning we saw it anew. Pratchett was always proud to be associated with fantasy and science fiction. Even towards the end of his career, when much of the literary establishment had accepted him and his books were praised as modern classics, he never stopped attending conventions and signings. He always saw himself as a genre author first and foremost and was annoyed when anyone implied they were above such things.

He defended his fanbase with even more ferocity. Mainstream coverage of Pratchett's books, even when the tone was broadly positive, would

---

2. A favourite being, 'The baby has known the dragon intimately ever since he had an imagination. What the fairy tale provides for him is a St George to kill the dragon.'

almost always take potshots at the average Discworld fan. His books were 'nerd-fests' (*City Life*), read by fans 'down at heavy metal HQ' who also enjoyed 'sexual inadequacy and ram-raiding' (*NME*), who were 'nerdy-looking, anorak-wearing' folk (*The Observer)* and 'the kind of people that find *Red Dwarf* funny'[3] (*Q*). Whenever a photographer turned up at a book signing, they would ignore the quite reasonable-looking bank manager who'd nipped in on his lunch break and head straight to the enthusiasts wearing pointy wizard hats or dressed as Death.

The general consensus seemed to be that the average Pratchett reader was an awkward 14-year-old boy with chronic acne and no friends. For the most part that was a gross generalisation, though even Pratchett had to admit that sometimes they had a point. Since the mid-1980s Terry had received stacks of fan mail, either via his publishers or sent directly to his home at Gayes Cottage. Lyn had become his default PA, eventually giving up her own teaching career to support her husband. Every day she would sort through the fan mail, filter out anything she felt crossed the line into inappropriate[4] and bring him the day's post with his elevenses. It was Lyn who first noticed the high percentage of teenage boys and young men writing to her husband, and on one occasion found that three of them shared the same name – Kevin. She slipped the letters into the folder of approved mail and wrote 'Kevins' on it. Terry and Lyn would think of certain types of Pratchett fan as 'Kevins' for ever more.

Pratchett knew the Kevins. He had been one himself; an awkward teenager shaking hands with authors at conventions and asking their advice, hungrily seeking out new books on SF and fantasy and people to discuss them with. He knew that the Kevins were the ones who devoured his books on the day of publication and wrote to him asking for more details; who queued up at cons and signings with huge piles of his ever-increasing backlist. They were the ones who would stay Pratchett readers throughout their lives and, like pimply vampires, pass on the bug to ever-increasing circles of new Kevins.

---

3. Which is an odd comment … *Red Dwarf* is funny, and was a favourite of Pratchett's at the time.
4. Possibly the reason Pratchett always maintained his fan mail was rather tame compared to other authors.

Terry instinctively understood such Kevinism, and knew how it deserved to be treated. The letter he had received from Tolkien when he was 19 had meant the world to him, and he tried to reply to his own fan mail as much as he could. During the early 1990s, he claimed that all but the weirdest messages (which thanks to his wife's diligence mostly never reached him) received some kind of reply, and part of every day was spent answering the letters brought up with his tea and sandwiches, replying by hand in the early days, and later on typed sheets headed with a picture of Great A'Tuin. Fans would send him photographs of themselves outside pubs called The Shades,[5] and include homemade badges dedicated to Unseen University's rowing team or the Ankh-Morpork City Watch. They wrote their own versions of the Discworld drinking song *A Wizard's Staff Has a Knob on the End* or Nanny Ogg's *The Hedgehog Song* from *Wyrd Sisters*,[6] they asked for maps and spin-offs, and suggested ideas for cookery books and games. They often asked for a signed photo, a request which Terry politely refused, sending a letter instead, pointing out that author photos were, in his opinion, rather pointless.

Letters from librarians were very common, usually praising Terry for elevating the reputation of the job with Unseen University's resident orangutan – such letters invariably used the word 'ook!' somewhere. Librarians, parents and teachers thanked him for turning their book-averse kids on to reading, saying that children who would previously run at the sound of a turning page were working their way through the shelves of his books at the local library, and often weren't stopping once they reached the end of his section.[7] Such letters could sometimes contain a passive aggressive tone, which Pratchett was amused by more than annoyed, usually along the lines of: 'I think it's marvellous that young readers enjoy your work because that means we can get them into libraries and introduce them to real books.' (This was quoted in a 1993 essay written for *The Author* magazine called 'Kevins'.)

---

5. Which, if they're anything like their namesake in Ankh-Morpork, should probably be avoided.
6. About a small, spiky mammal that, um, struggled with a particularly taboo sort of intimacy. Terry dedicated *Witches Abroad* to the numerous fans who had written their own lyrics to the song, saying 'and why not?'
7. Presumably, the fantasy author Fletcher Pratt benefited more from this than most.

Especially common were the 'where do you get your ideas from?' letters, often from budding writers who had insightful questions about process and structure, or entry-level curiosity about how books are written and published. Pratchett tried his best to provide honest and useful advice in the spirit of paying forward, a tradition he had practised diligently ever since he'd mentored Janice Raycroft at the *Bucks Free Press* in the early 1970s. Authors had found the time to meet and advise him when he was a budding writer, and he felt a responsibility to do the same. At first, he gave critical feedback on stories and writing samples (but would balk at a draft of an entire novel), though later these would be returned unread after one too many accusations of plagiarism from angry amateurs, many of whose work Terry had never even seen. The more persistent hopefuls then moved on to bother Colin Smythe, whose archives are full of unpublished Pratchett imitations.

As well as the nascent writing talent, the mailbag included innumerable requests for help with school projects, some from genuine fans asking well-thought-out questions, others under reluctant instruction from an English teacher, asking something along the lines of 'how do you become a writer?' and, genuinely, 'are you on flexitime?'. Such letters usually took the form of a sheet of numbered questions, leading Pratchett to assume teachers were handing out a template. The letters came in so often that he eventually put the answers to all the most common questions, along with biographical information, into a numbered list of his own, and sent copies back with a short covering letter. The sheet, known as 'The Terry Pratchett Answers', covered everything from 'where do you get your ideas from?' and 'how did you get published?'[8] to 'sales and front covers and stuff', 'films', 'odds and ends' and 'what's it all about then, eh; this writing business?'.

Terry's fanmail was such that he was constantly fighting a two-month backlog, which only increased with the growing popularity of electronic mail. Pratchett was, naturally, an earlier adopter of email and his address, tpratchett@unseen.demon.co.uk, was widely circulated in those more

---

8. Here Pratchett makes his usual claim that he sent a manuscript off to a publisher, rather than the more accurate version of 'developing a relationship with an existing publisher by interviewing them for the local newspaper, and handing them his book to read once he'd gained their trust.'

lawless days of the web, even turning up in a 1994 book called *E-Mail Addresses of the Rich and Famous*. It did nothing to help improve the volume of his correspondence, which he started to acknowledge in the jacket biographies of his novels, describing his job as someone who 'writes books in between answering the mail'.

Electronic communication began to overtake the 'snail mail' of posted letters, and Pratchett's undeniable nerd appeal meant many web pioneers were fans. The alt.fan.pratchett newsgroup went live on the newfangled world wide web in 1991, a system so boxfresh that before the 1994 *Discworld Companion* could explain online discussion forums, it first had to explain 'the internet'.[9] The alt.fan.pratchett (or AFP) forum became the cornerstone of online activity for Discworld fans for many years, developing into a lively and close-knit digital community (and later a sprawling and virtually unmanageable one) connecting Pratchett readers across the world. Fans discussed the books in detail, analysing the most obscure references and jokes (and often explaining them back to Americans). The forum eventually gave rise to a website, lspace.org – still active at the time of writing – as a depository for facts and analysis about Pratchett's work and an explainer of the endless AFP in-jokes and clichés that dominated the discussion. Terry himself joined AFP in late 1991 – he was, after all, an online enthusiast who enjoyed discussing his own work – and would often contribute to debates and settle arguments. He was contactable through the site, which did his postbag no favours, though many of the messages were just demands to know if he really was the real Terry Pratchett. The question 'does Terry really post here?' became such a cliché of the AFP community that eventually memes and jokes referencing the phrase became more common than the actual queries.

The many thousands of readers who received a reply, in whatever format, were extremely appreciative, and it helped strengthen the bond between author and fan. Many of those relationships lasted decades. In the early years Pratchett would often maintain a correspondence with fans whose letters he enjoyed, and greet them warmly at signings. Fans would often be converted into friends and find themselves invited to visit

---

9. Yes, I know. The internet and world wide web are not the same thing. But we're going to be here all day if we get into that.

his home, receiving the occasional phone call asking their opinion on this or that new joke, or checking a continuity detail on the assumption that their knowledge of Discworld's streets and history would probably be better than his. A timely letter could create a fan for life. One woman, commenting on a Pratchett Facebook group in the days after the author's death, was asked how Terry's work had impacted her. She said:

> The first book I read was *The Carpet People* and at school we had the opportunity to write to an author and I couldn't believe that Terry wrote back to me. I had to stand in assembly and read it out … I was the only one in my year that had the privilege to hear from my author.

Twenty years on, she was still reading his work.

Interacting with fans, whether digital, postal or physical, was a crucial part of the job to Pratchett and he tried to fulfil his obligations as best he could. Every publication was followed by a two-week signing tour of the UK (and later Europe, Australia and the States), in which he would try to sign everything put in front of him by anyone who came to queue, though he was not above a withering put down to fans who presented large piles of books. 'Have you ever heard the words "sad person"?' he asked a girl at the head of a queue in Croydon in 1996 when she handed over a carrier bag full of things to sign. He still signed them all. It was not unusual for him to stay at a bookshop for hours after closing time to deal with the size of the queue, periodically resting his wrist on an ice pack to hold off cramp. Fans would bring him home-baked cakes and, after the publication of *Witches Abroad*, jugs of banana daiquiris. He attended conventions for most of his writing career, and accepted that later, when he was Britain's most successful fantasy writer, he would be the centre of attention. Sometimes he'd enjoy the fuss and sometimes he'd slink off to find the real ale bar present at every British SF convention and hide in a corner, hoping to chat to an author he'd known for years rather than having his hand wrung by well-wishers. He cultivated a sincere and mutually respectful relationship with his readers that is common for cult authors, but virtually unknown among best sellers. It was a responsibility he took extremely seriously.

That readership was expanding all the time. In 1992 the book chain W. H. Smith claimed that ten percent of their sci-fi and fantasy sales came from Pratchett novels. By 1998 it was one book in every fifty, regardless of genre. By the end of the decade six-and-a-half percent of *all* new hardbacks sold in the UK were his. A new Terry Pratchett paperback was expected to sell somewhere in the region of 400,000 copies, with hardbacks hovering around the 40,000 mark. Considering Gollancz and Transworld between them usually published two of each annually, this meant total sales of around 880,000 per year in new releases alone. *The Times* reported that Terry Pratchett was 1996's best-selling living British author, a feat he would continue to accomplish year on year for the rest of the decade.[10] When *Carpe Jugulum* was published in 1998, the advice in *The Bookseller* to proprietors pondering how many copies of the latest Discworld they should order was 'think of a number, and then double it'.

An author selling almost a million books a year clearly had an audience that went far beyond SF nerds and teenage boys, and Terry noticed that his correspondents were becoming more varied. Often Kevin's mum was writing to say she had borrowed her son's copy of *The Colour of Magic* or *Wyrd Sisters* after hearing him laughing like a drain in his room. Pratchett estimated that slightly more than half his readers were women, and of those the demographic skewed towards what he'd refer to as 'ladies of a certain age'.[11] The 14-year-old schoolboy Kevin of 1989 could be a teacher or a journalist by 1999, and though he may have put his Star Trek uniform on eBay he was usually still reading Discworld. Josh Kirby's distinctive covers could be spotted clutched by commuters on trains and buses across the country. Not that a Kirby cover necessarily meant a Pratchett novel – the success of the Discworld had brought about a boom in comic fantasy, and Kirby found himself in great demand to provide artwork for the likes of Tom Holt and Robert Rankin, as well as several anthologies. If Kirby wasn't available, publishers would find an artist who could work in the same style. The format Corgi had been using for Discworld paperbacks since 1985 was widely imitated, and the market

---

10. Though weirdly not the one that earnt the most. Irvine Welsh was the UK's second best-selling author of 1996, but earned almost £1 million more. A successful movie adaptation can do wonders for your bank balance.

11. That certain age being more or less the same age as him.

was flushed with comic fantasy novels with busy, colourful artwork and the title and author's name floating in a box in the middle of the madness. The overwhelming popularity of the Discworld had a knock-on effect on a whole industry.

Remarkably this did little to shift the perception of Terry's work. A sniffy 1992 interview in *The Mail On Sunday* said that, to many, the author's name would still be met with a response of 'Terry who?'. In 1996 Pratchett was interviewed for *The Telegraph* by future British prime minister, Boris Johnson, whose reaction to the Discworld's enormous sales can best be described as bewilderment: 'I am still baffled by the scale of his success', concludes Johnson, adding, 'but then if I did understand the formula, I'd crib it.'[12] Two years later, and following many millions of books sold, James Delingpole, again of *The Telegraph*, was still asking about the 'stigma' attached to Pratchett's work. A snippy Terry Pratchett replied with, 'What stigma?'.

By the mid-1990s Pratchett was a very wealthy man. It was something most interviewers couldn't resist asking about. Those that came to Gayes Cottage were often disappointed to find that the place wasn't opulent; that Terry's office space was an adapted bit of corridor, and that his daughter attended a local comprehensive. The *Mail On Sunday* journalist who conducted the 'Terry who?' piece noted in surprise that Rhianna wasn't allowed £4.50 to buy a particular tropical fish for her aquarium ('"£4.50! For a fish!" said her father'), and that there was no 'big, plush motor-car outside the door'. His dismissive and condescending manner resulted in Lyn banning all journalists from their house.

Pratchett had been financially comfortable since Transworld entered the picture in the mid-1980s, and his £306,000, six-book deal with Gollancz in 1988 had elevated him beyond merely comfortable and into well off. Once the royalties started to roll in from an ever-expanding backlist, the leap from well off to enormously wealthy happened within a few years. Terry came to money late in life, which affected how he saw and spent it. He was happy to expand his cottage and greenhouse, insisted on paying for dinner when he went out with friends and – probably his biggest extravagance of all – flew business class when he travelled, but

---

12. Whether this is a desirable attitude for a prime minister is left for the reader to decide.

that was more or less where he drew the line. He would never aspire to fly first class, for example, considering it a titanic waste of money, and would rather ransack the kitchen looking for a lost train ticket than buy a new one; at least until Lyn pointed out that time spent looking for a lost ticket was time spent away from his keyboard, and was thus *costing* money he could be earning. Terry's upbringing had been modest and he had learnt thrift from his parents. Later, as a journalist and press officer, he had earned enough to get by, and put away a small amount of savings in a building society account, but no more than that. It was a conscious choice to have just one child – Terry and Lyn simply couldn't afford to support another member of the family and, apparently, he expressed a pang of regret that his wealth had come too late to affect this decision. When Pratchett went from comfortable to millionaire, it happened so late in his life, that his hard-learned thriftiness was unaffected.

Pratchett recalled two incidents that brought home to him the reality of his wealth. The first was in the late 1980s, walking into a branch of W. H. Smith, trying to decide between two videos and realising he could get both. The second, and more significant, came in 1994 when he slipped outside his front door, hit his head and with the ensuing concussion clean forgot where he'd put a cheque his agent had recently sent him. He called Smythe and asked for the cheque to be cancelled and reissued, and was told that this would be no problem, but of course he would lose some substantial interest by delaying. Pratchett didn't think this was much of an issue … until it was pointed out that the cheque he had misplaced was for half a million pounds.[13]

He was a millionaire by 1993 when the family said goodbye to their beloved Gayes Cottage, their home since 1970, which Terry had upgraded and extended as much as was possible given the age of the building. Terry and Lyn found a seventeenth-century manor house in the village of Broad Chalke, near Salisbury in Wiltshire, which they referred to as a 'Domesday Manorette'. It had large grounds, a separate chapel which Terry gleefully converted into his study and library (and after the *Mail On Sunday* incident, was the only part of the house journalists were allowed

---

13. Important note – this is a Pratchett anecdote, and 'half a million' is a suspiciously impressive figure. Smythe remembers it being a slightly smaller, though still significant sum.

to see), and a tennis court which was left unused until eventually being turned into a large greenhouse for exotic plants. The house had been listed at £500,000, but Terry was able to negotiate the price by paying in cash. It was a point of pride that he wouldn't be beholden to banks, despite his accountant lobbying for various mortgage schemes that would generate income through interest. Owning his own home outright was probably the most important by-product of wealth. Aside from a few high-interest accounts, Pratchett preferred to sit on and enjoy his money, rather than send it out to work for him on the stock market or in investments, and considered financiers to be fundamentally untrustworthy. By the early 1990s it was clear that royalties from his books were such that, should he ever find himself unable to write, his income would continue indefinitely. His work ethic had guaranteed him security for life.

Though Pratchett had views that nodded to the left of the political spectrum (one acquaintance described him as 'quietly anarchist'), believed in a society that helped its poorest and mistrusted concentrations of power, especially, bureaucracies, he refused to apologise or feel guilty about his wealth. Partly that was a hangover from his upbringing – you worked hard for your money, you earned it honestly, and you were proud to have done so. A theme in many of his books is money as a 'way of keeping score', as it was for him. His wealth brought him freedom and stability – and a certain amount of luxury – and it allowed him to keep doing the thing he loved the most – writing. Yet his money was also a tangible marker of his success, and success was a tangible marker of how much people enjoyed his work, and that itself was a tangible marker of his talent. From the young boy living in a cottage with no electricity to the best-selling author living in a 500-year-old manor house with its own grounds, his approach to money never changed: 'I'm not a rich man,' he told *The Scotsman* in 2012, 'I'm a poor man with a shitload of money.'

Chapter 14

The Nineties and Discworld Mania

S uccess and money were never the intended end points of Pratchett's writing; they were a by-product of a solid work ethic and strong sense of quality control. Pratchett was absurdly productive across this era, publishing twenty-three novels between 1990 and 2000, and the burgeoning range of Discworld products didn't end with books. This was the era of 'Discworld-Mania' and the decade saw three more video games, two animated television series, audiobooks (both abridged and unabridged), two albums of music, crafted models of hundreds of characters, two half-hour television specials, T-shirts, jewellery, candles, maps, companion books, roleplaying games and quiz books, and that was just the official output. Outside of the products sanctioned by Pratchett himself were the fanzines, websites, badges, cross-stitch patterns, scarves and some pretty faithful costumes. Discworld was a fan-focused industry. It might have been inspired by the books, but it was spreading far beyond them.

None of that would have been sustainable had Pratchett not maintained quality control in his primary product. Though he worked on other projects throughout his career, he was savvy enough to understand that the Discworld was the rock (or possibly carapace) on which his success was built. Beginning in 1986 with *The Light Fantastic*, he would publish at least one new entry in the series every year – bar one – for the rest of his life. Discworld entered the decade in good shape – Pratchett had established his principal players and had started to sketch the world in some detail, though both of 1990's entries to the canon are relatively slight – unsurprising given the author's simultaneous focus on *Good Omens* and the *Bromeliad* novels.

August 1990 brought the shortest book in the series. Like *The Unadulterated Cat*, *Eric*, or to give it its full title *Faust Eric*, was a collaboration, co-credited to Pratchett and his illustrator, Josh Kirby.

Kirby had little direct input into the story, but since the whole plot was hung on set pieces designed to suit his style, the book can be seen as a genuine collaboration and the cover displayed the names of author and artist. The idea had come from Gollancz, who recognised quite rightly that Kirby's artwork had become synonymous with the Discworld, and wanted to see if it could be taken further. A fully illustrated 40,000-word Discworld novella, printed in full colour, was proposed. Pratchett was keen on the idea, though Kirby took some convincing – he was used to spending a few weeks on a piece and then moving on to the next project, enjoying the variety and freedom it gave him. *Eric* would involve sixteen new double-page illustrations – several months' concentrated work, which Kirby worried would be exhausting. He was won over in the end, and his artwork is easily the most enjoyable aspect of the whole project. *Eric* contains some of the best work in Kirby's thirty-year-plus career, especially the Tsortean Horse scene, picturing characters emerging from a giant wooden horse via a hole positioned artfully just under its tail.[1] Best of all is a double-page vista of the entire Discworld – turtle, elephants and all – something Kirby had been desperate to paint since *The Colour of Magic*.

Outside of the illustrations this is one of Pratchett's least interesting works, though it zips along amusingly enough. He knew he needed a disc-trotting plot full of strange and fantastic landscapes for Kirby to draw, and the easiest way to achieve that was to resurrect Rincewind, whom he had intended to leave permanently trapped in the Dungeon Dimensions, literally and metaphorically, following the events of *Sourcery*. Pratchett saw the character as a hangover from an earlier period of his writing, and had no real wish to bring him, or his psychotic Luggage, back into the fold. However, a good craftsman knows the tool to fit the job, and a Rincewind story was the easiest way to give Kirby the landscapes he needed.

The great tragedy of *Eric* is that the most common edition of the book has no illustrations at all. On 16 August, a hardcover and a large-format paperback, both with wonderful full-colour artwork, were published by Gollancz, but it would be two decades before an illustrated edition of

---

1. No-one ever claimed that 'funny' was the same as 'subtle'.

the story would be available again. The following year a standard-sized paperback emerged, which did away with Kirby's artwork everywhere except the cover. Neither the author nor artist was especially pleased about this, and Pratchett was convinced the idea was pointless since the story had been written specifically to be illustrated. He was proven wrong when the more-affordable paperback quickly hit 100,000 sales. Subsequent editions – including every version published in the United States – even replaced Kirby's cover art. It wasn't until 2010 that an edition featuring the complete artwork, with Kirby's name once again credited alongside Pratchett's, finally became available.

That year's other Discworld offering was more narratively satisfying, though, like *Eric*, it was a relatively lightweight addition to the canon. *Moving Pictures* echoes *Pyramids*, in that it takes one high-concept idea – in this case old Hollywood and the birth of cinema – and squeezes as many jokes and references from it as possible; taking in the Marx Brothers, Fred and Ginger, *Singin' In The Rain*, *Casablanca*, *Gone With The Wind* and hundreds more. It's a solid romp, full of fantastic gags (the best of which is probably the nod to *King Kong* towards the book's climax, depicting a giant woman climbing a tall building holding a struggling ape) with an unsettling Lovecraftian undertone, but it is ultimately unmemorable by Pratchett's high standards.

Moving Pictures is the end point of a certain type of Discworld novel. Though Terry was capable of quite marvellous character development, as seen with the likes of Death, Vimes and Granny Weatherwax, he was occasionally guilty of using stock templates, especially with regard to younger adult progtagonists. When a fan wrote to Pratchett to ask if the book's hero, Victor Tugelbend, would return in another novel, Terry replied to say that he viewed such characters as movie stars, reappearing in several books but playing different roles. To him Victor, *Pyramids*' Teppic, the eponymous hero of *Mort*, and perhaps even initially Carrot in *Guards! Guards!* were all roles played by the same actor. This is also true of their less-than-developed female co-stars; *The Light Fantastic*'s Bethany, *Sourcery*'s Conina, *Pyramids*' Ptraci, *Moving Pictures*' Ginger and *Mort*'s Ysabelle; or nerdy sidekicks such as Twoflower, Nijel or Eric. Many Discworld villains and bit-players can also be seen in this way. Following *Moving Pictures*, Terry would start to grow beyond such limited characterisation.

The following year saw mid-period Discworld find its feet, with the publication of *Reaper Man* in the spring, and *Witches Abroad* in the autumn. The former is one of Pratchett's most poignant pieces of writing. In the book, Death discovers that he himself is now due to die, and resolves to spend the rest of his time working among humans. He reinvents himself as a farmhand called Bill Door, and falls into a dignified and understated romance with an elderly farm owner, Miss Flitworth. A secondary plot, involving a zombie wizard, has a lot of fun with horror clichés and makes an especially savage point about consumerism with the arrival of a demonic shopping mall, but aside from some great lines and likeable characters it feels like an unnecessary distraction. Pratchett would later admit that he wished he had used the two plots for two separate novels. The final scenes, where Bill Door takes Miss Flitworth dancing on the day he knows she will die, are probably the most moving pieces of writing Pratchett had yet published.[2]

Witches Abroad revisits the witches of Lancre, this time freeing them of their Shakespearean conceit and sending them, as the punny title suggests, to foreign parts. Here Pratchett leans into the groundwork he set up in *Wyrd Sisters*, in which the importance and shape of stories, fairytales and myths are unpacked and examined. His affection for the three witches shines from the page, and there's plenty of fun to be had in the sending up of *Cinderella*, *Sleeping Beauty*, *Little Red Riding Hood* and more. There's more here than Grimm parodies[3] though. *Witches Abroad* is a story about the expectations that are put upon us, and about not becoming the thing we fear the most. Pratchett had gradually increased Granny Weatherwax's power from the village witch of *Equal Rites* into a formidable magic user, and her character is driven by the iron discipline necessary to keep her power in check. The book ends with Granny confronting her own sister in a tense and emotionally layered stand-off, as Pratchett continued to add depth to his principal actors.

---

2. Reaper Man has some fun with typography, with the two stories represented in different fonts. At one point the celestial being, Azrael, replies to Death with the word 'YES', which appears in a text size 400 times bigger than the standard type and fills the width of the page. In the hardback edition Pratchett made sure this appeared at the top of the left-hand page, so the reader would be surprised when they leafed over. Unfortunately the significantly more common paperback version reset the type and ruined this rather excellent piece of comic timing by putting it on the facing page where the reader can see it coming.
3. Or, if you like, Hans Christian Ander-puns.

He would spend the rest of the decade cycling through a handful of returning (rather than recast) characters, as Discworld mania propelled each book to the top of the charts. There was the City Watch 'howdunnits' (*Men At Arms, Feet of Clay, Jingo, The Fifth Elephant*), the storybook adventures of the witches (*Lords and Ladies, Maskerade, Carpe Jugulum*), travelogue romps courtesy of Rincewind (*Interesting Times, The Last Continent*) and examinations of humanity told via Death and his somewhat stern and self-important granddaughter, Susan Sto Helit (*Soul Music, Hogfather, Thief of Time*). As a rule, spring would bring a more cerebral story, while the pre-Christmas release would be a lighter adventure. Each book continued to deepen the Discworld, pulling it closer to the reality we know and further from the thinly sketched, generic fantasy landscape of the early stories.

The '90s also yielded one more stand-alone novel. In many ways 1992's *Small Gods* was as important as *Equal Rites* had been five years earlier. The combination of rage and humanity that marked *Truckers* is present here, though the two plots couldn't have been further from each other. *Small Gods* is the first of Pratchett's adult books to lead, not from its jokes or its characters, but from its theme – the gulf between faith and religion. It's a story into which Pratchett poured years of baffled frustration with church dogma, and a seething rage at the horrors that man could carry out in its name.

It started as a book about a tortoise. Pratchett pinpoints the genesis of the plot in a 1989 article he contributed to *20/20 Magazine*. Unpacking his own pet from its winter hibernation sparked the thought that a tortoise might make a good character for a story. Research into the subject turned up an old Greek legend about a playwright who had been killed when an eagle dropped a tortoise on his head. Terry's mind began to work – why would an eagle, which usually drops tortoises onto sharp rocks to crack their shells, drop one onto a man's head when there was so much open ground to choose from? His conclusion was 'it must have been on purpose'. But why? 'Because the tortoise was controlling it and wanted to be dropped on the man.' But a tortoise wouldn't have reason to hate a playwright, would it? What kind of person might someone really hate? 'A priest.' And why would the tortoise hate a priest? 'Because the tortoise is actually God, and no-one is likely to hate priests more than their god.'[4]

---

4. This is perhaps the point in the thought process where Pratchett heads in a direction very few would even approach.

It's a brilliant example of how Pratchett could reverse engineer a plot from a single idea, using a combination of his imagination and decades of randomised research.

Small Gods would call on a lifetime of such reading. Though never religious himself (see chapter one), Terry had always made sure his atheism was well-researched. By the age of 14 he had read the *Old Testament* all the way through, and found it both horrifying and compelling (as opposed to its sequel which he found well-meaning, full of sound advice but, aside from the trippy fever-dream of Revelation, a little bland). At the same time, he'd fallen in love with the works of Charles Darwin and rationalism. In *Small Gods* he takes the swollen balloon of religious doctrine and pricks it expertly. Here, God did not create men: God was created *by* men. Enough belief can bring forth a god, and they are given their shape and purpose by the worshippers who dream them up. God works for *us*, not the other way round. There is true nastiness in *Small Gods*, probably more so than in any previous (and many subsequent) Pratchett novels, but it is the nastiness of humanity, which can twist the good-natured faith of ordinary people and use it to accumulate power. The brilliant twist of *Small Gods* is in making the ridiculous turtle, on which Terry's fantasy world rested, into a symbol of rationalism against a dogmatic church which believes the world is a globe, and enforces that view with the same terrifying zeal as medieval Catholicism.

It's more complex than rationalism = good, religion = bad, however. The central character of Brutha practises a gentle and genuine faith in a god he believes wants the best for people, and the book can be read as a treatise on what religion can or should be, versus what it usually becomes. In *Small Gods* Pratchett isn't angry at gods (it would be over a decade before he tackled that subject in *Nation*, more of which later), which he argues fill a need in the human psyche. He is furious with those that propagate evil in their name. Angry, thoughtful, blisteringly clever, while still managing to be extremely funny, *Small Gods* is a remarkable novel, possibly Pratchett's first genuinely *great* one, and a point in his canon where he noticeably 'levels-up'. It would begin a run of excellent form.

As the decade progressed it was clear that the magic of Discworld was starting to leak out of the pages of the books. Terry was always wary of authorising spin-off media and merchandise; as a sci-fi fan he was well aware of the level of junk that could be passed off as official merchandise, and had no desire to see Rincewind depicted on a cereal box, or Nanny Ogg on a pair of underpants. Pratchett and Colin Smythe were approached continually about such marketing opportunities, and rarely entertained them. One typical offer, kept in Smythe's archive, was from a company pitching to make Discworld hosiery and underwear, shoes, action figures, hats and Granny Weatherwax tea. Pratchett hated these ideas. He was always careful about who was granted rights to the Discworld for TV, movie and game adaptations, as it carried the risk of taking the merchandising of his characters out of his hands. You only have to look at the spin-off empire that built up around J. K. Rowling's *Harry Potter* franchise to see how tacky and ubiquitous merchandising of a literary property can become. Pratchett's feeling was that he didn't need the money, so any Discworld memorabilia would need to be worth having for its own sake.

One of the first companies that *did* gain a license was a tiny Essex-based studio called Clarecraft, which specialised in fantasy figurines and had previously worked with the Tolkien estate. Co-founder Isobel Pearson had been one of those early converts who had encountered Pratchett's work via Nigel Hawthorne's reading of *The Colour of Magic* on Radio 4 back in 1984. Isobel and her husband, Bernard, contacted Colin Smythe with the idea of creating collectible Discworld figurines in 1990. A rough model of the Luggage was produced during a meeting with Pratchett and Smythe in London; it was enough to pique Pratchett's interest, and he faxed through rough character sketches of Rincewind and Granny Weatherwax for them to work from.[5] Bernard Pearson was dispatched to a Covent Garden bar to present the author with a wax prototype Rincewind for approval. Not only did Pratchett love the figure, which captured his character's hangdog, permanently put-upon expression, but the two men liked each other almost immediately. They were similar in age and Bernard had worked as a village policeman for years, a job that mirrored many of the experiences Pratchett had as a local journalist around the same time. They also shared a love of the countryside and rural life, not to mention a fondness for a pint of real ale and a well-

---

5. Wary of Josh Kirby's rather loose interpretation of Granny on the cover of *Equal Rites*, Pratchett wrote 'no warts' on his sketch.

pickled onion. Clarecraft was given an enthusiastic go-ahead to start producing figures, beginning with Rincewind, the Luggage, Granny and Death. The pieces were an immediate hit among fans, and soon became the small studio's main stock-in-trade. The Pearsons and their team – including a young artist called Leigh Pamment who created models of many Discworld figures, and would tragically die in a train accident in 1996 – created hundreds of pieces, each one workshopped with Pratchett himself, who always had trouble letting go of the reins of his creations. Over the years the Pearsons would model most of the characters in the books, from the major players such as Vimes, Nanny Ogg and Death, down to the incidental bit parts, including Herne The Hunted – who was the god of small, furry animals mentioned very briefly in *Wyrd Sisters* and *Lords and Ladies* – or Death's manservant, Albert, dressed as a pixie, as depicted in *Hogfather*. Pratchett enjoyed throwing the Pearsons challenges, such as the pewter Hobb of the Furrows medallion, which brought luck to cabbage growers, or the anorankh, a silver necklace in the shape of an anorak which was born from the accidental muddling of the words 'anorak' and 'ankh' by a contributor to alt.fan.pratchett. Such trinkets were unlikely to swell the Pearsons' coffers, but represented everything that was good about their collaboration with Pratchett; capturing the spirit of Discworld without ever exploiting it.

The Pearsons were the first of a handful of Discworld fans who, like the writer Dave Langford,[6] would be drawn into the industry surrounding the series, becoming firm friends and collaborative partners, eventually forming a sort of Discworld 'brain trust', and helping to manage the various extensions of the franchise. Many years later, after Pratchett's death, such figures would be named part of the Order of the Honeybee, and be tasked with protecting his legacy. Bernard, especially, would become a key presence in Discworld life, a close friend of Terry's and a familiar figure within fandom. Pratchett would immortalise him as the larger-than-life Sergeant Jackrum in his 2003 novel, *Monstrous Regiment*.

The next recruit to team Discworld turned up around the same time as the Pearsons. An Oxfordshire-based civil servant and amateur dramatics

---

6. One of Langford's main roles was to use his encyclopedic memory to ensure that jokes didn't get repeated. Occasionally – as in a *Hogfather* gag involving a man riding behind a woman and hanging on in, er, the wrong place, which originally cropped up in *Equal Rites* – one slipped through.

enthusiast called Stephen Briggs approached Pratchett and Smythe about adapting *Wyrd Sisters* for the stage. That year, 1990, Briggs' company, Studio Theatre Club, became the first anywhere in the world to stage a Discworld play. Pratchett attended the opening night of the show's four-night run at the Unicorn Theatre, Abingdon, and found himself laughing fractionally before a punchline, which he worried might be distracting for the actors. He was delighted with the production, though felt that Briggs' adaptation suffered from sticking too slavishly to the source material, and worried that non-fans might find the play a little baffling as a result. Fortunately there were, by now, so many Discworld fans that concerns for the layman weren't really applicable, and all four nights sold out. Terry met the cast backstage, taking along bottles of champagne and Clarecraft models of the three witches. That night he and Briggs met in person for the first time, and Pratchett was surprised to note that the writer, who was also playing the role of Duke Felmet, was a dead ringer for another Discworld character, the Machiavellian Lord Vetinari. The pair got along well, and Pratchett happily authorised Briggs' request to adapt *Mort* the following year. Stephen Briggs would eventually adapt twenty-three of Pratchett's books for the stage, often being sent the manuscripts in advance, meaning Studio Theatre Club was able to stage performances of new Discworld novels in the same month they hit the shelves.

Since that first performance, productions of Pratchett's work – written by Briggs and others – have been staged in twenty-two countries and in several languages.[7] These have ranged from the National Theatre's spectacular, high-budget production of *Nation*, right down to countless school drama–club stagings of *Guards! Guards!*, *Mort* and many more. Professional companies had to jump through as many hoops as Colin Smythe could think to throw at them, but Pratchett was happy to let almost any amateur group perform his work, providing they sought permission to do so and gave a small donation to his preferred charity, the Orangutan Foundation. As a result, Discworld plays have been staged on all seven continents, including a version of *Wyrd Sisters* performed by staff at an Australian research base in Antarctica in December 2004

---

7. Terry and Lyn once travelled to Prague to gamely sit through a performance of *Maskerade* done entirely in Czech, a language neither of them understood. They quite enjoyed it.

in celebration of the winter solstice. Pratchett would try to see as many productions as he could, including the endearingly low-budget ones, but even he drew the line at travelling to the South Pole.

Stephen Briggs would become one of Pratchett's most consistent collaborators, and was responsible for several Discworld spin-offs. He maintained the accuracy of his plays by combing through the books, and quickly became an expert on the franchise. Pratchett would telephone him, alongside David Langford and Discworld superfan Pat Harkin, when he needed to know which-street-met-which in Ankh-Morpork, and what pubs you'd pass as you walked along them. It was Briggs who suggested that the city might be mappable. Pratchett had always been against mapping the Discworld, feeling that putting definite lines around his world could hem his creativity. The Discworld, after all, needed space to accommodate anything its creator wanted to parody or reference. He also felt that mapping the Discworld would see him falling into the same traps as the bad fantasy novels that inspired the series in the first place. Most of these came with the standard line-drawn map showing the compulsory 'wiggly river' and 'pointy mountains' established by *The Lord of the Rings*.[8] The city of Ankh-Morpork, however, was different.

The idea had a practical benefit – Pratchett was midway through writing *Men At Arms*, a sequel to *Guards! Guards!* set entirely within the borders of the city, and it was becoming clear that he needed to maintain consistency across the books, if only to keep the more tedious end of fantasy fandom from pointing out the continuity errors. Briggs faxed a rough version over to Pratchett, who was satisfied enough to give it the go ahead. The result was months of painstaking work by Briggs (his wife claimed that by the end of the process she could have walked around Ankh-Morpork with her eyes shut), with Pratchett making occasional adjustments and suggestions that often meant – since Briggs was working with pencil, paper and Pritt Stick – having to start all over again. This included an eleventh-hour decision to move Short Street, the main thoroughfare through the city, to an entirely new angle, causing a despairing Briggs to agree through gritted teeth, and trudge back to his desk, muttering darkly.

---

8. That said, Pratchett loved the maps in Tolkien's masterpiece.

The Streets of Ankh-Morpork, featuring Briggs' remarkably detailed 'mapp' redrawn beautifully by the artist Stephen Player, was published by Corgi in time for Christmas 1993.[9] It was the most elaborate Discworld spin-off yet, boasting a metre-square street plan and a short introductory text by Briggs and Pratchett, folded to mirror an ordnance survey map. This was a beautifully detailed work, full of hidden touches. It was also the first example of an outside source influencing Discworld directly. Much of the layout was Briggs' work, as were many of the street names, and Pratchett would use the map to guide the action in all future stories set in the city. *The Streets of Ankh-Morpork* was a huge success, climbing to number four in the bestseller *non-fiction* list – which for a map of an entirely fictional city is quite some achievement – and winning an artwork award from the British Science Fiction and Fantasy Association.[10] The project was so successful that the next step was obvious.

Despite its creator's earlier insistence that it couldn't be done, *The Discworld Mapp* was published in 1995, with the legwork again being done by Briggs, under Pratchett's direction, and Stephen Player once again translating the detailed draft into a beautifully drawn map of the world. Two more 'mapps', *A Tourist Guide to Lancre* and *Death's Domain*, followed in 1998 and 1999, though neither sold as well as the first two, with the final mapp receiving a print run which was less than half of the first. Rather than true maps, the *Lancre* and *Death's Domain* fold-outs featured detailed aerial views with artwork handled by another addition to the Discworld family, Paul Kidby.

Kidby was a graphic artist from London, who had been sent a Discworld novel by his sister and quickly became a huge fan of the series, convinced his artwork was a natural fit for Pratchett's style. At the time he was working as a commercial illustrator for the magazine company Future Publishing, providing artwork for the likes of *SFX*. A journalist friend slipped Pratchett some examples of Kidby's work during an interview, and samples were also sent to Colin Smythe and Pratchett's publishers. None of these approaches met with success, which Kidby

---

9. This author vividly remembers receiving it in his stocking that year and spending the whole day poring over the details.
10. Presumably because getting the map of a fantasy city into the non-fiction chart deserves some sort of special prize.

reasoned might be because he'd sent generic fantasy illustrations rather than specific Discworld artwork. It didn't help that Pratchett already had an effective working relationship with Josh Kirby, whose work and style had become synonymous with the series. Nevertheless, Kidby felt strongly enough about his ideas to try approaching Pratchett once more. He and his then-wife, Sandra, attended a 1993 book signing at W. H. Smith in Bath, handing an envelope of new Discworld drawings directly to the author. A few weeks later the Kidbys were surprised to receive a phone call from Pratchett, who had been stunned by the artwork and said it was exactly how he'd pictured many of his characters. He invited the 29-year-old artist to his home to discuss future projects. As with Pearson and Briggs, this began a long and fruitful association between artist and author. Josh Kirby's work may have matched the imaginative and chaotic spirit of the early Discworld, but Kidby's pieces represented the characters in a more naturalistic way, and felt truer to the maturing tone of the books. Kidby soon became Pratchett's 'artist of choice' for Discworld projects, though Kirby was still called upon for jacket art and more high-profile pieces, and the Kidbys and Pratchetts became close friends.

The final member of Team Discworld was a softly spoken young fan called Rob Wilkins. He drifted into Pratchett's orbit in 1993, the same year as Kidby, and though his impact wasn't as immediate as the unholy trinity of Pearson, Briggs and Kidby, ultimately his involvement would be the most significant. Pratchett met Wilkins at a book signing at the Oxford branch of W. H. Smith, and they bonded briefly over hobbyist electronics and the lengths both had gone to push the humble ZX Spectrum to its limits. They stayed in touch, as Pratchett often did with fans he took a shine to, and they bonded further at the first Discworld convention in 1996, where Pratchett gave the younger man the nickname 'Captain Capacitor' due to his love of soldering computer parts together. Wilkins was taken on by Colin Smythe Ltd as technical director in 1998, greatly improving the company's web presence, as well as helping with Pratchett's increasing workload. By Christmas 2000, he had become Pratchett's full time personal assistant. Wilkins would remain by Pratchett's side for the rest of the author's life, later describing Terry as his best friend, and saying that he'd only worked *for* Pratchett on his first day – after that he'd worked *with* him. After Pratchett's death it was Wilkins who became the face of Discworld, described by Neil Gaiman during the making of the *Good Omens* TV show, as 'Terry's representative on Earth'.

The models and mapps were the beginning of a growing empire of Discworld spin-offs, all carefully controlled and approved by Pratchett. Discworld mania was booming and between them Bernard Pearson, Stephen Briggs and Paul Kidby – with Terry's direct involvement – would develop the cottage industry that surrounded the franchise and its fans. Bringing Pratchett's work to life became a full-time career for all three. Briggs created T-shirts, bookmarks and posters as a 'spare room business' on top of his fictional cartography and dramatisation skills. The Pearsons produced hundreds of models and trinkets with their team at Clarecraft, and later under various other guises, while Paul and Sandra Kidby sold artwork through their website, PJSMPrints.co.uk.

Briggs also steered through *The Discworld Companion*, an encyclopedia and reference work summarising nearly every character, building, country, religion and landmark mentioned in the books. Pratchett added to or rewrote almost every entry, and contributed more detail from his notes, including teasing plot points that wouldn't manifest in the novels for years, if ever at all. The *Companion* first appeared in 1994 and was revised three times, with the most recent edition published in 2012. Terry found it the most useful of his spin-offs, reaching for the *Companion* whenever he needed to remember the names of Nanny Ogg's fifteen children or the capital city of Klatch.

Elsewhere, a fiendishly difficult quiz-book, *Unseen University Challenge,* devised by the fiendishly clever David Langford, was commissioned by Gollancz in 1995, with a sequel (*The Wyrdest Link*) following belatedly in 2002. A lavish artbook, *The Josh Kirby Discworld Portfolio*, collecting Kirby's covers and illustrations, was published in 1993, while the more modest *The Pratchett Portfolio*, collecting Kidby's work, hit the shelves in 1996. That year also saw Corgi start publishing Briggs' play scripts as paperbacks, starting with *Wyrd Sisters* and *Mort*. By then, the Discworld machine was so huge that even the scripts received reasonable reviews in the press and sold respectably.

A tradition of publishing annual Discworld diaries or almanacs began in 1997 with *Discworld's Unseen University Diary*, a year planner augmented with new writing by Briggs (and later Bernard Pearson and his team) – steered, tweaked and approved by Pratchett – complete with Paul Kidby illustrations. The diaries provided fans with bonus Discworld material every year, and though it wasn't all written by Pratchett, the author approved each new diary, often contributing upwards of 10,000 words of new content and tweaking Briggs' work. His editor at the time, Jo Fletcher, remembers that Pratchett would always over-deliver on his contributions.

In 1993, Corgi began a programme of abridged audiobooks (referred to at the time as 'books-on-tape'), narrated at Pratchett's specific request by the comic actor Tony Robinson. Robinson was an inspired choice. His portrayal of the hapless Baldrick in the sitcom *Blackadder*, a character which had directly inspired Corporal Nobbs in *Guards! Guards!*, had made him a household name, and his children's shows, *Blood and Honey* and *Maid Marion and her Merry Men* shared a subversive tone with Pratchett's work. He had a personal investment too; he and his daughter Laura had read *The Colour of Magic* together during a particularly hard time in his life. Corgi began with the *Bromeliad* trilogy and the first three Discworld novels, and the tapes were immediately successful. Robinson would go on to record all but three of Pratchett's books and the two men became friends, though the author's occasional presence in the recording studio, scowling about the sheer amount of material lost in the abridgement process – sometimes up to two-thirds – could be off-putting.

Those that preferred their Discworld presented in full – footnotes and all – were catered for by Isis Audio Books, which won the contract to produce unabridged versions of the first eight Discworld novels, beginning in 1995. These were performed by *The Young Ones* and *Comic Strip* actor Nigel Planer. An unabridged recording was not to be taken lightly, as Planer remembers, and would involve two-and-a-half days of intense performance per book. 'I was particularly proud of them being unabridged,' said Planer. 'They don't change a word, which was a problem sometimes because those early books had not been copy edited very well, and there were plenty of mistakes and typos in them, so we had to do some small edits to make something make sense.' Planer would record all of the unabridged Discworlds up to and including 1998's *Carpe*

Jugulum.[11] His schedule meant he was unable to record the following year's *The Fifth Elephant*, and at Pratchett's recommendation Isis Audio hired Stephen Briggs who, as the author's stated choice, held onto the gig for the next decade and a half, and recorded every Pratchett novel from that point until the release of 2015's *The Shepherd's Crown*. Pratchett would always look after his friends. Discworld fans would spend years debating whether Robinson, Planer or Briggs gave the best interpretations of the different characters.

By the mid-1990s, with the mania in full swing, Discworld had become a truly multimedia operation. Three video games emerged across the decade, starting with *Discworld* in 1995,[12] the result of several years' hard work on behalf of the developers, Perfect 10. The game had a budget of £400,000 and was made in collaboration with Pratchett, who wrote much of the script. It featured a voice cast led by Eric Idle as Rincewind – who ad libbed to the point that playing the game sometimes felt like Monty Python's Discworld – as well as former Doctor Who Jon Pertwee and Pratchett regulars Nigel Planer, Tony Robinson and Stephen Briggs. As an avid gamer himself, Pratchett was keen to make sure this was done properly, and involved himself at almost every stage. He was so involved with the game that fans who found themselves stuck on this or that scene would ask his advice at signings, and he was usually able to tell them how to solve whatever puzzle was troubling them. Pratchett was satisfied enough with *Discworld* that he took a more hands-off approach to its sequel, *Discworld II: Missing, Presumed ...!?*, and 1999's *Discworld Noir*, which shifted the gameplay format away from a platform puzzler to a more immersive mystery with a darker tone, creating new characters and departing from the books. Again, the game was created with Pratchett's direct involvement at the scripting stage.

---

11. With the exception of *Equal Rites* and *Wyrd Sisters*, which were given to Celia Imrie as the producers wanted a woman's voice. According to Planer, Imrie hadn't enjoyed the experience, and by the time of *Witches Abroad* it was left to Planer to do the honours. His Nanny Ogg is brilliant.
12. The cover was done by Josh Kirby meaning that, as he needed to match the visuals of the game, for the first and only time he was forced to draw Rincewind as he was described in the book: younger, with a short scrappy beard and dark hair, rather than the white-haired, Gandalf-styled wizard of the book jackets.

Perhaps the oddest spin-off to come out of the era of Discworld mania was *From The Discworld*, a 1994 soundtrack album written and produced by prog-rock veteran Dave Greenslade. It was based loosely on Pratchett's suggestions and, at one point, featured 17-year-old Rhianna Pratchett on keyboards. It has some interesting moments, including a dramatic opening, set to Tony Robinson reading the first paragraph of *The Light Fantastic*, but is otherwise inessential at best, and painfully naff at worst. The plasticky sounds of the synths and cheesy programmed drums have dated terribly, and the jolly version of *A Wizard's Staff has a Knob on the End* is probably unforgivable. Alas, critics at the time tended to agree. *Scotland on Sunday* called it 'awful', going on to describe it as 'regressive prog rock, reeking of seventies excess and overblown theatricality'. Stuart Maconie, writing for *Q* magazine, described the tunes as 'ploddingly dull ... it may be the most calamitously unfunny lapse of taste on a record since [Benny Hill's] *Ernie (The Fastest Milkman In the West)*.'

Plays, albums, video games and models are all very well, but the Holy Grail of spin-off media will always be the movie adaptation, a format conspicuous by its absence during Discworld's '90s pomp. *Mort* almost made it several times – starting around the late 1980s – and the book's journey to Hollywood and back would make a fascinating documentary should the key players ever be coaxed into talking. Pratchett had always said that the fourth Discworld novel, with its straightforward, standalone plot would make the best movie of all of his books. Hollywood, however, never seemed to quite grasp the idea, with one exec reportedly suggesting that the story be rewritten to exclude the character of Death entirely.[13]

Pratchett and Smythe enjoyed several years of expensive lunches as various producers pitched for Discworld properties and were rebuffed. To Pratchett it wasn't about the money – he had plenty of money – it was about seeing it done properly. A movie deal was finally announced in July 1996, with New Line Cinema – who five years later would go on to make Peter Jackson's *The Lord of the Rings* trilogy – partnering with a British company, Scala Productions, on a version of *Mort* with a planned budget of £25 million. Script duties were to be courtesy of Pratchett and British

---

13. Less than two years later, the Grim Reaper featured prominently in the hit movie *Bill and Ted's Bogus Journey*, leading to some withering comments from Pratchett at Hollywood's expense.

writer/director Paul Bamborough. Pratchett would be asked about the movie in almost every interview he gave for years afterwards, and would usually say it was 'progressing', but that he was 'keeping his nose out of it'. The plan was to have Death as a CGI skeleton for some of the film, and a human actor playing him at other moments. Various star names were thrown around for the role, though Pratchett remained tightlipped about his preference, aside from a (probably) jokey suggestion of Danny DeVito. Unfortunately, Hollywood has its own special purgatory and *Mort* was doomed to stay there, as various producers, directors and writers came and went, and the rights to the project were passed through a merry-go-round of execs.

Its most startling near miss came in 2010, when Disney's Ron Clements and John Musker, directors of classic movies *The Little Mermaid*, *Aladdin* and *Hercules*, expressed interest in adapting *Mort* as the studio's next animation project. Pre-production was sufficiently advanced that an animation team was assembled but alas, the plug was pulled. Disney never comments on cancelled films, but it was widely believed at the time that Clements and Musker hadn't been able to secure the rights to the book, which now technically resided with Paul Bamborough's Camel Productions. The only clue to how Disney's *Mort* might have looked comes from one of the studio's in-house animators, Sue Nichols, who leaked a Christmas card sent around to colleagues during that period. Though she was contractually prevented from revealing which project she was working on, the card featured a smiling skeleton with blue dots in its eye sockets, dressed as Santa Claus. The following year Pratchett and Smythe sued to recover the rights, claiming that they should have reverted long ago, in order to free the project up for another studio. As of 2019, *Mort* has remained frustratingly unfilmed.

At the same time that Hollywood was trying – and failing – to get Pratchett's work onto the big screen, the BBC was considering a lavish mini-series of *The Colour of Magic*. A company called Catalyst obtained the rights to the first two Discworld books in 1995, and the project got tantalisingly close to fruition. The team behind the 1980s BAFTA-winning, part-animated, televised comic strip *Jane* would direct and produce, with Gary Kurtz, producer of *Star Wars* and *The Empire Strikes Back* as executive producer, and a script written by up-and-comer Rob

Heyland, who had worked on the hit drama *Cracker*. Heyland's script works hard to tie the overarching story of the two books together, opening with Rincewind and Trymon, the villain of *The Light Fantastic*, being taught at Unseen University in a scene that could come straight from a *Harry Potter* movie. The dialogue is a little clunky in places, but in others the script feels sumptuous and grand, and captures Pratchett's wit well. Sadly the BBC, as Smythe puts it, 'pulled the rug', and *The Colour of Magic* joined *Mort* and *The Bromeliad* in development hell for the remainder of the decade.

It was Cosgrove Hall Films, the studio behind the animated *Truckers* show, that would finally get Discworld to the screen. The idea of an animated series based on the books came from Channel 4's commissioning editor Lucinda Whiteley, who had wanted to bring a Pratchett adaptation to the channel for years, pitching it to Cosgrove Hall via their distributors. It was an easy process from that point; after *Truckers* Pratchett had told the studio's Mark Hall that 'all he had to do was ask' when it came to future projects. The rights for *Mort*, Hall's first choice, were tied up in Hollywood, but it was decided that *Wyrd Sisters* and *Soul Music* – straightforward parodies of *Macbeth* and the music business – would make decent starting points. Cosgrove Hall assembled an excellent cast for both series, with Jane Horrocks, June Whitfield and Annette Crosbie as *Wyrd Sister's* three witches and Les Dennis as Verence, while *Soul Music* would feature Neil Morrissey as Mort and Graham Crowden as Ridcully. The biggest coup was casting horror legend Christopher Lee as Death, whose leaden tones suited the character perfectly. *Wyrd Sisters* was broadcast in May 1997, in a Sunday teatime slot, but was hamstrung by tepid reviews and struggled to find an audience. The books were read by adults but the show looked cartoonish, and unless you were a Discworld fan it was difficult to know who it was aimed at. Many of the jokes, which would sing on the page, fell foul of clunky timing on screen, and the quality of the animation looked cheap and dated. Channel 4, who had been waiting to see how the series did, held off on plans to air *Soul Music*, which went straight to video[14] and was eventually broadcast two years

---

14. A *Soul Music* soundtrack album, comprised of 1950s rock 'n' roll parodies, became the second Discworld CD in three years to be largely ignored by fans and critics.

later, at the hardly prime time slot of 2.30 am. The experience poured water on television's desire to bring the Discworld to life for some years.

To appreciate the extent to which Discworld mania flourished, we have to look outside of the official spin-offs. Fan activity was driving a healthy secondary industry, which Pratchett was more-or-less happy to endorse, so long as it didn't spill into a fully commercial endeavour. In 1996, a fan called Julia Froggatt was featured in her local paper, *The Chester Chronicle*, after her online business supplying Discworld cross-stitch patterns started to take off. Another fan began selling unofficial Unseen University scarves, half green and half purple to represent the 'greenish purple' of Octarine, the colour of magic. Discworld fanzines had been around since the late 1980s, when *Tales of the Broken Drum* was introduced as a Pratchett zine, and quickly swelled to cover comic fantasy in general (essentially meaning it also covered Robert Rankin, Tom Holt and anything else with a Josh Kirby cover). By the mid-1990s there was a boom of Discworld zines, from the professional and comprehensive *Discworld Chronicle* to the more ramshackle-looking, but feature-packed *The Wizard's Knob*. Fansites and newsletters mushroomed across the web, with names such as *Klatchian Mist* and *The Discworld Multi-User Dungeon*. In 1997 a young fan called Jason Anthony, who would later legally change his middle name to Rincewind, set up the *Discworld Monthly* online newsletter, an absurdly comprehensive update on new releases, plays, press coverage and events, and one of the few operations that, at the time of writing, is still going strong. Within a year he'd acquired 10,000 subscribers, swelling to nearly 20,000 at the newsletter's peak. The following year an American fan, Joe Schaumburger, started a similar newsletter, *Wossname*, on the other side of the Atlantic, still being published at the time of writing by dedicated fan Annie Mac, who took the reins following Schaumburger's passing. Meanwhile an unofficial Discworld fanclub, The Guild of Fans and Disciples, had been formed with Terry's blessing in 1994 and was run out of the home of superfan, Jacqui Edge in Lancashire. Within a year the entirely homespun G.O.F.A.D. had 350 members. By the end of the decade it had over 4,000, by which time it was being overseen by another fan, Elizabeth Alway. The guild had its own quarterly newssheet, *Ramtop to Rimfall*, edited by Alway, which would run until the club quietly dissolved in 2006. Terry was delighted by this sort of activity. It was exactly how he felt fantasy and SF fans should be behaving and he encouraged them enthusiastically, writing to the letters page of *Ramtop to Rimfall*, or answering fan questions in *Discworld Monthly*.

It was only a matter of time before an attempt was made to bring fans together in person. The first organised Discworld fan-gathering, a convention in all but name, was thrown by Bernard and Isobel Pearson in 1995, which they called the Clarecraft Discworld Event, held on a blisteringly hot summer's day in Woolpit, Suffolk. Terry was, naturally, the guest of honour, though the event was really just a large market for Discworld and related merchandise. Several hundred people attended and a good time, by common consent, was had by all. A 'mini-convention' was proposed for the following year by Discworld fan Paul Rood, who was inspired by a friend who had just returned from a gathering of P. G. Wodehouse fans. Rood was swamped by so many enquiries after posting about the idea on alt.fan.pratchett, that the 'mini' was quickly dropped. He approached Pratchett for permission to throw the bash, and was given the go-ahead after Terry, who knew a few things about fantasy conventions, was satisfied that the organisers more or less knew what they were doing. He helped with the odd bit of advice and a handful of contacts, and was persuaded to carry flyers on his next signing tour, despite grumbling at the size and weight of the package when the postman delivered them. Pratchett said at the time that he expected the event to sell less than half of its 850 tickets.

The first official Discworld Convention was held on the weekend of 28–30 June 1996, at the height of the Euro '96 football tournament, at Sacha's Hotel in Manchester. Despite Pratchett's fears, a healthy crowd of over 800 people enjoyed a mock episode of *Blind Date*, an 'Ephibian slave auction', a gala dinner with a speech by the guest of honour (one T. Pratchett, of Wiltshire), a costume masquerade (which convention veteran Pratchett dubbed 'respectable'), a Q&A with the author, and a Discworld quiz in which Pratchett's team were flummoxed by a question about the as-yet-unpublished *Hogfather*. 'How could you know that one?' demanded Pratchett. 'We know everything!' came a voice from the audience. Proceedings finished with the bizarre ceremonial dunking of Paul Rood in a paddling pool full of custard, presided over by the baffled but happy-looking author.

The weekend was a great success. What surprised Pratchett most was the number of convention-goers who'd never been to such an event before. A look around the trading floor confirmed his hunch that his audience had a comfortable fifty-fifty gender split and the Kevins, though present, were far from dominant. All of human[15] life was there. It gave the Discworld convention (dubbed DWCon) a family-friendly atmosphere. As Pratchett would later say, every attendee had turned up expecting to be the only person there. What they found was each other. Anyone could be a Discworld fan, and sometimes it felt like just about everybody was.

---

15. And possibly some non-human.

Chapter 15

A Little Respect

By the mid-1990s, it was clear that Gollancz and Corgi's plans had paid off. Though there were still – and always would be – pockets of resistance that saw Pratchett as a niche concern, the ubiquity of his books had transformed him into a household name. If you didn't read Terry Pratchett novels, you certainly knew someone who did. The snobbishness from the literary establishment would never go away entirely, though. Colin Smythe tells a story on his website about nipping into the large and extremely respected Hatchards bookshop in central London to buy a copy of Pratchett's 2000 novel, *The Truth*. It had been number one in the *Sunday Times* bestseller list for weeks but was nowhere to be seen on the bestsellers' table, or indeed anywhere in the front section of the shop with the other top-selling books. Smythe was told that, despite the evidence of basic mathematics, Hatchards didn't consider *The Truth* to be a true bestseller and besides, the sci-fi and fantasy section jealously guarded the Pratchett books. This tells us a lot about how Pratchett's work was perceived at the height of his fame – and arguably the 'height of his fame' stretches from about 1995 to the present day – Waterstones and W. H. Smith would be happy to line their window displays with the latest Discworld, but the snobbier end of the literary community would never consider his success as valid, while the nerdier end would always consider him one of their own. The general public, meanwhile, bought his books in the millions.

Nerdy he may well have been, but the 1990s made Pratchett a celebrity. It was a state of affairs to which he adapted in his own way – by carefully and cleverly cultivating what we'd now refer to as a 'personal brand'. The Pratchett of 1985 may have dressed like a driving instructor, but the Pratchett of the mid-'90s dressed largely like Johnny Cash. He was fond of wearing all black or, occasionally, white and khaki green, and very early in his 'celebrity' life took to wearing a black fedora hat for almost any public occasion. He wore a gold skull ring and later would carry a black cane topped with a silver Death's head. The glasses become smaller and neater. The look wasn't just an affectation or a style choice.[1] Pratchett had never been a natty dresser; from the shapeless hooped sweaters of the 1970s to the flat-cap-and-tinted-specs chic of the 1980s, his sense of style ranged from non-existent to objectively terrible. While at the CEGB, his idea of 'business attire' had been a piano-key tie. This new man-in-black look was a calculated creation. Terry Pratchett the author was himself a character, separate from the private man who shared his name and face. He'd often joke that all he needed to do was to take off his hat and he'd instantly become an anonymous, bearded man in glasses. At Discworld conventions, which after the success of the first event would be held every other year, it was well known among fans that the man in the hat with a badge that said 'Terry Pratchett' was a public figure who would welcome a handshake and a request for an autograph or a photo;[2] while the short, bald man who happened to *look a lot like* Terry Pratchett, but whose badge bore another name, was in the mood for being left alone. The carefully rehearsed quotes and anecdotes were all part of this. Pratchett was playing a role in public; that of the eccentric fantasy author. It was a version of himself he gave to his fans, and was happy to share, but it wasn't the real man. Neil Gaiman's foreword to *A Slip of the Keyboard* describes an encounter with a person who'd met Pratchett at an event and thought him a 'jolly old elf'. They had fallen into his trap. In private, Pratchett could be much snippier, and indeed a common phrase used by those who knew him best was of someone who 'didn't suffer fools'. His assistant, Rob Wilkins, describes the blazing rows the pair would have on an almost daily basis: ('We had an argument every day,' Wilkins said during a filmed fan Q&A in 2017. 'Every day I quit, and every day Terry sacked me. The door nearly came off its hinges on many occasions as I slammed it behind me.') Briggs, Pearson and Kidby all reported similar clashes. ('He did not suffer fools,' wrote Pearson in 2016's *The Terry Pratchett Diary*, 'as I often found to my cost'), and at one time or another all of Pratchett's editors found themselves on the wrong end of a waspish reply. One contemporary of Terry's, who knew

---

1. At least you hope not – in 1997 *SFX* readers voted Pratchett the worst dresser in sci-fi.
2. Especially if you bought him a drink.

him well in the '80s and '90s, described him as 'a very complex character' who 'behaved so differently in front of various people that there are going to be some extraordinary contradictions depending upon whom you speak to.' The 'jolly old elf' and the 'man in black' were there to distract people from an intensely private person. That's not to say Pratchett was a monster behind closed doors – his friends remember acts of enormous generosity, and the arguments he could have with his editors, or with Wilkins, Pearson and the rest, were always creative in nature, never personal – the result of both sides passionately wanting the work to be the best it could be. He was a man who very much lived the ethos he presented in his writing, which stressed the importance of basic human decency. As Granny Weatherwax would have it in a powerful speech in 1998's *Carpe Jugulum*, he refused to see people as 'things'.

Whatever was happening behind closed doors, public Pratchett was every inch the media professional and an ambassador for his own work. In 1995 he was interviewed on the daytime chat show *Pebble Mill* by Alan Titchmarsh. Pratchett, dressed in olive and white, is relaxed in front of the camera, cracking a few well-practised oneliners and dealing patiently with a host who appears completely out of his depth talking about video games and CD-Roms, and whose most incisive question about his guest's work is, 'are you a bit like Tolkien then?'

Yet, even in this shallowest of interviews we can see Pratchett fighting to be more than 'the guy that writes funny fantasy books'. He doesn't exactly flinch when asked to describe the Discworld, but there's certainly a flicker of annoyance. From the publication of *The Colour of Magic*, right up to the end of his life, interviewers tended – despite having Britain's most successful living author in front of them – to assume much of their audience needed the fundamentals of his famous concept explaining. Turtle. Elephants. Flat world. But to Pratchett, the books had become far, far more than what he described as 'the business with the turtle'. He would almost always answer the 'what is the Discworld?' question by explaining the idea of real people in a fantasy environment, but would usually be pulled back to spell out 'the business with the turtle' all over again. In the introduction to Paul Kidby's *The Art of Discworld* he admits to sometimes wishing he'd left out the turtle all together.[3]

---

3. Which would have been hard luck for the elephants.

In the run up to the millennium, Terry was beginning to be regarded as 'an important and influential figure'. In the same year as the *Pebble Mill* interview, he was approached by Channel 4 about filming a travelogue as part of its 'Short Stories' series. The result, *Terry Pratchett's Jungle Quest*, saw the author head for the rainforests of Borneo to meet orangutans in the wild and draw attention to the ecological issues threatening them. Pratchett took the same hands-on approach to the documentary as he did with all of his projects, shaping the 'story' and writing the narration himself. The popularity of Discworld's Librarian had created an unexpected association between author and ape, and he was glad to help raise the profile of a species which, as he says in the documentary, is often overlooked in favour of their more 'outgoing' cousins, the chimpanzees and gorillas. Eventually he was asked to become a trustee of the Orangutan Foundation, and made sure all amateur performances of Discworld plays made a contribution to the charity.

The half-hour documentary is wonderful. Pratchett's script is warm and informative while being packed with zingers. The footage of the bearded author coming face-to-face with Kusasi, a huge orangutan with the swollen cheek pouches of a dominant male, is compelling television. Pratchett crouches, visibly spellbound, as a creature which he admits could pull his arm out of its socket sits peacefully before him, eating fruit and having its picture taken, before walking slowly back into the forest. *Jungle Quest* was easily the most successful thing Pratchett did on television that decade. Sir Alec Guinness, writing in his diary, said it was 'the best thing I have seen on the box all year'. Having met the approval of Obi-wan Kenobi, Terry Pratchett happily added documentary filmmaking to his skill set, and filed it away for later.

In 1996, the men's lifestyle magazine *GQ* approached Terry about interviewing the technology billionaire and Microsoft founder, Bill Gates. It's a fascinating piece, in which Pratchett's skills as a journalist are clearly evident. The pair discuss the evolution of tech and the potential impact the internet might have in a world where any piece of information can be passed off as valid. Pratchett uses the example of Holocaust denial being presented online as a legitimate historical study. Gates's response is typically idealistic, saying that the internet would be self-policing, and that reliable sources would be clearly marked as such. Looking back on the interview, from an era blighted by accusations of 'fake news' and the spread of popularist politics via social media, it's remarkable how perceptive Pratchett's comments are. They show a typical understanding of how false information spreads, and the potential impact it can have if left unchecked.

In 1997, Terry appeared in *The Sunday Times Rich List* for the first time with the paper claiming he was worth in excess of £20 million.[4] That February he received the closest thing the English middle class has to beatification, when he appeared on Radio 4's *Desert Island Discs*. Once again, he attempted to calmly explain that his work was about much more than a giant turtle, and host Sue Lawley gave him ample room to discuss his childhood and route into literature. He chose an eclectic list of songs for the show's hypothetical island sojourn,[5] including rock singer Meat Loaf, folk group Steeleye Span, comedian Bernard Miles and pieces by Mozart, Vivaldi and Berlioz. His luxury item was New York's Chrysler Building, and when pressed for a book to take with him, said he would look for something called 'Edible Plants of the South Seas'. A few months later came the final proof of Pratchett's acceptance into mainstream British culture – someone chose the Discworld as their specialist subject on *Mastermind*.[6]

His popularity wasn't restricted to the UK. Australia and New Zealand, in particular, warmed to his work fairly early in his career. Pratchett's first trip to Australia was in 1990, and was another experience that drove home to him quite how far his life had progressed. In his guest of honour speech at the 2004 Worldcon, he described looking down on the clouds of the Pacific from his business-class seat, sipping his brandy and, feeling something of a fraud, wondering what went right. He landed to a welcome that surprised and delighted him, finding decent-sized crowds of warm and generous people at every convention and signing. Pratchett

---

4. This was partly calculated on the *Mort* movie deal and the residuals and future earnings it was likely to contain. Pratchett hit back by claiming he wasn't even worth £10 million, and refused to be drawn further

5. A concept brilliantly parodied in *The Last Continent*, a book he would have been working on at the time.

6. For several years Pratchett and Smythe had been told that Discworld was actually banned as a specialist subject on the show. The lifting of the ban was further evidence of the books' ubiquity.

fell in love with the country and its citizens, and would return at least once a year, often extending a promotional trip into a family holiday.[7] He even considered buying a second home in Tasmania, a six-bedroom house with ten acres of garden and a literal hundred-acre-wood for a snip of £130,000, but in the end decided that booking occasional holidays was a lot less hassle than maintaining two homes on opposite sides of the world. In 1998 he celebrated his love of Australia by stranding Rincewind there. *The Last Continent* saw the hapless wizard stuck in a baking hot, spider-ridden country of red dust and beer-swilling sheep rustlers called Fourecks, a Discworld avatar for the 'land down under', full of Aussie folklore and tweaks to the nose of the country's national character, done with obvious affection.

Pratchett's work also spread beyond the English language, with translations appearing in several countries. By the end of his life, his novels would be published in thirty-seven different languages. Translating the novels, with all of their clever wordplay, was no easy task. Translators would spend hours workshopping new jokes and checking them with the author. The title of *Mort*, for example, ceases to be a pun when it's read in French, and would be a book simply titled 'Death'. In the end, French publishers went with the less imaginative *Mortimer*.[8] The best foreign titles were those that spun their own puns, such as the Estonian version of *Equal Rites* being titled *Charming Equality*. The Dutch translation of *Witches Abroad* is called *Witches Up In the Air*, using the common Dutch phrase *in de lucht*, meaning something that is unresolved (as in 'I don't know, it's still up in the air') while *Wyrd Sisters* in German is called *Macbest*.

In many parts of Europe Pratchett was selling nearly as well as he did at home. He was very popular in the Czech Republic, home of the first Discworld fanclub and newsletter to be produced entirely in a language other than English. Terry developed a close friendship with his Czech translator, Jan Kantůrek, who worked hard to preserve the humour in the

---

7. Although it should be noted that to Terry a holiday was simply a period of time where he could write, uninterrupted by fan mail and phone calls, between drinking cold beer and the odd bit of sightseeing.
8. Translations for many of the titles are provided on Colin Smythe's excellent website, colinsmythe.co.uk, under the heading 'Translations re-translated'.

books. Pratchett was so impressed with Kantůrek's work that he allowed him to draft his own footnotes to the stories, an honour no other translator shared. Serbian Discworld fan, Dejan Papić formed his own publishing company, Laguna, in order to have Pratchett translations available in his country, eventually becoming the leading publisher in the Balkans and opening his own chain of bookshops, a literary empire entirely founded on *The Colour of Magic*.

Perhaps the most curious treatment of Pratchett's work came in Germany, where his publishers, Heyne, would take outrageous liberties with the text and artwork. Germany was the only European country where Terry's books had been available consistently since the beginning of his career. It's odd then that during the 1990s, as his popularity swelled, his new German publishers would be so careless with their product. The company's first edition of *Mort* used, for reasons no-one could quite work out, Josh Kirby's jacket art for *Wyrd Sisters*. Heyne then asked Smythe to supply fresh artwork for the later book. The request was refused, so for a while the German editions of both books carried exactly the same jacket illustration. Heyne had a strange habit of ignoring the bespoke illustrations created for the novels, and simply used whichever of Josh Kirby's pictures they could get their hands on. An edition of *The Carpet People*, so beautifully illustrated in Germany under the publishers Sauerländer in 1971, was published by Heyne using artwork Kirby had done for James Corley's sci-fi novel, *Benedict's Planet*, featuring an alien figure wearing a long robe. A double volume containing *The Colour of Magic* and *Sourcery* had a jacket intended for Robert Rankin's *The Sprouts of Wrath*, suggesting that the Discworld contained British policemen and a Morris Minor car. When confronted, the publishers pointed out that at least the cover featured a man in a wizard's hat. Most baffling of all was a version of *The Dark Side of the Sun* which used a painting Kirby had done for his *Voyage of the Ayeguy* series, showing an alien figure being crucified on a beach. The last straw came when an edition of *Pyramids*, published in 1991, was found to contain an advert for instant soup, half way through the novel, in the actual body of the text. A furious Pratchett refused to sign another contract with the company.

In 1998, just a few months after celebrating his fiftieth birthday, Pratchett was awarded an OBE in the Queen's birthday honours list, for services to literature. This came as something of a surprise, and initially he thought it was a joke. Publicly, he made light of it, claiming he had always denied writing literature of any kind. Privately though, he was pleased and, despite his notorious distrust of authority, never seriously gave any thought to turning it down, as Roald Dahl had done. To Pratchett this was legitimation, not just of him, but of the genre he represented. He broke the news on alt.fan.pratchett, where he addressed his delight and surprise:

> Will I ever win a major children's book award? No – not gritty, not relevant, too popular.[9] The Booker? ... I'm on a different planet. And then suddenly there comes this OBE, out of the official honours system, which I'd never, ever considered had anything to do with me. I find it very strange and curiously democratic.

That summer Terry, looking dapper in a morning suit and accompanied by his wife, daughter and mother, travelled to Buckingham Palace to receive one of his country's highest accolades from the Prince of Wales. Also receiving honours that day were Geoff Hurst, from England's winning 1966 World Cup squad, the Olympic athlete Linford Christie, entertainer Bruce Forsyth and the pioneering DJ John Peel; the latter leading Pratchett to joke that there must have been some sort of two-for-one deal on short, bearded, balding men. Terry found the occasion fascinating, from the hidden toilet door quietly shown to guests if they needed the facilities, down to the military brass band playing songs from the musical, *Les Misérables*, which Pratchett couldn't help but find amusing considering the show's theme of downtrodden masses rising up against inherited wealth and power.

Throughout this period Pratchett's books were evolving and it's no coincidence that his sustained success was built on a world that continued to move forward both literally (thanks to a swimming turtle) and thematically. It's a cliché to say the series gets darker as it goes along, but it certainly took on a more serious tone. It happened quickly as well. There were only two years between *Soul Music*, a romp through

---

9. He was entirely wrong about this.

rock 'n' roll clichés and puns about Elvis and Def Leppard, and *Feet of Clay*, which wraps a compelling police mystery around a treatise on the nature of the self. It's to Pratchett's credit that while the books shift in tone, they never stop being funny. He was always quick to defend the humour in his work, arguing that 'serious' and 'funny' were not mutually exclusive properties in a book – the opposite of 'funny' wasn't 'serious', the opposite of funny was 'not funny', and his work was never that.[10]

As the new millennium got closer, Pratchett took a last victory lap around the characters that had sustained the series for most of the decade. Rincewind's antipodean-style adventures in 1998's thoroughly entertaining romp *The Last Continent* would be the last time the character would headline his own novel. Rincewind had been an excellent companion for Pratchett fans, guiding them deeper into the author's worldview, but after nearly fifteen years it was difficult to see where he could go next. The failed wizard had saved the entire world – twice – but his major role was as a tour guide for the reader, and that wasn't the sort of book Pratchett was interested in writing any longer.

Later that year came *Carpe Jugulum*, the last adult Discworld novel to follow the exploits of the witches of Lancre. Both Granny Weatherwax and Nanny Ogg would feature heavily in the later Tiffany Aching series, but neither would be at the centre of the action again, nor would the books follow their thoughts or perspectives. As fond of Granny as Pratchett was, she had become too powerful. An indestructible character is rarely an interesting one. *Carpe Jugulum* is probably Granny's greatest test, with the old witch facing a family of vampires that can control minds; though to Granny the real enemy is already inside her head – her gnawing fear that she will 'go to the bad' and lose sight of right and wrong. *Carpe Jugulum* is among Pratchett's darkest works. In a scene near the start of the book Granny is called to minister to a heavily pregnant woman who has been kicked by a cow. As Death arrives to claim a soul, it's clear that Granny can make a decision and save either the mother or the child. Every storybook instinct tells us that she will save the child. The hero will *always* save the child. There is a similar scene in *Maskerade*, where Granny plays cards with Death over the life of either a baby or cow, and

---

10. Alright, apart from *Night Dweller*.

of course it is the baby that is saved. In *Carpe Jugulum*, Granny allows the baby to die. Not only that, she bans the husband from killing the cow that kicked his wife and killed his child, saying the couple will need it. It's a practical and logical outcome, completely in keeping with Granny's character, but for the audience it's jarring. Later, the old witch delivers a powerful statement on the nature of sin, and humanity's need to treat people as 'things'. *Carpe Jugulum* is as close to a morality tale as Pratchett gets.

His final novel of the century, and the last in the transitional phase at the end of what can loosely be called mid-period Discworld, came as the real world braced itself for a new millennium. November 1999's *The Fifth Elephant* is closer in tone to the post-2000, more grown-up Discworld, and though Commander Vimes would return in several more novels, this would be the final time that Captain Carrot was featured as a central character. He would fade into the background noise of the City Watch, alongside Corporal Nobbs and Sergeant Colon in future stories. Carrot, the last man standing of Terry's stock 'movie stars', was conceived as the central protagonist of 1989's *Guards! Guards!*, though the more cynical, damaged Commander Vimes had quickly overtaken him as the driving force of the books. Still, Carrot's arc as the true heir to the throne of Ankh-Morpork, and his relationship with the werewolf officer, Angua, were important elements of all the Watch books so far. It was another narrative strand that Pratchett was letting go. Carrot was now a supporting player in Vimes' story, and the whole 'true king' plot that simmered through *Men at Arms* and *Feet of Clay* was dropped for good. Such tangles with destiny had never suited Discworld – that was one of the central themes of the series – but now Pratchett was growing beyond even the *subversion* of those tropes. Instead *The Fifth Elephant*, which had the slightly-less-punny working title of *Überwald Nights*, tackles the theme of religious fundamentalism, with the culture of the Dwarves paralleling fundamentalist Islam, Hasidic Judaism and Coptic Christianity in a way that would feel extremely prescient just a few years later. It's rich and complex, and a world away from the Discworld of, say, *Witches Abroad*, just as that book was a world away from *The Light Fantastic*.

Pratchett knew that the Discworld was the foundation of his fortune, but he had refused to let it be an albatross around his neck. Across the decade, he had managed to evolve the series into something far more interesting, and had skilfully taken his audience with him as he did so ... though to some he would always be the nerdy writer associated with 'the business with the turtle'. Still, for those willing to look, it was clear that a line in his work had been drawn. In 2000, *The Truth*, the twenty-first Discworld novel, was the first since 1992's *Small Gods* to feature a cast of completely new characters. It was a story he'd wanted to write for years – of the Discworld's first newspaper, and a distillation of those years of his life dedicated to local journalism. He'd played with the concept in the late '80s, and had originally intended his 'newspaper novel' to follow *Eric*, though this was put aside in favour of the more marketable *Moving Pictures*. However, it was a story he always intended to tell, and he even seeded the plot with an entry for the lead character, William de Worde, in the *Discworld Companion*, six years before he would appear in print. *The Truth* is a labour of love, borne from conversations between Pratchett and his editor at Gollancz, Jo Fletcher, a former local journalist herself. De Worde, the founding editor of *The Ankh-Morpork Times*, finds himself in dozens of situations taken directly from Pratchett's – and sometimes Fletcher's – own lives; from talking down a potential suicide on a high roof to the endless supply of humorously shaped vegetables sent in for consideration.

What's especially interesting about *The Truth*, is what it *isn't* about. In many ways it isn't even a fantasy story. Yes, it has the usual cast of dwarves, trolls, vampires and werewolves, but really that's just dressing. This is a story about a newspaper and it could easily have been set in Victorian London. Ankh-Morpork had changed from the filthy medieval city of the earlier books to a complex – if admittedly still filthy – pre-industrial society, teetering on the edge of a recognisably modern world. Years later fans would refer to *The Truth* as the start of a loosely connected series of books often referred to as the 'Industrial Revolution' sequence.

A key passage comes about a third of the way in, when the city's ruler, Lord Vetinari, invites himself to see the newfangled printing press. Vetinari lists the magical calamities that had befallen the city in recent years, referring to events in several of the previous decade's books. He demands to know if the newspaper office had been built on an ancient magical site, or is likely in some way to cause tentacled monstrosities to once more threaten the nature of reality. The answer is no. It's a very funny scene but it can also be seen as a message from the author – 'I'm not doing that sort of thing any more'. *The Truth* is not necessarily a more serious book than, for example, *Moving Pictures*; both take a form of media and wring it for jokes and clichés, and both are in their own way equally funny. *The Truth*, however, is handled in a more grounded way. The characters are more well-rounded, the stakes are lower, and it delivers its messages with a dollop more panache. The transition between the Discworld of the 1990s and that of the millennium is more a hazy series of gradients than a sharp line, but *The Truth* is the closest thing there is to a turning point.

The late '90s and early 2000s also reached a turning point behind the scenes. In 1998 Pratchett and Smythe ended their longstanding relationship with Gollancz, Terry's publisher in hardback since *Equal Rites* in 1987, though the company would still work on spin-off media such as diaries, calendars and quizbooks. Hardback rights for the next three novels were handed to Doubleday, an imprint of Transworld, which had published Pratchett's paperbacks since *The Colour of Magic*. The deal was worth 'millions, but not many millions', according to the company's head of adult publishing, Patrick Janson-Smith, when interviewed by the *London Evening Standard*. Almost all of Pratchett's novels from *The Last Continent* onwards would be published by Doubleday, whose children's division had already proved themselves with their handling of the *Bromeliad* trilogy and the *Johnny* books.

There were several reasons for the change, and Pratchett insisted that money was the least of them. It was Transworld/Corgi's paperbacks that had truly put Pratchett on the map. Corgi's handling of *The Colour of Magic* had been the first pebble in the avalanche of his success. The hardcovers grabbed the headlines, but it was the Corgi paperbacks you saw on every tube, bus and train. It made sense to unite his hardcover and paperback publishers under one roof. Transworld was also a global company, and the new deal covered all territories worldwide outside of the US (a market which remained a tough nut to crack).

In 1986, when Pratchett had first signed his publishing deal, Livia Gollancz, the daughter of founder Victor, was still in charge of her father's company and the company represented much that he loved in

SF fandom. It connected his work to the books he'd been obsessed with
as a boy. Things had changed over the years, however, and much of the
core team had moved on, including Malcolm Edwards with whom he
had originally signed. The imprint had also been sold twice over; once
to an American company, Houghton Mifflin in 1989, and then again to
the British-based Cassell in 1992. Cassell itself had only recently been
sold off by its parent company, CBS, and was still finding its feet as an
independent. Terry still had a strong relationship with his immediate
team, especially his editor, Jo Fletcher, but decision-makers further
up the chain were becoming a problem. To say Cassell mismanaged
Pratchett's account would be something of an understatement. Print
runs shrank, meaning some Pratchett products would sell out quickly
and be replenished frustratingly slowly. Worse, the company badly
neglected fans overseas. Cassell would ship the minimum number of
copies of a new book to shops in Australia to ensure they maintained
copyright under Australian law, which specified that a British title must
be published within thirty days of its UK release or else be offered to
a domestic publisher. The few copies would then sell out quickly, and
a full release would not materialise for some weeks. Twice, Pratchett
arrived for signing tours to find Australian bookshops didn't have
enough books to meet demand. He was furious. Cassell's neglect cost
the company the UK's bestselling living author and 40,000 domestic
sales per year. 'The whole team were bitterly upset', says Jo Fletcher.
'They had put an enormous amount of effort into building him up and
they were devastated.'

Pratchett and Fletcher were extremely close, having known each other
since the 1980s. Fletcher, a fellow fantasy author, had been one of the
'HP Lovecraft Holiday Fun Club' thanked in the acknowledgment page
of *Equal Rites*, and Terry had been delighted when she took over his
account at Gollancz. When he decided to jump ship, he was adamant
that she knew the decision had nothing to do with her. She recalls:

> I was called into the managing director's office [on the morning of
> the announcement] and handed a letter saying that what I was about
> to hear was absolutely nothing to do with me. Not even my 'most
> dulcet tones and fervent, passionate entreaties' would have made

any difference, because the seeds were sown long before I joined the company. He said it had no bearing whatsoever on the books that remained, and he was absolutely sure that we'd work together again. This was a business decision, and the decision had been made … it was a lovely letter and I was really upset.

It was ultimately for Fletcher's benefit that Gollancz were allowed to keep the various Discworld ephemera of quizbooks, artbooks and other spin-offs, with the annual tradition of Discworld diaries beginning soon after.

Transworld, for their part, were respectfully modest about their acquisition. 'If it was another publisher we'd be slightly more euphoric,' Janson-Smith told *The Bookseller*, 'but we have quite a sentimental feeling towards Victor Gollancz.' Pratchett's team released a statement describing the parting as 'amicable, if sad'.

The sharpest and saddest point of change in Pratchett's world came in October 2001, when Josh Kirby died at the age of 72. The news came as a shock as Kirby had been in good health and was still painting every day. He had died in his sleep of natural causes, at his home in Diss, Norfolk, where he lived alone. A neighbour had found him two days later, after becoming concerned that Kirby wasn't answering his phone. His last Discworld cover was 2001's *The Wyrdest Link*, Dave Langford's spin-off quizbook, featuring the Librarian posing as BBC quiz host Anne Robinson. Writing in the Discworld Convention programme the following year, Colin Smythe said of Kirby: 'His work was truly unique, and no one can fill the gap now left.'

However, the sad truth was that someone *had* to fill the gap.[11] Pratchett had always been unswervingly loyal to Kirby. Earlier research by Gollancz had suggested sales might increase with another, less obviously fantasy-orientated cover artist, but Pratchett was convinced that Kirby's style had been instrumental in his success and refused to budge, leaving Gollancz to tinker with new ways of displaying Kirby's work in more 'accessible' styles, much to the artist's annoyance. Now a change had to be made. Pratchett wouldn't be drawn on the subject at the time, but it was widely assumed that Paul Kidby would land the gig, having been acting as

---

11. Though presumably Germany's Heyne would have just used the cover of *Wyrd Sisters* over and over again.

Pratchett's 'artist of choice' for the Discworld for nearly a decade. One wonders if Kidby wouldn't have inherited the position soon, anyway. It's an uncomfortable thing to admit in the light of Kirby's death, but the changing tone of the books meant that his work, so perfectly in tune with the Discworld of the '80s and early '90s, had begun to feel at odds with the more serious themes and less anarchic storytelling in Pratchett's later writing. Kidby's style, meanwhile, was more naturalistic and could be more serious and also have a softer, more fairytale feel. Loyal as Pratchett was, even he might have had to admit, eventually, that his books no longer felt in sync with their covers. However, the circumstances in which the baton was passed between the two couldn't have been sadder and no-one would have wished for it to have happened the way it did. Kirby's passing was another watershed moment, marking the end of an era in Pratchett's career. The next full, adult Discworld novel to be published, *Night Watch* in 2002, would feature jacket art by Paul Kidby, who delivered a homage to Rembrandt's painting *The Night Watch*. Hidden in the background, in the position where Rembrandt had inserted a picture of himself, is a beautifully observed portrait of Josh Kirby.

Chapter 16

Rats, Cats, Chalk and Cheese

Night Watch wasn't actually Paul Kidby's first Discworld cover. On 18 October, 2001 *The Last Hero* was published which, repeating the trick of *Eric* a decade earlier, was a novella augmented with full colour illustrations of Kidby's work. In many ways, *The Last Hero* can be considered something of a throwback. As with *Eric,* Pratchett had opted for a globe-trotting adventure that would give Kidby scope to pick the ball up and run with it. Though in narrative terms the stakes couldn't be higher – the whole world is threatened – tonally this a lighter story than Pratchett had written in some years. Cohen the Barbarian and his band of elderly former heroes have decided to blow up the home of the gods as revenge for letting them grow old, but don't realise that, for reasons best described as 'plot', their actions will destroy the whole Disc. It's up to Rincewind, Carrot and a stowaway Librarian to save the day, flying to the centre of the world in a spacecraft designed by the genius polymath, Leonard da Quirm. Their route takes them under the Disc and past the elephants, via a crash landing on the Discworld's tiny, dragon-infested moon. It was the sort of story Pratchett simply didn't write anymore. It was also a final outing for Rincewind and Carrot as major protagonists who, having had their last proper stories told in *The Last Continent* and *The Fifth Elephant,* act basically as action heroes here,[1] with no real character insight or development.[2] This was old-school Discworld, skewering the tropes of bad fantasy in a way that Pratchett hadn't really concerned himself with since the early '90s, and can be

---

1. In Rincewind's case, somewhat reluctantly.
2. I wish I had more space to write about the books, because there actually *is* some really interesting stuff going on in *The Last Hero,* especially concerning Cohen's anger and sadness that he has been allowed to achieve everything there is to achieve and hasn't died yet. There's also the character of Evil Harry Dread, based on Pratchett's former head teacher, Harry Ward, and Mrs McGarry, a barbarian heroine based on an old teacher of Jo Fletcher's.

seen (along with Vetinari's speech in *The Truth*) as the capstone on an era of comic fantasy. It is a last hurrah for an entire style of writing; one final, full-throated fantasy parody, before Pratchett got on with all that 'contributing to literature' that had evidently so impressed the Queen. The fact it was released as *The Lord of the Rings* movies were about to break box office records – making the story hugely marketable – was either canny timing or good luck.

Adding to the throwback vibe was the fact that *The Last Hero* was published by Gollancz, whose owners Cassell had been acquired by a larger publisher, Orion Books. The new owners, who had tempted back Pratchett's original editor, Malcom Edwards, from HarperCollins.[3] There's a lovely symmetry in one of the Discworld's key behind-the-scenes figures returning to work on such a celebratory project; the old gang back together for one last adventure. The concept had been dreamed up between Pratchett and Jo Fletcher, as a tribute to the beautifully illustrated fantasy books both remembered reading as children, and with Fletcher at Gollancz, there was never a question of giving it to Transworld.

Though an expensive project, with its stunning Kidby visuals, *The Last Hero* was a huge success and earned back its advance within six months. Having learned a lesson from *Eric*, Pratchett ensured that when *The Last Hero* debuted on paperback it was with illustrations presented in full – in fact the paperback was given extra artwork, plundering Kidby's back catalogue for relevant images of Death, Rincewind and the Disc. Aside from audiobooks, *The Last Hero* hasn't appeared in print anywhere in the world without Kidby's artwork.

In 2001, Pratchett also returned to children's fiction after five years writing exclusively for the adult market. In November, just a few weeks after Josh Kirby's death, Doubleday published *The Amazing Maurice and His Educated Rodents*, the first Discworld novel to be aimed at younger readers. The story of how a devious talking cat and a troupe of magically augmented rodents trick towns out of their money by faking a plague of rats and employing a handy 'stupid looking kid' to lead them away, was

---

3. Smythe later said that had Edwards still been at Gollancz in 1998 the Australia debacle would never have been allowed to happen, and Pratchett may well have stayed with the company.

first mentioned in *Reaper Man* as a parody of the *Pied Piper of Hamelin*, and had been ticking away in the author's head ever since. Despite (or perhaps because of) its intended audience, *Maurice* is one of the darkest of Pratchett's tales. Its villain, a rat king, is one of the Discworld's few genuine monsters, a malevolent spirit comprised of the minds of dozens of rats tied together at the tail, moving as one. The talking rats *literally eat each other's dead bodies*, and there are echoes of genocide in the talk of 'exterminating vermin' that, when you take into account the rodent nature of the characters, brings to mind Art Spiegelman's chilling graphic novel, *Maus*, a retelling of the Holocaust with cats and mice.

Pratchett's books for younger readers always explored their themes more directly than his adult fiction; in *Maurice* we're asked to consider what it truly means to be sentient and self-aware. There's a phrase Pratchett uses in several of his books when a character becomes aware of their individuality – 'the darkness behind the eyes'. Maurice and the rats, until recently just animals acting on mindless instinct, have now learned to separate the world inside and outside of their own heads. The same thing happens to the character Myria LeJean in *Thief of Time*, published just six months earlier. What it truly means to be alive and conscious was clearly preying on Pratchett's mind.

The Amazing Maurice and His Educated Rodents is a dark and richly textured book. It is also, despite the unfamiliar sight of chapter headings, a Discworld novel. This means, happily, it remains extremely funny. Writing for younger readers removes any need Pratchett had to restrain himself. *Maurice* has fart jokes, daft puns and the brilliant idea that the rats name themselves after phrases they like on discarded food packing, hence 'Peaches', 'Ham 'n' Pork' and, best of all, 'Dangerous Beans'. That Pratchett makes this last character the intellectual centre of the story is as good an indicator as any as to how well he was able to balance the profound and ridiculous elements of the tale. Reviewers fell over themselves in praise. The respected SF magazine, *Locus* called it 'hilarious, moving, scary, impishly vulgar, and wickedly wise'. Neil Gaiman, writing in the *Financial Times Weekend* said it was 'by any terms, an astonishing novel', while, writing in *The Guardian*, Francis Spufford labelled the book 'ethically challenging, beautifully orchestrated, philosophically opposed to the usual plot fixes of fantasy'.

The following year something happened that Pratchett had always claimed was next to impossible – *The Amazing Maurice* was awarded the Carnegie Medal. Though carrying a prize fund of only £5,000, a trifling amount for someone like Pratchett, the Carnegie is one of the most prestigious awards for children's literature in the world, often considered the 'children's Booker'. The prize is awarded by the UK's Chartered Institute of Library and Information Professionals – librarians – and to an old 'library boy' like Terry, there could be no higher authority. He said at the time that he was stunned – the book had been submitted for consideration by his publishers without his knowledge, as he hadn't seen the point.

In retrospect, his incredulity feels a little suspect. After all, *Johnny and the Dead* had been named 1993's Best Children's Book by the Writers' Guild of Great Britain, while *Johnny and the Bomb* was awarded the silver position at the 1997 Smarties Prize. Both had made the Carnegie shortlist. Since then Pratchett's stock in the literary world had risen considerably, bolstered by his OBE. Discworld fan and Booker Prize-winner, A. S. Byatt had claimed that *Thief of Time* deserved the Booker itself, and many people had agreed with her. In 2000, a group of academics, including Pratchett's old friend Ed James, published *Terry Pratchett: Guilty of Literature*, a collection of detailed academic analysis of his work. The days of Pratchett books being dismissed as nerdy fluff had – for the most part – been left behind. What's more, *The Amazing Maurice* was a demonstrably excellent novel. Its prize-winning potential could not have escaped the author's notice, so it's reasonable to view Pratchett's 'stunned' reaction with a little suspicion. However, whether expected or not, it would be a hard heart that would deny him his moment. Ten years earlier, a judge at *The Guardian*'s Children's Literature Award had pondered whether one of his books could really be considered 'good literature'; now the panel chair for one of Britain's most prestigious prizes was calling his latest novel 'an outstanding work of literary excellence'.

On awards night, when he accepted the medal, he shocked the audience by peeling away its gold surface to reveal a large chocolate coin, from which he proceeded to take a bite. He'd had the fake award prepared especially,[4] and had expertly palmed the real medal as soon as it was

---

4. Pratchett had known he'd won the Carnegie for at least a month, though he'd been sworn to secrecy. He had been bursting at the seams to talk about it.

handed to him, switching it for his replica. It got his speech off to a unique start.

This was Pratchett's first major award, and there was a feeling that he was being honoured, not just for a single novel, but for a whole body of work. In his speech, he hailed the prize as a win for the overlooked fantasy genre, and also for children's literature which portrayed a rounded and realistic view of humanity, even if some of its characters happened to be talking rats. The Carnegie judges had praised the book for highlighting 'the danger of allowing stories or fantasy to replace reality', a theme Pratchett leaned into in his speech, in which he argued that the very best fantasy was about 'more than just wizards waving wands' and that evil had to be defeated in ways more effective than throwing a magic ring into a volcano.

Some critics detected a hint of astringency in Pratchett's speech. *The Scotsman* said that the author 'hovered dangerously on the precipice of bitterness at his having been ignored by the literary establishment for too long', and was keen to acknowledge the apparent digs at Tolkien, and J. K. Rowling's *Harry Potter* series. Those that knew Pratchett best were convinced that there was no bitterness and no malice intended. 'Because he had a very distinctive way, and because he could be very sarcastic, sometimes his attempts at being funny weren't appreciated,' said Jo Fletcher. 'He was *thrilled* about the Carnegie. He wasn't the jolly old gnome that people liked to portray him as, but he wasn't bitter and twisted.' That said, it certainly stung that the establishment had ignored his work for so long. Pratchett was undoubtedly pleased with his double win for 'Best SF/Fantasy Author' and 'Worst Dressed Person in SF' at the 1997 *SFX* awards, but it hardly counted as industry respect.[5] The Carnegie was something very different. It was coveted and respected, and just three years earlier its latest recipient had been complaining on his own online newsgroup that he was never likely to win one.

The market for children's literature had changed dramatically since Pratchett's last children's book, *Johnny and the Bomb*, was published in 1996. The following year, *Harry Potter and the Philosopher's Stone* made

---

5. In 2001 *The Bookseller* gave Pratchett a special award for 'services to bookselling', but he regarded that as a pat on the head for shifting units and keeping the industry afloat, as opposed to an acknowledgment of his skills.

its cheerful way onto shelves, and by the millennium J. K. Rowling's franchise had turned the industry upside down. It had taken her just a few years to dethrone Pratchett as the UK's bestselling living author. Her fourth book, *Harry Potter and the Goblet of Fire*, sold as many copies in its first day as a new Pratchett would in an entire year. By the time *The Amazing Maurice and His Educated Rodents* emerged, Rowling's sales were in the hundreds of millions, and the film franchise based on her novels was about to push them higher. As Colin Smythe says on his website, the success of the Potter books 'changed that market out of all recognition'. Rowling had managed to do what decades of miscellaneous books about 'penniless orphans with strange powers and a mysterious destiny' had failed to do – she had made fantasy *cool*. Naturally she spawned hundreds of imitators, and her success boosted the sales of other fine fantasy authors. Philip Pullman's breathtaking *His Dark Materials* trilogy had become a phenomenon of its own, and the third volume, *The Amber Spyglass*, had claimed the Carnegie the year before *Maurice*. Daniel Handler's *A Series of Unfortunate Events* and Eoin Colfer's *Artemis Fowl* books had also sold in their hundreds of thousands. If publishers in the 1990s were keen to find 'the next Discworld', by the early 2000s they were *desperate* for the 'next Harry Potter'. Pratchett's return to children's fiction, whether by accident or design, meant that an absolute master of the genre had re-entered a market now primed to accept him. The Carnegie Medal was proof of this, even in the form of a huge chocolate coin.

Despite the award, it was obvious that Pratchett was no longer top dog in the field. The *Potter* books were an untouchable phenomenon that redefined what 'literary success' could mean. Terry had been dethroned, and the media was now obsessed with setting Pratchett and Rowling against each other. In 1999 he had been invited to write a piece for *The Sunday Times* on the rise of fantasy, pegged to the release of Rowling's third book, *Harry Potter and the Prisoner of Azkaban*. In the article he describes the Potter series as part of a fine old tradition of British fantasy; of Tolkien, Lewis, E. Nesbit, Diana Wynne Jones, Susan Cooper and Alan Garner. He concluded his article by calling her work 'beautifully cooked'. Pratchett, always keeping a weather eye on the industry, had spotted the ascending Potter phenomenon before the wave had crested, and had read *Philosopher's Stone* out of curiosity. The unexpected success of the series, and the crossover elements inevitable in two populist fantasy worlds (wizards, witches, a magic school, trolls, goblins, broomsticks and pet dragons) rang alarm bells, and he decided against reading the rest of the series in order to stave off plagiarism accusations in either direction. His instincts were sound. By 2001, he was regularly being asked by younger fans whether the Discworld festival of Hogswatch had been inspired by Rowling's Hogwarts school. It didn't help that, by genuine coincidence, Paul Kidby's artwork portrays the Discworld wizard Ponder Stibbons as looking almost identical to Harry Potter. To younger fans, introduced to the genre via the Potter books and now branching out, the fact that Pratchett had coined Hogswatch in 1976, or that Kidby had been drawing Ponder since 1995, simply wasn't on their radar. Why would it be? The accusations were laughed off, and the misapprehensions corrected, but the comparison was irritatingly common. Even the BBC's Andrew Marr, interviewing Pratchett on his Sunday morning current affairs show, introduced his guest as a writer 'following in the footsteps of J. K. Rowling and Philip Pullman'.

Unfortunately the Carnegie speech, with its implied and possibly misjudged comment about fantasy being more than 'wizards waving wands', was the signal for a sensationalist media to try and spark a wizarding war. Rowling became a constant presence in all of Pratchett's press. He was no longer 'Britain's best-selling living author', he was now 'the man who *used to be* Britain's best-selling living author'. He was asked his opinion of Rowling's work constantly and learned to choose his words carefully, always being respectful of her writing, pointing out that he had only read the first Potter book, but that he considered both Rowling and himself to be competent authors who got lucky standing on the shoulders of giants. Occasional attempts to goad him into agreeing that Rowling had been influenced by the Discworld were always skilfully batted away. They were both, after all, fantasy writers. Neither had invented the idea of a school for wizards, and both were borrowing from the same sources – centuries of fiction about magic, mythical creatures and strange worlds.

Only once did Pratchett publicly allow himself to be drawn on the issue. In July 2005, Rowling was profiled in *Time* magazine. In the piece she said that she wasn't a fan of fantasy, hadn't initially realised that was what she was writing and considered her work to be a subversion of old tropes. *Time* used this as a jumping-off point for a weirdly misinformed rant on the subject, saying that prior to Rowling, fantasy had been stuck as 'an idealised, romanticised, pseudofeudal world, where knights and ladies morris-dance to "Greensleeves".' Pratchett wrote a letter to *The Sunday Times* – which had covered Rowling's comments – taking issue with the article's sniffy and dismissive attitude, and need to push some authors down in order to build another up. He quite rightly pointed out that the 'subversion' *Time* was attributing to Rowling had always been at the heart of the very best fantasy. The letter focused largely on the *Time* feature itself, rather than Rowling specifically, but did include one undeniable broadside at the author – did someone writing a book about wizards, dragons and goblins really not think she was writing fantasy?

The letter caused an immediate stink, making headlines across the world. The BBC website declared 'Pratchett Attacks Rowling', a headline that Terry had spent the last few years trying to avoid.[6] The reaction from hardcore Harry Potter fans was something akin to a kicked bee's nest. 'This just makes me feel sick. On her birthday for crying out loud.'[7] screamed one fan on the *Snitchseeker* online message board, 'I'm never buying any of his books. Ever.' Pratchett was subject to much online hate, and received the occasional death threat as a result, usually from young American Potter obsessives who had no idea who he was. The following day he posted on alt.fan.pratchett in an attempt to clarify his comments, emphasising that his beef was with the *Time* journalist, not with Jo Rowling or her work.

The notoriously press-averse Rowling kept out of the debate and the feeling would have been mutual had interviewers not continually raised the issue. Pratchett, alas, did not have the luxury of avoiding interviews if he wanted to publicise his work. He would remain cautious, often saying 'my lawyers have advised me not to comment' or 'I have to be careful what I say here' whenever the subject was raised. Still, there is nothing to suggest that Pratchett actively disliked Rowling, or in any

6. As this was resolutely untrue, the ever vigilant Colin Smythe was able to force a backtrack from the BBC, who downgraded the headline to the *slightly* more sedate 'Pratchett takes swipe at Rowling'.
7. Unfortunately this is true – the letter had been printed on 31 July, Rowling's fortieth birthday.

way begrudged her success. The pair had met at least once, during an awards ceremony. Rowling had complained that she was unlikely to ever win a major literary award and – according to the author Charles Stross, who had heard Pratchett repeat the anecdote – Terry had replied, 'Jo, me neither: we'll just have to cry ourselves to sleep on top of our mattresses stuffed with £20 notes.'

Pratchett's next children's book appeared in spring 2003. *The Wee Free Men* was the story of a 9-year-old girl with the deliberately incongruous name of Tiffany Aching. Like *The Amazing Maurice and His Educated Rodents*, it was a subversion of a well-established storybook trope – a little girl must travel into fairyland and steal back her baby brother from the queen of the fairies. It's a combination of elements taken from centuries of folk tales and classic literature, most obviously Lewis Carroll's *Alice's Adventures in Wonderland*, but also *The Wonderful Wizard of Oz*, *Peter Pan*, the *Narnia* books and the classic 1980s movie, *Labyrinth*. Pratchett had hated the *Alice* books when he'd read them as a child. He'd found the tone smug and condescending, and the self-consciously weird imagery grating. It bothered him that the books were hung on such a passive heroine. His young witch, Tiffany Aching, was an antidote to the posh and prissy Alice. She's the youngest daughter of a farmer, has been raised to work hard, and is an expert at making cheese. Such details are the mud on the boots that made Pratchett's child characters feel properly grounded. Tiffany's practicality is what sets her apart. Like *Equal Rites'* Esk, with whom she shares literary DNA, Tiffany accepts no nonsense, though she's more practical and less of a dreamer. Pratchett would go on to write five books about Tiffany, allowing her to grow in character and age. Another thing Pratchett disliked about children's books was characters that stayed frozen in time. Tiffany is 9 in *The Wee Free Men*, and a young woman of 17 by the time she makes her final appearance in *The Shepherd's Crown*. It's a pleasant reminder of how much Pratchett had grown as a writer. In his thirties he had struggled to write relatable young women, but as a man in his fifties he was able to make a teenage girl feel effortlessly real. After the publication of *The Wee Free Men* he was even made an honorary Brownie Guide, in recognition of having written 'a real girl'.

Tiffany, initially intended as a one-off character, became one of Pratchett's favourites to write. He said that with Tiffany, as with Sam Vimes, he could trust the character to know what she was doing – all he had to do was create the scenario and he instinctively knew how Tiffany would think and react. The narrative seemed to unfurl itself. Pratchett would later create a personification of this process: Narrativia, the goddess of creative writing. In later interviews he would often thank 'my lady, Narrativia' for the flashes of inspiration midflow on which a plot might turn.[8]

Just as *Equal Rites* had been a snapshot of Pratchett's life in the '70s and '80s in the homely Gayes Cottage, Tiffany's homeland of The Chalk was a reflection of the Wiltshire countryside he and Lyn had made their home since the mid-'90s. Terry had grown up in the chalklands of the Chiltern Hills and he felt a deep connection to his adopted home of Broad Chalke, near Salisbury. He only needed to look out of his window and he could see Tiffany's homeland, clear as day – a landscape of farms, sheep, ancient standing stones (Broad Chalke is just a few miles from Stonehenge), old shepherds' huts, huge, ancient carvings in the side of the hills, running hares and fossils. It's the ancient heart of rural England, and visiting the area feels like treading through the countryside of the Discworld itself. Terry's land was in the bones of the Tiffany stories, just as Tiffany could feel the land in *her* bones.

The books saw Pratchett indulge his love of folklore, and he frequently referenced facts and tidbits he'd picked up across a lifetime of research. In *The Wee Free Men* Tiffany talks about Old Mrs Snapperly, an elderly woman thrown out of her house and left to die a street beggar when winter came, because locals thought she was a witch. The story comes straight from an interview Pratchett had done with a new age witch for the *Midweek Free Press*, back in 1973. The same piece also casts suspicion on the rumours that witches dance naked in the night air, given the English climate – an aside that crops up several times in Discworld novels. A reference to old men calling foxes 'Reynard' was first

---

8. A good example is in *Thief Of Time*, when Pratchett was trying to think of an identity for the fifth horseman of the apocalypse, whom he had already given the everyday persona of a milkman called Ronald Soak. He claimed it was sheer coincidence that soak backwards was Kaos – the perfect apocalyptic name.

reported as an overheard conversation in a *Bath Chronicle* Weekender piece and is repeated almost verbatim in *The Shepherd's Crown*, while the superstitions and symbolism around hares found in *I Shall Wear Midnight* come directly from a book review Pratchett wrote in 1974 (see chapter four). In many ways the Tiffany books are Terry's most personal and there's a sense that he found writing tales of The Chalk comforting; a landscape as close to home as he could find anywhere on Discworld.

The Amazing Maurice and His Educated Rodents was the start of perhaps the best run of form of Pratchett's career. November 2002 saw the release of *Night Watch*, a novel rated by many (including Neil Gaiman) as the best in the Discworld series. In the story, Sam Vimes is ripped from his own time and sent hurtling back to a darker, nastier era, when Ankh-Morpork was a police state, mired in corruption with revolution in the air. It's an era the character had already lived through once, and must do so again as he assumes the identity of his own mentor, the doomed Sergeant Keel, and guides his younger self through the coming revolution, which he knows will end in a bloodbath. It's comfortably the most gripping of Pratchett's books, and the usual simmering anger that propels every Vimes story explodes into boiling rage here. There's still time for the odd gag – this is Discworld, after all – and the references to everything from time travel movies to *Les Misérables* are artfully done, but the humour had never taken a backseat to the narrative in the way it does here. At times *Night Watch* is a gripping thriller, with one of the few Pratchett endings to leave the reader blinking back tears.[9] The reaction to *Night Watch* was immediate and gratifying, showing the clear water between Pratchett and his contemporaries.

The goodwill was beginning to spread across the Atlantic too, as America finally began to catch on. *The Washington Post* carried a lengthy review that began by calling Pratchett 'arguably the leading comic novelist of our time, and a master of contemporary fantasy'. A short but positive write-up even appeared in *The New York Times*, a particularly difficult nut to crack evidenced by the fact the words '*New York Times*! YAY!' are written on a faxed copy of the review in Colin Smythe's archives, presumably by Pratchett's US press officer.

---

9. Or possibly sobbing. Ahem.

The following year, *Monstrous Regiment* continued late-period Discworld's darker, more serious tone with a story about gender stereotypes and the futility of war. These were subjects Pratchett had tackled before, but here they were done by an author arguably at the peak of his narrative powers. The story of a young girl who disguises herself as a boy to join the army and rescue her brother from a doomed war, is another of Pratchett's angriest and best. *Monstrous Regiment*, with its previously unseen location and new cast of characters, was scarcely a Discworld novel at all. Indeed, Pratchett had seriously considered setting it in Europe during the eighteenth-century Peninsular War, but found that with a little work he could match it to Discworld's tone, though at times only just. Preparation for the book had involved in-depth historical research, since his editor at the time had voiced doubts that a woman could get away with passing herself off as a man during a war. Pratchett, immersing himself in contemporary accounts and spending several days doing research in queer-focused bookshops, found evidence that over a thousand American women may secretly have fought in the Civil War, while in Europe women in disguise had achieved high ranks in various armies, especially in the time of Napoleon. In the end the decision to set the story on Discworld made sense, and not just commercially (Pratchett claimed his books sold roughly the same whether they were set atop Great A'Tuin or not). It further deepened the franchise, and expanded what could be done within the world. It also allowed him to bring supernatural elements into the plot, making it a broader and richer piece of storytelling.

The two novels, *Night Watch* and *Monstrous Regiment*, were as dark as Discworld would get. Both are furious stories, rigid with anger at the way authority can mistreat the people it purports to protect. In both books the common soldiery become cannon fodder, and bluff military types – either power-crazed rulers or petty bureaucrats – are happy to expend lives to further their agenda. Both mirror events in the real world so closely (the Peterloo Massacre in *Night Watch*, the horrors of colonial warfare in *Monstrous Regiment*) they barely count as satire at all. The 'business with the turtle' had never been less relevant.

Not that Pratchett had abandoned his sense of humour. *Going Postal*, in 2004, the tale of a convicted con man, Moist von Lipwig, forced by

Lord Vetinari into resurrecting Ankh-Morpork's decrepit post office, has a frothy but brilliantly executed plot that ticks like a Swiss watch, though the old anger surfaces in places. The 2007 sequel, *Making Money*, in which Moist is forced to take over the running of the city's largest bank, balances an equally frothy plot which darts expertly around, with thorough and prescient attacks on the finance industry. By the time it arrived in paperback in 2008, with the international banking crisis in full swing, readers realised just how on the money[10] Pratchett had been.

In 2005 Doubleday published *Thud!*, the thirty-fourth novel in the Discworld series, and one that set the tone for many of the books to come after it. *Thud!* is a compelling murder mystery that engages the futility of war at a political level just as *Monstrous Regiment* had done from the frontlines. It also picks up a thread about religious fundamentalism first explored in *The Fifth Elephant*, published six years earlier and now, thanks to the post-9/11 so-called War on Terror, extremely relevant. Sam Vimes is, as ever, powered by righteous fury, but there's enough sheer Discworld sparkle here (and enough Fred Colon and Nobby Nobbs) to keep the story treading lightly when it needs to.

Thud! marks a significant point in Pratchett's journey. After decades of moving between publishers, toying with different cover formats, attending Worldcons and getting hugely frustrated with the Hollywood machine, *Thud!* was the first Pratchett novel to make *The New York Times* bestsellers' list, an achievement such a long time coming that Terry's US editor, Jennifer Brehl, wept on the phone when she called to tell him the news. Publicly, Pratchett had made light of his failure to make a dent in the US market, but those that knew him best knew it bothered him. It was, after all, a significant territory and the home of many of his genre heroes, not least Mark Twain and Harry Harrison. The Englishness at the heart of Discworld hadn't put off the Australians, Czechs or Serbians, but the gatekeepers of US literature struggled to see past it – *The New York Times'* anglophobic evisceration of *Good Omens* had been a case in point. Though most of Pratchett's books had received a US release of one form or another, there was always a sense that his publishers didn't know how to market his work. While he often had a US agent or editor who

---

10. Sorry.

championed his writing, they would inevitably be answerable to someone further up the chain who simply didn't *get* Terry Pratchett. In the early years of the Discworld, the books were published with dreadful generic 'fantasy' covers, done by the same artists who worked on straight fantasy by Raymond E. Feist or Robert Jordan, with no hint of the subversion or humour to be found inside. The books tended to be published ad hoc and out of order, meaning there was no manageable marketing plan that synced with the rest of the world. The marketing of Discworld novels in America was sometimes baffling, such as the press synopsis for *Lords and Ladies,* which referred to a group of morris dancers as a 'football team'. Distribution in the US was so poor that the books Pratchett signed at conventions were invariably the imported British editions. The haphazard publishing schedule also meant he was usually ineligible to win the more prestigious American SF awards. Pratchett was one of the first Worldcon guests of honour to have never been given SF's coveted Hugo Award.

By 2000 a new team was in place at publishing giants HarperCollins, Terry's US publisher since 1994, and his editors and agents were finally able to convince the company that an author selling millions every year, around the globe, was worth backing. Slowly, the situation began to improve. Pratchett had always been a cult author in the US, but that cult began, steadily, to grow as a well-branded and marketed backlist, with stylish, redesigned jacket art, came into print, and new novels synced with their UK publication dates. In 2004 Pratchett was the guest of honour at Worldcon. By 2005, he was a *New York Times* bestseller and by 2009, America was hosting dedicated Discworld conventions of its own.

He could not reasonably be called a cult author any longer, though part of his continued success was his refusal to stop acting like one. His relationship with his fanbase was still that of a genre writer, and at events, including the posh parties thrown for this or that Discworld anniversary, he would always prefer to spend time chatting with fans – a number of whom he insisted should always be invited – than with press or industry types. There was no denying he had achieved a status that went beyond 'popular writer'. As Jo Fletcher says, 'He had become a front-of-the-shop, piled-on-the-tables author. Like Stephen King stopped being a horror author and became "Stephen King", Terry Pratchett stopped being a fantasy author and became "Terry Pratchett".' His books weren't just extraordinarily successful, they were usually critically acclaimed as well (though there would always be a few that resisted). It didn't hurt that he was writing at a level far above his earlier work. Few could read a complex and moving book such as *Night Watch*, or an enthralling young adult adventure story like the Tiffany Aching novel *A Hat Full Of Sky*, and not find them gripping and impressive.

In 2006, the final piece in the long-awaited puzzle of Discworld spin-offs fell into place – over Christmas Sky TV broadcast a live action Discworld mini-series, an adaption of *Hogfather*, made with a lavish budget and big TV stars. The film, which had been made by Manchester-based production company The Mob with Pratchett's close involvement (he's credited as 'mucking about' with the script) was extremely faithful, and pleasingly sumptuous-looking. *Terry Pratchett's Hogfather* was a huge success for the channel – enough to commission a second mini-series, an adaption of *The Colour of Magic*. Pratchett had long since bought back the rights from Catalyst, the company responsible for the abandoned attempt to adapt the book ten years earlier. Discworld superfan David Jason was cast as Rincewind after lobbying hard for the role,[11] (and despite having played Albert – far better casting – in *Hogfather*) with production set to begin the following year.

Pratchett, meanwhile, was collecting honorary doctorates like a schoolboy collects football stickers, and had even been invited to the White House. To cap things off he was awarded a *Blue Peter* badge to mark the BBC's new dramatisation of *Johnny and the Bomb*, something he'd coveted since childhood. The council estate kid from Forty Green, the country bumpkin press officer, the real-ale swilling, nerdy fantasy author with his army of anorak-wearing Kevins, could now legitimately consider himself a bonafide national treasure.

---

11. He was, of course, the wrong Trotter brother for it.

Chapter 17

The Embuggerance

On Tuesday, 11 December 2007, Terry Pratchett released a statement via Sandra Kidby's website, PJSMPrints.co.uk – usually reserved for selling Discworld artwork and memorabilia – under the title 'An Embuggerance':

> I have been diagnosed with a very rare form of early onset Alzheimer's … . We are taking it fairly philosophically down here and possibly with a mild optimism … . Frankly, I would prefer it if people kept things cheerful, because I think there's time for at least a few more books yet :o)

The statement went on to reassure fans that two new books, *Nation* and *Unseen Academicals*, were on the way and that all commitments and appearances were going ahead as planned. It also included a plea that any offers of help came only from people that really, really knew what they were talking about.

The response was immediate – a predictable, but nevertheless appreciated outpouring of sympathy and support from fans swept into Terry's inbox, with some 150,000 emails within the first few days. The statement made headlines around the world, becoming a 'top of the hour' announcement on TV news bulletins, and appearing on the front pages of newspapers. It feels trite to say that life would never again be the same, when the subject at hand is a degenerative and incurable brain disease; for Pratchett, though, this would become more than simply a matter of his personal health. Alzheimer's would come to define his professional life and legacy in ways he could never have anticipated.

Experts agreed that Pratchett's variant of Alzheimer's disease, posterior cortical atrophy (PCA) would probably have started developing around a decade before his diagnosis. Later Terry and his personal assistant, Rob Wilkins, would trace the first symptoms back to 2005 when Pratchett became convinced that the letter 'E'[1] had vanished from his keyboard. Try as he might, he couldn't see it. Wilkins also noted that 2005 was roughly the start of an, at first barely noticeable slide in his spelling and typing. For a proficient touch typist and trained journalist these were, in retrospect, worrying signs, but Pratchett was approaching his sixties, and naturally chalked up such errors to encroaching old age.

In truth, his health had been in decline in minor ways for a few years, which – accompanied by what you might call 'the natural wastage of time' – masked and distracted from the slow emergence of his PCA. In 2004, after suffering attacks of angina, he underwent angioplasty surgery to treat abnormally high blood pressure, a relatively minor operation in which a stent is inserted into the arteries in order to widen them. There were complications during the procedure when Pratchett reacted badly to the dye injected into his bloodstream, causing arterial bleeding. He remembers waking up during the operation and having hallucinations of a man selling sandwiches at the side of the room, leading his surgeon to wonder why the patient was shouting about his lunch. The incident actually made the papers at the time,[2] though the coverage was poorly informed and largely overblown. Pratchett was put on blood pressure medication after an unsuccessful experiment with beta blockers, and his heart problems settled down.

By 2006 it was becoming increasingly clear to Terry, not to mention Lyn and Rob, that *something* was amiss. He was constantly losing his car keys and other small items, would struggle to locate the socket for his seatbelt, and found himself having problems tying a tie or putting on an inside-out jacket. He began to experience what he would refer to as 'Clapham Junction days', when he was overwhelmed by the constant need for his attention on this or that project and felt he couldn't cope with the increasing demands on his time. That year, David Pratchett, Terry's father, died from pancreatic cancer, following a year-long illness. Driving home from his final visit, Terry scraped the side of his Jaguar along a wall. He put the incident down to the distractions of grief, especially since he'd had tears in his eyes, but after another small accident parking

---

1. Or possibly 'S', the letter changed with the telling.
2. Though not the part about the sandwiches.

his car, he agreed to hand over his keys, worrying that he might not be safe behind the wheel.

After ruling out eyesight problems, his GP diagnosed him with 'ischaemic change', the medical term for the natural ageing process on human brain cells. The diagnosis was something of a relief. However, it wasn't long before another Clapham Junction day occurred and caused Terry to consider that something more serious might be wrong, and he returned to his doctor. This time he was given a mini-mental state examination (MMSE), which is the basic test for Alzheimer's, but the results didn't suggest anything that would explain his memory and coordination problems, and the disease was ruled out. He was sent to a specialist for an MRI scan and ultrasound. The scans showed up 'grey spots' in his brain indicating areas of dead brain cells. A specialist thought this was the legacy of a transient ischaemic attack, better known as a mini-stroke, the result of a blood clot in the artery to his brain, which had likely occurred two years before. The diagnosis made a lot of sense, since this would date the mini-stroke not only to the time he was treated for angina and high blood pressure, but it also coincided with the point he had first noticed problems with spelling and coordination. He was prescribed statins to lower his cholesterol and ordered to change his diet. He was told that, in all likelihood, his brain would rewire itself, with functioning brain cells taking up the slack of those that had died off. Alarmed, but satisfied with a diagnosis that seemed to make sense of all his symptoms, Terry got back to work.

He had no intention of slowing down and 2007 was extremely busy. Most years were. The American success of *Thud!* represented the full opening – at long last – of a whole new market, and the promotional trail for his latest novel, *Making Money*, was one of his most gruelling yet. It took in signing tours of Russia and the USA, the latter including a prestigious visit to the White House, where a number of authors were to be honoured by First Lady, Laura Bush over breakfast, with a lunch held later at the Library of Congress in Washington. At this event, and then again in New York, Pratchett talked about his mini-stroke, though the revelation wasn't especially commented upon. He gave an interview about it to the *Daily Mail*, which reads like a man quietly trying to raise awareness about an issue he'd rather not have had to deal with. His tone is jolly as he discusses his symptoms, and his knack for dropping 'off-the-cuff' oneliners and inserting prepared zingers into his interviews is still very much in play.

However, the symptoms weren't going away, and despite what specialists had told him, they seemed to be getting worse. During a signing tour of Italy, the wife of the British ambassador had noticed that his shirt was buttoned wrongly. When he returned home to continue work on his next book, he found his typing had deteriorated to the point it was now easier for him to dictate to his PA. It was enough for Terry's GP to seek a second opinion, and he was referred to Addenbrooke's Hospital in Cambridge. Specialists went back over his scans, and subjected him to more tests. This time, the diagnosis was PCA. Terry had been diagnosed, at the age of 59, with early-onset Alzheimer's Disease.

PCA is a very rare form of Alzheimer's, and tends to manifest itself in young patients, with 'young' for an Alzheimer's sufferer typically meaning anyone under 65. Alzheimer's is caused by a build up of proteins in the brain, forming 'tangles' between nerve ('brain') cells, cutting them off from one another. Eventually the isolated brain cells die, causing enough damage to impair various functions, including memory, sight, hearing, spatial awareness and speech. Typically the disease begins in the hippocampus, a tiny area of the temporal lobe shaped rather delightfully like a seahorse, which is part of the brain's memory centre. This is why, for most sufferers, the memory is the first thing to be affected. There are various causes of Alzheimer's, though current medical thinking has yet to arrive at a definitive one. For some the cause may be genetic, for others it can be tied to general bodily health and the risks of ageing, and for some, it's sheer bad luck. The disease is progressive, meaning it will only ever get worse. Alzheimer's is rarely fatal in itself, but most sufferers will eventually die from complications arising from their condition, such as blood clots to the brain, breathing problems and a vastly increased vulnerability to infection. A patient with late-stage Alzheimer's requires round-the-clock care. There are several treatments that can slow the progression of the disease, but there is, as yet, no cure. Alzheimer's is a slow death sentence, in which a person's personality and memories gradually fade. The process can take many years, or progress extremely quickly. Average life expectancy from diagnosis is around seven years.

PCA, the variant of Alzheimer's Terry had been diagnosed with, is slightly different to the more common form of the condition. Rather than the hippocampus, PCA targets the back (posterior) of the brain, the area that controls spatial awareness and processes information provided by the eyes. For example, our eyes can tell us that a computer keyboard is on the desk in front of us, but it is the rear part of our brain that tells us what it is, and makes sure our fingers can find it. One of the standard tests for PCA involves copying a simple line drawing – the eye can see the picture, but struggles to process the information in a way that means it can recreate it. PCA is often referred to as the most preferable strand of Alzheimer's to have – though this attitude annoyed Pratchett no end – as it leaves many of the brain's functions intact for longer. Sufferers have decent memory recall, can hold conversations and think creatively. It's fairly common for people coming into contact with someone with PCA to not even notice its effects. Pratchett often said that, in the early stages of his diagnosis, had no-one told him he had a form of Alzheimer's, for much of the time he wouldn't have known himself.

What do you do when you have been told you have a form of Alzheimer's Disease? How do you cope knowing you've just been handed a slow but inevitable death sentence? What happens *next*? What Terry desperately wanted to hear, from the very second of his diagnosis, was that there was a 'golden path' ahead of him. That someone could tell him exactly what steps there were to take, and show him what he should do. He needed direction and he needed answers. Unfortunately, matters were not quite so straightforward. In fact, in the short term, the situation was infuriating. Following his diagnosis, the unit at the hospital in Cambridge closed for the night, and he had no other option but to go home. Later, when he was invited to give the prestigious Dimbleby Lecture, he described the day of his diagnosis. It's common that after receiving bad news people experience a moment of bewilderment, a ringing in their ears or a dark silence that blocks out whatever their doctor says next, as their brain tries to take in the magnitude of what they've heard. Terry Pratchett's reaction was different. Just for a moment his doctor was surrounded by a glowing red fire; as was a second doctor he passed on his way out of the building. Inside Pratchett, a white-hot rage was growing, and it would continue to grow hotter. Only the calm medical advice of some extremely knowledgeable fans, and the practical, solid reassurance of his family got him through the next few days. For her part, Lyn was actually relieved – she had suspected that her husband had a brain tumour. Terry said he would actually prefer that. Brain tumours are curable.

The problem was that there *was* no 'golden path', as there might be available to, say, a cancer sufferer, who might be told that there was a rocky road ahead, but at least they would know where the road was. Terry was left dangling. There were only two Alzheimer's specialists in Pratchett's area. One had no experience of PCA, and the other would only take patients of 65 or over. And since only specialists can legally administer Alzheimer's treatment, it meant there was no-one available locally who was qualified to prescribe him the relevant medication. In fact, as it turned out, the NHS couldn't supply the necessary medication *at all*. A drug called donepezil, which went by the trade name Aricept, had been shown to slow the progress of the disease, but Aricept was a relatively recent discovery, and, as such, was extremely expensive. Though the rules have now been changed, in 2007 the NHS wouldn't supply Aricept to anyone suffering with an early, or mild form of the disease. It was, however, legal to obtain it yourself if you knew how to work the system, and since Terry was well connected and very wealthy, he was able to procure the drug relatively quickly. The fact that a drug, which could potentially extend quality of life, was out of reach to tens of thousands of patients was intolerable for someone with Pratchett's sense of injustice. The fizzing, simmering rage was ready to boil over.

Terry needed a focus for his rage. He needed to feel he was moving forward, and he needed to gain a sense of control of his disease. As such he made three important decisions within days of his diagnosis. On hearing the news, Rob, Terry's PA, asked who they should tell. The reply was 'everybody'. His publishers would need to know, as would the people with whom he had business relationships. Some things would have to be cancelled or postponed. The news was going to get out. The solution was to be democratic about the information and control the story – on 11 December, Terry's short blog was shared on the PJSM Prints website, informing the whole world of his diagnosis. That was decision one. Decision two bore fruit the following spring when Pratchett announced he was donating a million dollars to Alzheimer's research.[3] This was his way of fighting back. He had been appalled by what he'd learned about government spending on dementia, which in 2008 amounted to around £11 for every person in the UK who had the disease. The figure for cancer research was £289 per head. Prior to making the donation, Pratchett visited Downing Street to lobby Labour Prime Minister, Gordon Brown, whom he would later say had personally made him a cup of tea. Not willing to play favourites, later that year Terry would meet with David Cameron, and address the Conservative Party Conference in Manchester on the subject of Alzheimer's research.

The third major decision was to do everything in his power to raise the profile of Alzheimer's. He was going to make it an acceptable topic of conversation and destigmatise the condition. He compared his work to how the Dimbleby family helped to remove the stigma around cancer by announcing that Richard Dimbleby had died of the disease in the 1960s. One oft-repeated mantra of Terry's was 'to slay the demon, you have to say its name'. He embraced the role of unofficial spokesperson for Alzheimer's Disease, appearing on chat shows and current affairs programmes, putting the promotional energy usually reserved for a book launch into talking about his illness. He agreed to let a BBC documentary crew follow his progress throughout 2008, as he met with consultants, investigated new treatments and spoke to fellow sufferers. His intention was to take the fight to Alzheimer's by any means necessary, using all of the influence and respect a 'national treasure' had at his command.

That year – 2008 – was full of arbitrary landmarks and anniversaries. April saw Terry's sixtieth birthday, and Rhianna Pratchett excelled herself by getting the folk band Steeleye Span, a favourite of her father's since he was a young man, to play an open-air concert near Terry and Lyn's home in Wiltshire to celebrate.[4] Sky's adaptation of the first two Discworld novels was broadcast in spring as *Terry Pratchett's The Colour of Magic*, to even more acclaim and success than 2006's *Hogfather*. The

---

3. Pratchett tended to use the nice, round number of 'one million dollars'. Unfortunately, the UK press tended to quote figures in sterling, which at the time was the less impressive sounding figure of 'slightly shy of £500,000'.

4. The group would go on to record a concept album based around the Tiffany Aching book, *Wintersmith*. It is easily the best of the three Discworld-themed albums available.

aforementioned David Jason, a man quite comfortably in the 'national treasure' camp himself, starred as Rincewind, Sean Astin, the former child star who had recently played Sam Gamgee in Peter Jackson's *Lord of the Rings* movies, played Twoflower, and Tim Curry hammed it up marvellously as Trymon. That autumn saw Terry and Lyn's fortieth wedding anniversary, and the twenty-fifth anniversary of the publication of *The Colour of Magic* and thus the Discworld series itself. The latter event was marked by a special party at the Royal Society, which doubled as a launch for Pratchett's latest book, *Nation*.

There's nothing special about sixty, forty or twenty-five of course, they're just numbers. To paraphrase *Good Omens*, keep counting and you're bound to get to them eventually. Taken together though, they seemed to give 2008 a particular significance in Pratchett's life,[5] marking the end of another era. Sadly 2008 never really felt like a year of celebration. It was dominated by Terry's disease, which became the lead angle in every interview he gave, and every article and review written about him or his work. This was something he had encouraged. He allowed himself to become 'Mr Alzheimer's', partly because he felt deeply that people were not aware enough of the disease, and partly because it gave him a sense of momentum and allowed him to feel he was being proactive against his own illness. Still, it was tiring, as the journalist Frances Hardy, writing in the *Daily Mail*, remarked: 'When I broach the subject of his illness with a pointed, "How are you?" he sighs a tad wearily. He's done nothing but talk about dementia, every permutation and implication of it, since September last year, and he's practically run out of things to say.' A few months later, Deborah Orr, writing in *The Independent*, visited Pratchett's study in the chapel, on the grounds of his Wiltshire house and agreed that enough was enough with the Alzheimer's chat, writing in her piece: 'Actually, I think it's a bit of a shame that the diagnosis of a progressive brain disease does more for a man's public profile than the amassing of a distinctive and valuable body of work does.' Orr does her best to steer the interview back to Terry's writing and latest book, but

---

5. Actually, taken together they make 125. For those that believe in the numerological theory that numbers have significance and carry messages from higher powers, 125 is supposed to be a symbol of optimism and a sign to keep going through hardship. Make of that what you will. I'd make nothing of it whatsoever, but each to their own.

by now, having done nothing *but* talk about his disease for months on end, he seemed unable to help himself. 'I absolutely beg Pratchett to stop saying interesting and provocative things about his medical situation,' she says. 'He pays no heed.'

It was probably the ubiquity of the coverage that contributed to a slight sense of unease as the 2008 Discworld convention got underway, an event Pratchett usually looked forward to immensely. Fans, used to greeting the guest of honour at some point, worried he may be less available this year, or that he would be a shell of his former self. Terry, the king of this particular hill, played up to his audience's fears marvellously. Taking to the convention stage for the first time that year, he undercut the tension by pretending to forget his name before reading it from a piece of paper in his pocket. It was a masterstroke of diffusion.

However, footage from the same convention, which appeared in the two-part documentary, *Terry Pratchett: Living With Alzheimer's* released the following year, shows that all was not well. Terry had given his traditional 'bedtime story' reading, giving fans a sneak preview of *Nation*. Reading is often a problem for PCA sufferers and Pratchett is seen losing his thread as he complains about 'shadows' on the page preventing him from seeing the words. It was a painful reminder that, despite the author's attempts to put on a brave face,[6] PCA was still lurking below the surface. For the first time, fans at the convention were told that Terry would, from now on, be signing his name only, and would no longer make out dedications in books.

Pratchett had spent the whole year energetically dealing with his disease, and doing his best to dispel any thought that 'the embuggerance' had invalided him, saying in almost every interview that if someone didn't *know* he had Alzheimer's, there's no way they could *tell* he had Alzheimer's. For the most part this was true. On one occasion a doctor based in London, having spent the day with Terry, contacted the specialist treating him to say he genuinely believed there had been some mistake, and that this man couldn't possibly have any form of dementia. Terry was still capable of being quick of tongue, and though he could sometimes come across as awkward and short-tempered, well, Terry had *always*

---

6. Though he hated being called 'brave' and would be withering to anyone who tried it.

been awkward, and occasionally short-tempered, especially if he was in the throes of a new book. When he had first started seeing specialists in an attempt to diagnose his condition, his wife and PA had warned the doctors that many of his symptoms taken together were also a chronic condition known as 'being an author', and more specifically known as 'being Terry Pratchett'.

In fact, the various measures he had put in place since his diagnosis appeared to have brought about some improvement, and his mood remained largely positive. Terry was regularly tested in an attempt to track the advancement of the disease. In 2008 he was scoring twenty-nine out of thirty on the tests issued by his doctors. By 2010 that score had dropped, but only by three points to twenty-six. The Aricept, of course, was the most likely source of help, but Terry was also toying with other less straightforward remedies. Lyn had heard that turmeric could be effective at slowing the disease, and made him a daily tincture that occasionally left him with a yellow moustache. She also stuffed him so full of vitamin tablets he practically rattled. On the other end of the scale was the 'Loony Helmet', a frightening-looking sci-fi prototype of black cubes and wires, designed by a South African GP living in the north of England called Dr Gordon Dougal. The helmet sent bursts of infrared light into the brain of the wearer, in theory stimulating cellular growth. Once Bernard Pearson had cast a mould of Pratchett's unusually domed head in order to make sure the helmet sat comfortably, it was used twice a day. The Loony Helmet[7] features prominently in *Terry Pratchett: Living With Alzheimer's*. In the programme Dr Dougal certainly seems pleased with his invention, which he says was successfully used on his stepfather, apparently giving him a new lease of life and, according to Dougal's mother, 'restoring his libido'. Even more endearing than a man inventing a helmet that improves his elderly parents' sex life, were the reactions of Terry and Rob to the kit. The two tech nerds, who had bonded over their customised ZX Spectrums, had no idea if the device would work, but both instinctively felt that it was exactly the sort of thing they should try. Pratchett would always be open to new treatments and drugs, provided

---

7. This was Pratchett's name for the device, though it's a shame Dr Dougal didn't adopt it for future marketing purposes.

they had some scientific rigour behind them, even having the metal fillings removed from his teeth on the advice of an expert who said it could slow down the effects of the disease and, in any case, would do him no harm. In a 2011 interview with Madison.com, a website dedicated to news in the Wisconsin city where that year's US Discworld Convention was to take place, Terry admits that some new medication was turning his pee blue, something which alarmed patrons sharing a urinal with him in an English pub.[8] This colourful side effect indicates that Terry was likely taking Methylene Blue, an Alzheimer's drug being trialled in the US which was, at one point, being hailed as a game-changing 'wonder drug'; but which could indeed turn a patient's urine the colour of a particularly exotic cocktail.

In early 2008, Terry had finally been assigned to a specialist, Professor Roy Jones, one of the founders of the Research Institute for the Care of Older People (RICE), based in Bath, a city Terry knew well. He would visit the RICE centre twice a year as his disease ran its course. Professor Jones and his team would administer a series of practical and mental tests, including word games, memory tests and drawing tests. The tests showed, as you would expect, that Terry had a higher-than-average IQ. He couldn't resist showboating on the word games, and when asked to name as many animals beginning with the letter N or shopping items as he could, he would deliberately go so fast, and into such ludicrous detail that the psychologist testing him would eventually stop tracking his answers. His doctors theorised that, though the PCA was certainly impacting his thought processes and the activity in his brain, one factor mentioned in his original diagnosis remained true – his brain was likely 'rewiring' itself, with other brain cells taking up the slack of those cut out by the disease. Sadly, all concerned were aware that this was a bodge job. It could keep him going for a while, but eventually he would run out of brain to rewire. This was made painfully clear in the practical section of the test, where Terry was required to copy some basic line drawings – intersecting pentagons, a curly spring shape and a simple drawing of a house with a 3D, side-on perspective. His attempts to copy the shapes

---

8. Pratchett used this as an opportunity to pretend he was an alien by turning to the person next to him and saying, 'I'm really enjoying my visit to your planet.' Later, this side effect turns up in *The Long Earth*, as the result of taking anti-nausea medicine.

sit uncomfortably on the page next to the originals. The intersecting pentagons are missing several lines, the spring is lacking a loop, and the little drawing of a house has no perspective aspect at all; it's a flattened house, such as might be done by a 4 year old with a crayon. It's with an added pang that, for a fan, the picture most closely resembles the description of the Tooth Fairy's castle in *Hogfather*.

What makes this all the more poignant, of course, is that Pratchett had been a skilled artist. The illustrations he had provided for *The Carpet People* back in 1971 were full of character, depth and perspective, and are expertly inked. The versions he hand-coloured are absolutely exquisite, full of detailed shading and wonderful use of colour. He created several satisfyingly sci-fi images for the cover of *The Dark Side of the Sun*, and had drawn dozens of clever cartoons for his columns in the *Bucks Free Press*, *Bath Chronicle* and *Psychic Researcher*. Collectively, these showed off several different skills and techniques. While it's a mercy that the nature of PCA meant that Pratchett was able to continue to write – he would author or co-author eleven novels in the eight years following his diagnosis – it's heartbreaking that his gift as a visual artist should be one of the first things sacrificed to his disease. It's with no small irony that 2009 would see Doubleday publish a new edition of *The Carpet People* that restored Pratchett's original illustrations for the first time since 1971.

Chapter 18

The Knight's Tale

There's an in-joke in the Discworld City Watch series that sees the character of Sam Vimes promoted endlessly. He begins 1989's *Guards! Guards!* as the alcoholic and dysfunctional captain of the Night Watch. By 1998's *The Fifth Elephant* his full title is His Excellency, His Grace, Commander Sir Samuel Vimes, The Duke of Ankh. To this is tagged the title of Blackboard Monitor, a throwaway joke which, three books later, ends up being significant. Pratchett always said that Vimes was one of the characters he most related to. His passage through life echoes Pratchett's own – raised as poor as a church mouse, marrying above his station, overachieving beyond his wildest dreams and eventually being given an honorific once considered unthinkable. The universe, as any Discworld reader knows, has a sense of humour about these things, and having watched Pratchett overburden his character with titles, it decided it was time for life to imitate art. Thus, in December 2008, with Terry already preening after being given a degree and visiting professorship at Trinity College, Dublin, a press release from Buckingham Palace announced that Terry Pratchett was to receive a knighthood, granted in the Queen's New Year's honours list.

Pratchett was flabbergasted when he'd first heard the news. His OBE had been unexpected enough, and he rather felt he'd risen about as high as anyone was going to allow. And yet, just shy of ten years later he found himself kneeling in his morning suit as Her Majesty the Queen placed his knighthood insignia medal around his neck. *The Independent* wrote: 'In a period of personal adversity, Mr Pratchett has shown genuine courage. The knighthood of this modest man is an example of what our honours system should be about – and the best reason of all not to scrap it.'

Despite the paper's focus on his recent 'embuggerance', officially Pratchett was being honoured once again for services to literature. A Radio 4 presenter who had the nerve to suggest that he had been knighted for any reason other than his writing, received a sharp reprimand during an interview with the author. That seems a little unfair. We can't know if 'Sir Terry' would have made an appearance in 2009 were it not for his work to raise awareness around dementia, but you suspect that his personal circumstances played their role. After all, despite being called the *Queen's* honours list, knighthoods are largely awarded from Downing Street, an address Terry had visited several months earlier. The prime minister must have been impressed. He had, after all, made him a cup of tea.

Professor Sir Terence David John Pratchett of Broad Chalke, Wiltshire, Knight OBE and Blackboard Monitor,[1] wasted no time in acting the part. As a knight, he decided, it was essential that he had a sword, and if he was going to have a sword, it was going to be made exactly to his liking. He approached a local blacksmith, Jake Keen, to help him forge his weapon from scratch. The pair gathered iron ore from a field in the nearby village of Tisbury, liberated some clay from the foundation of Rob Wilkins' house, and found hay and sheep dung from Terry and Lyn's grounds in Broad Chalke. They baked the ingredients to make a crude shaft furnace, which they used to smelt the iron ore. Terry, wanting something particularly special, also added material from the Sikhote-Alin meteorite, which had crashed to Earth in the Soviet Union in 1947, the year before he was born, creating genuine thunderbolt iron. He then worked with an experienced swordsmith, Hector Cole, to create his own unique weapon, made partly from iron found in the landscape he loved, and partly from iron that had fallen from space. The following year the new Sir Terry was told by a fan that he was also entitled to his own coat of arms. Unfortunately the College of Arms – who deal with such things – wouldn't allow him to add hippos to either side, as with the one he had created for Ankh-Morpork. The official coat of arms of Sir Terence Pratchett (etc) features, in the archaic language of heraldry: 'a Sable an Ankh between four Roundels in saltire each issuing Argent' (that's a shield showing a silver ankh on black), with a crest depicting 'On Water Barry wavy Sable Argent and Sable an Owl affronty wings displayed and

---

1. Trinity College actually supplied him with a personalised board eraser for his lectures, with this title engraved onto a brass plate and screwed to the handle.

inverted Or supporting thereby two closed Books erect Gules' (roughly, an owl and some books perched atop a helmet). The motto is '*Noli Timere Messorem*', the correct translation of the dog-Latin motto Pratchett gave to Mort in the Discworld novels. Roughly translated it means 'don't fear the reaper'. The owl, perched above the ankh is, of course, a morepork.

Amid the whirlwind of press coverage and fuss that surrounded the knighthood and work to promote Alzheimer's awareness, it's easy to lose track – as much of the press did – of the fact that in autumn 2008, Pratchett published one of the best books of his career. *Nation*, a story ostensibly aimed at the young adult market, was the first non-Discworld novel Pratchett had written since *Johnny and the Bomb*, eleven years earlier. The idea had first come to him in 2003 while reading about the 1883 Krakatoa eruption, which caused a giant tsunami to rip across the Pacific, claiming an estimated 36,000 lives. Unfortunately, his timing was horrible. In December 2004, a tsunami caused by powerful seismic activity in the Indian Ocean caused the deaths of nearly 230,000 people from fourteen countries. It was clear that the plot Pratchett had in mind would now be in terribly bad taste, and the idea was put aside for several years.

The irony is that *Nation* is not a book about a natural disaster. It's a book about being angry with the gods. In the story, Mau, a young man belonging to a non-specific island tribe called The Nation, returns from his coming-of-age ritual to find a giant wave has destroyed his village and killed everyone he knows. Stranded on the island with him is Daphne – the daughter of a minor British royal, whom Mau thinks is a 'ghost girl' because of her pale skin and white clothes – who is shipwrecked after the tsunami. The pair forge a bond, as refugees from the surrounding islands are drawn to The Nation, forming a new society. Into Mau, Pratchett pours decades of anger at how faith, tradition and pointless, ancient values dictate the way the world works. Mau never completed his coming-of-age ritual, and thus is considered to have no soul, yet he speaks directly to the god of the dead, and the spirits of his ancestors, screaming 'shall not happen' over and again as the threats of more deaths arise. *Nation* is an extremely powerful story, and though not without some delightful humour, is easily the most serious of all of Pratchett's books. The scenes where Mau returns to find the drowned bodies of his entire tribe and diligently buries them at sea, working in a trance and watching himself from inside his own head as he commits the corpse of a baby to the dark waters, are disturbing and evocative, and unlike anything else in Pratchett's canon.

The author had much to be angry about. His father had died during the writing of *Nation*, having endured the pain of pancreatic cancer for over a year. Terry did his best for him, but David Pratchett did not have a comfortable end to his life. Terry's mother, Eileen, as is often the way, followed her husband within a couple of years, dying of a stroke. Though much of the work on *Nation* had been completed by the time of Terry's PCA diagnosis, the previous year had seen him pinballing between specialists while dealing with a health condition that had caused problems with the most basic of tasks. At one point, soon after learning of his condition, Terry believed that *Nation* might be the last book he would write, and his schedule was cleared to ensure he could finish it; though of course rumours of his imminent demise turned out to be greatly exaggerated, even by Terry himself.

Pratchett said that *Nation* was fuelled by much of the anger and frustration of that period, and it seeps into the book like ink into paper. He had said that *Nation* was a book he *had* to write, that it was a story that dragged him along behind it, running to keep up. It's an extraordinary and beautiful tale, full of rage and darkness, that is also capable of a wonderfully light touch as the two young people at the centre of the plot fall in love in a quiet and unassuming sort of way. The love story leads to a bittersweet ending that mirrors Philip Pullman's *His Dark Materials* in the inevitability of its separated sweethearts. It was arguably, perhaps even *unarguably*, Pratchett's finest work, and was widely praised as such on its release. *Nation* won Pratchett Published Writer of the Year at the Brit Writers' Awards, the Michael L. Printz Award for Excellence in Young Adult Literature, bestowed by an association of libraries in the USA, the 2009 Boston Globe-Horn Book Award for Excellence in Children's literature and the *Los Angeles Times* Book Prize for Young Adult Literature, though it was curiously ignored by the Carnegie panel. The following year, Pratchett was also given a lifetime achievement award for outstanding contribution to children's literature by the Writers' Guild. Like Pullman's epic, *Nation* was adapted into an impressive stage show by London's National Theatre, running over the coveted Christmas season.

The treatment of religion in *Nation* picks up a thread that runs through Pratchett's work, most notably in *Truckers*, *Small Gods*, *The Amazing Maurice*, and to a lesser extent, *Hogfather* and *Monstrous Regiment*. Specifically, it comes to the fore in the third volume in the *Science of Discworld* series, *Darwin's Watch*, co-written with scientists Jack Cohen and Ian Stewart, which deals directly with creationism as a threat to any era wishing to call itself an age of reason. Pratchett made no secret of his rejection of the dogma and rules of mainstream religion. He considered himself a humanist, a loose term for people who embrace the compassion and empathy characteristic of real faith – especially the Christian values of forgiveness and tolerance – but do so against a backdrop of scientific rationalism and basic human decency rather than spirituality or a belief in the uncanny. Humanism is atheism dressed up for church on a Sunday. Pratchett had been involved in the British Humanist Association since the 1990s, and would work occasionally with the organisation as they campaigned against Christian doctrine impacting British law, including a high-profile debate about the right to die, which reached the House of Lords. It would be a cause with which Pratchett would be increasingly associated.

His atheism had softened over the years. Ed James, writing in *Terry Pratchett: Guilty of Literature*, remembers that as young men the pair had been militant in their rejection of God in all forms, but notes that only he has remained quite as aggressive in his stance. Over the years Pratchett's view on religion became more speculative, and his PCA seemed to move his thinking further away from the absolutist view of the Richard Dawkins' brigade. In a 2009 interview with *The Times* he spoke of experiencing a moment of complete calm shortly after his diagnosis, finding himself whistling as he pottered in his garden.

When the character of Death speaks in the Discworld books, his words aren't actually heard in a literal sense, but rather arrive inside the head of the listener without having troubled their ears. In that moment of calmness, the voice of Terry's father unfolded in his head in the same way, telling him not to worry and that everything was happening as it was supposed to. He told the *Times* journalist that he didn't think what he'd had was a religious experience, but felt he could now understand those who did have them. The anecdote was a relatively small section in a wide-ranging newspaper feature, but was seized upon by the media, always looking for a clickbait-friendly angle. 'Terry Pratchett says he has found God' screamed the headlines the next day.

Pratchett was pretty sure he hadn't found God, joking that he could barely find his keys. He contributed a piece to the *Mail On Sunday* soon afterwards, which he called 'The God Moment', clarifying the story, and explaining his view of religion, tying his background into the bitter treatment of dogma in *Nation*, which he says was fuelled by a realisation at an early age that an 'act of God' that wiped out a family and a 'miracle', that saved one, must come from the same source. He went on to say that he believed the voice he had 'heard' that day had not been God's or his father's in a literal sense, but belonged to a spiritual part of the human mind that was capable of thinking in an abstract way, and could be spellbound by beautiful music or art. He argued that the potential for epiphany was generated from within. It's a view familiar to anyone paying attention to Pratchett's work, in which people create their gods, and not the other way around, and 'the darkness behind the eyes' separates human from animal. This nuanced article might have gone some way to clearing the matter up, had the *Mail's* website not run it under the headline, '"I create gods all the time – now I think one might exist", says fantasy author Terry Pratchett'.

If the accepted God of Christian dogma did exist, Sir Terry Pratchett was doing his damndest to get on his nerves. Tied inexorably into the conversation around Alzheimer's, was the question of death, both literally, and in the form of the 'living death', waiting as the disease took its course. Terry knew, as all dementia sufferers do, that progress of his disease was inevitable and that the rewiring in his brain would eventually run out of solder. Though his heart may still beat, there would be a point in the coming years when he would no longer be Terry Pratchett; when he could no longer write, or joke, or come back with a waspish retort. In keeping with the symptoms of PCA, it was also likely he would not be able to see, or at least not be able to comprehend what he was seeing. To Terry this idea was intolerable. This wouldn't be living in any form he would recognise, and given the choice – and he was determined to be

244   The Magic of Terry Pratchett

given the choice – he would prefer to peacefully end his time on Earth before things could progress that far. He was also very aware that, as far as the law was concerned, that wasn't going to be his decision to make. Increasingly, any conversation around dementia would become a conversation around what is usually called euthanasia or assisted suicide, or as Terry preferred to call it, 'assisted dying', and whether ethically, morally and legally, a person had the right to choose when it was time.

Terry became a passionate campaigner for the right to die. To him it was the height of cruelty to expect someone to endure in this world when life had become, for whatever reason, intolerable; and the height of insanity to prosecute those who might help the people they loved to end their suffering. Assisted dying quickly became as inevitable a part of any Terry Pratchett interview as Alzheimer's and 'the business with the turtle'. The subject first gained prominence in 2009, when the now *Sir* Terry lent his weight to a campaign by the British Humanist Association (now Humanists UK) ahead of a debate in the House of Lords to clarify the rights of people who helped their loved ones travel abroad in order to end their life legally. The question had arisen thanks in part to the publicity around the case of Debbie Purdy, a multiple sclerosis sufferer who feared her husband would be prosecuted should he help her to reach a country where euthanasia was legal. There were several other high-profile cases in the late 2000s that prompted debate around assisted dying, the most famous being that of Tony Nicklinson, a British man who developed 'locked-in syndrome' after experiencing a stroke. Nicklinson's wish to be allowed an assisted death was denied by the High Court, and he eventually died of starvation after refusing food in 2012. Pratchett kept a photograph of Tony Nicklinson in his study as a reminder to keep fighting. In August 2009, Terry contributed an article to the *Mail On Sunday* entitled 'Point me to Heaven when the Final Chapter Comes'. He discussed his time as a journalist, the horrors of deaths he had witnessed, and the elderly local nurses he met in the 1960s who would remember 'showing someone the way' or 'pointing them to heaven' when a patient's pain became too much. It was a concept that would crop up in his next novel, the Tiffany Aching story *I Shall Wear Midnight*. The article was one of the first times that Terry had spoken publicly about his own death, which he knew would probably occur within a decade, if he was very lucky. He said he wanted the opportunity to end his life at home, sitting peacefully in a chair in his garden, with a glass of brandy in his hand, and the music of the sixteenth-century composer Thomas Tallis playing on his iPod; specifically the beautiful choral piece *Spem In Alium.*

Early in 2010, Pratchett became the first novelist to be invited to give the prestigious Richard Dimbleby lecture, to be broadcast on BBC 1 to an audience of five million. The lecture had been introduced in 1972 in memory of Richard Dimbleby, the pioneering television journalist who would become the BBC's leading news broadcaster. Every year an influential public figure was selected by the Dimbleby family to give the forty-five-minute lecture on a subject of their choosing. Previous recipients included the Duke of Edinburgh, the Prince of Wales, the former Archbishop of Canterbury, Rowan Williams, and the technology pioneer, James Dyson. Pratchett was selected in anticipation that he would use the opportunity to talk about dementia. Instead, he wrote an at-times moving, at-times angry, always-compelling plea for acceptance and compassion for assisted dying.

Terry was honoured by the invitation, and was gratified to have the opportunity to talk at length on an issue that mattered so much to him on such a high-profile and respected platform. There was, of course, a problem. In the past, Pratchett had enjoyed public speaking, and had given many readings and guest of honour speeches at conventions across the world, delivering well-honed oneliners and dealing expertly with hecklers and well-wishers alike. His PCA, however, posed a significant issue. It was entirely possible, on his best days, that Terry could deliver the entire speech, but his condition was unpredictable, and it was equally likely that he would be unable to focus on the words in front of him. A few weeks before the lecture, which was to be filmed before an invited audience at the Royal College of Physicians, he asked Tony Robinson, the voice of abridged Discworld, if he would be on hand to step in, should he struggle at any point during the reading. Robinson, himself a noted Alzheimer's campaigner, agreed, but didn't seriously expect to be called upon. He arrived in good time for the speech, only to be told by a producer – described in Robinson's autobiography, *No Cunning Plan*, as 'ashen-faced' – that Pratchett was having a difficult day, and that he would be required to deliver the whole thing. This was a daunting prospect, but Robinson had recorded over forty Pratchett novels across two decades, and was familiar with the rhythms of his writing; and as a professional actor of stage and screen was used to coping with pressured performances. The lecture, which was entitled *Shaking Hands With Death*, went without a hitch. Terry was able to deliver an introduction before Robinson – introduced by David Dimbleby as a 'stunt Pratchett' – took the stage. Terry looked less hearty than he had in the *Living With Alzheimer's* documentary, but seemed robust enough. He had traded in his man-in-black 'urban cowboy' persona for a more learned, eccentric professor look, all crushed velvet and wildly bushy eyebrows, his previously neat beard allowed to grow out, bringing to mind Charles Darwin or John Dee. His speech included a few awkward pauses, but he eased into the short performance as it went on, visibly relaxing whenever he landed a solid laugh, before handing over to Robinson.

Shaking Hands With Death is an exceptional piece of writing, and though it was a shame that Terry couldn't deliver it himself, Tony Robinson is an actor and probably gave the reading more punch and power than the author could have done, even on one of his best days. In it, Terry describes the moment when, had there been any justice, his father should have died revelling in the memory of the sun on his face during his war service in far-off Karachi. It's a death Pratchett would give to a character in *I Shall Wear Midnight*, when the gruff and ailing Baron of the Chalk dies peacefully, with his face lit by a memory of sunshine from his childhood.[2]

The lecture argues eloquently for compassion for the terminally ill and their relatives, and the need to establish a legally empowered tribunal to assess each case on merit. Pratchett goes on to quote statistics about public opinion, and the words of the government's dignity ambassador, Michael Parkinson, before launching into the social history of the Victorians, the nature of God, and the experiences of a young *Bucks Free Press* journalist dealing with his first glimpse of death. It's also, perhaps surprisingly, a very funny piece of writing. Sir Terry Pratchett may have

---

2. This being Discworld, it's immediately followed by Death remarking 'WASN'T THAT APPROPRIATE?'

changed his jacket, but the leopard can never entirely, as the Discworld's Lord Vetinari would say, 'change its shorts'.

The Dimbleby Lecture had the intended effect. It was extremely well received and resulted in acres of column inches dedicated to arguments on both sides of the assisted dying debate. Though it also, perhaps unfairly, introduced the idea that Terry Pratchett was frail and perhaps struggling. The lecture did an ordinate amount of good in an important area that needed highlighting, though it possibly distracted from the idea that Pratchett was still a creative force.

He had joked that his 'Mr Alzheimer's' reputation might evolve into something a little darker following the Dimbleby Lecture, the most public statement he had made on the subject of assisted dying. He was right. He quickly became the media's go-to source for a quote whenever the subject raised its head in the news, via a new development, a new ruling or, inevitably a new death. Later that year he was asked by the BBC if he would be interested in following up *Living With Alzheimer's*, which had gained great acclaim and won a BAFTA for its creators. Commissioning editor Charlotte Moore suggested that his next film could look at the options for assisted dying available in Europe.

The result, broadcast in June 2011, was *Terry Pratchett: Choosing To Die*. The film was put together by the same team that worked on *Living With Alzheimer's*, and who would go on to make two more documentaries, *Terry Pratchett: Facing Extinction*, a return to the rainforests of Borneo and the state of orangutan conservation twenty-five years after *Jungle Quest*, and the posthumous docudrama *Terry Pratchett: Back in Black*. *Choosing To Die* had a very different and more serious tone to the other films. In fact, it could legitimately be seen as one of the most controversial pieces of television in the history of the BBC, garnering 7,000 complaints, including outraged explosions from Christian and pro-life organisations, Church of England notables, and a joint letter of complaint signed by four members of the House of Lords. An early day motion in the House of Commons, condemning the documentary and calling on the BBC to remain impartial on such issues, was supported by fifteen MPs. Those most offended by the film had loud voices and powerful allies. They were, however, largely drowned out by a greater roar of approval. *Choosing To Die* was critically acclaimed by viewers and critics, and was called a landmark piece of television by more than one source. It would go on to bag its creators another BAFTA.

Whichever way it's sliced, *Choosing to Die* is an extremely provocative and powerful piece of filmmaking. Pratchett explores the ideas and options available to people who may want to die, including an interview with the founder of Dignitas, the facility based on the outskirts of Zurich, Switzerland, which allows individuals to end their own lives legally in carefully controlled conditions. Pratchett, accompanied by Rob Wilkins, interviews several people living with terminal or progressive and incurable conditions. Some were determined to see their disease through, for either their own or their family's sake; others wished to end their lives but were unable to afford the tremendous fees needed to travel abroad to a country where euthanasia, though tightly controlled, was legal. Two men, Andrew Colgan and Peter Smedley, very different people with very different conditions, had arranged to travel to Zurich to end their lives at Dignitas.

Despite the accusations to the contrary, the documentary tried hard to maintain a balanced view on an extremely complicated moral issue. Pratchett is shown as a passionate advocate for the rights of the very ill to end their suffering on their own terms, but he is constantly confronted with compelling arguments to the contrary. One woman, the wife of a man with motor neurone disease, seems barely able to contain her rage on behalf of Terry's wife, when he tells her he would consider taking his own life against Lyn's better judgement. A surprising source of balance in the film comes from Rob Wilkins, who looks increasingly uncomfortable as the documentary progresses, despite Terry's steadfast insistence that assisted dying is a necessary right. At one point the pair are talking to Andrew Colgan, a 42-year-old science fiction fan suffering from multiple sclerosis, who has travelled to Zurich to die the next day. Sat with Pratchett and Wilkins in a bar on the eve of his appointment, Colgan, fully lucid, as you must be in order to undergo the procedure under Swiss law, describes how he has fallen in love with the city. Wilkins practically begs him to cancel his appointment, saying they can explore Zurich together and visit the large Hadron collider at CERN. Colgan insists that he needs to go through with his plans while he is still healthy enough to make the journey – he may never get another chance, dooming himself to see his disease through to its bitter conclusion.

Two days later, Pratchett, Wilkins and a cameraman are present as Peter Smedley, a gentle businessman in his seventies suffering from motor neurone disease, calmly, and with a great deal of dignity, drinks the chemicals that will first send him to sleep, and then stop his breathing and heartbeat. The camera stays on throughout the process. It is believed to be the first televised case of a person receiving an assisted death. The moment is extremely difficult to watch, and incalculably moving. It's an astonishing, important piece of television. Unsurprisingly, it is this footage that generated the most complaints, praise and column inches. Some called it brave and important, others accused it of being a high-brow snuff movie, exploiting the death of an old man. *Choosing To Die* was followed by a *Newsnight* live debate, made the front pages of several newspapers, and was discussed in Parliament. If Pratchett's aim was to inspire a national conversation around the issues of assisted dying, he had achieved it in spades.

Perhaps such a close examination of death is partly what inspired Terry to make as much use of the life he had left as he could. Despite the energy he was investing into social action, he was still primarily a writer and his work rate had barely slowed since his PCA diagnosis three years earlier. Following the publication of *Nation* in 2008, he had delivered a further three Discworld novels in consecutive years, *Unseen Academicals*, *I Shall Wear Midnight* and *Snuff*. The former – Pratchett's longest by some distance, and the only book that had ever necessitated an extension to his deadline – felt a little flabby, though had some excellent moments. The latter two could sit comfortably shoulder-to-shoulder with the rest of the series. Pratchett may have been struggling with reading aloud, but there was clearly no problem with his imagination.

One significant issue, however, was his typing. Pratchett's creative instincts, his naturally high IQ and the support of various treatments all combined to enable him to work, but the effects of the disease couldn't be entirely contained, and typing, even with the aid of a spellchecker, was becoming harder. He could dictate to Wilkins, but as dedicated as his assistant was, he couldn't be around every time Pratchett wanted to write. The solution, much to both men's delight, was technology.

Pratchett's first point of call was an application called Dragon, a dictation programme that had become, more or less, an industry standard. Pratchett and Wilkins, who had made their computers speak in 1981, were always going to love the idea of finally being able to talk back to one. Dragon was excellent for taking the minutes of a meeting, capturing memos or drafting emails and was an essential tool for many people with vision problems. What it struggled with was creative writing, especially – and with no small irony given its name – creative writing set in a fantasy universe. Fortunately, help was at hand. Pratchett had complained online that Dragon was simply not good enough, and been contacted by the team behind an application called Talking Point, which worked alongside Dragon but had a more sophisticated artificial intelligence that 'learned' a user. Pratchett was able to 'train' the programme by reading aloud from an Arthur C. Clarke novel and feeding the computer with his entire back catalogue to digest overnight. The result was a workable system that meant Terry could walk into his office and begin to write as soon as he opened his mouth. In interviews he even claimed that, should his hand-to-eye coordination be returned to its former glory, he would still prefer to speak his novels aloud. In fact, it was interviews that gave him his only real problem – he developed a habit of inserting the words 'comma' and 'full stop' into his sentences, leaving journalists unsure if he was joking.

Metaphorically, there was a ticking clock on the edge of Pratchett's peripheral vision, and despite the advancement of his PCA he appeared determined to maintain his ferocious work rate. Doctors couldn't tell him how long he would be able to work, and when Wilkins asked this question in *Living with Alzheimer's* Pratchett shut him down, saying he would rather not know. Despite the demands of campaigning and the far more serious demands of his illness, there would still be at least one new Terry Pratchett novel published every year, while he still lived. It was a record he had maintained since 1986 and had no intention of letting slip. He was determined to get as many of his ideas down on paper as he could. In 2011, Pratchett told the *Guardian*'s Alison Flood that he was working on three projects simultaneously. One was a young adult novel set in an alternative Victorian London, which would eventually emerge in 2012 as the likeable and entertaining *Dodger*, and another was his long-awaited autobiography, with the working title *A Life in Footnotes*.

The third project was the most unexpected. While archiving old material, Colin Smythe had come across the work Pratchett had done in the mid-'80s for his proposed science fiction series, about quantum Earths and the technology that allowed humans to step between them. Pratchett, reading his old notes and short stories, was pleasantly surprised at how compelling the ideas had been. Shortly afterwards he bumped into the science fiction author Stephen Baxter, at a dinner party thrown by a publisher, and found himself explaining the concept of what would become *The Long Earth*. Baxter was immediately excited by the idea, and the pair spent the entire evening with their heads together, discussing how the story could develop and ignoring their hostess. Neither could quite shake their excitement, and they continued to kick around ideas over the phone, eventually agreeing to collaborate on the series; it would be only the second time in his career that Pratchett had co-authored a full novel. Such a collaboration was far from business as usual for Baxter either, and his standards for co-authors were extremely high – his most recent, and indeed only, collaboration had been with the late Arthur C. Clarke.

Between them they sketched out a five-novel arc dealing with the impact of stepping technology on human society, the concept of infinite 'long' planets, and the life forms that could evolve along their axes. It was a big, classic 'what if?' science fiction idea, that asked questions about evolution and the exploitation and free distribution of resources and tech, with a solid human story at its centre. The duo made an excellent team; Pratchett's wild, improvised creativity and heart meeting Baxter's methodical intelligence. Baxter was good at the essential concepts of quantum, Pratchett was an expert in the instincts of people. The spark may have been Pratchett's, but the *Long Earth* sequence was, like *Good Omens*, a genuine collaboration, with the two authors going back over each other's work and tweaking until everything had been merged into a happy midpoint of the two minds. The opening scene of the first book, for example, involving a First World War soldier who strays into a parallel Earth, was Baxter's concept, but reads like pure Pratchett.

The Long Earth was published to much acclaim in 2012, and its sequel, *The Long War* followed in 2013. By the end of that year the pair had worked up complete drafts of three more books, *The Long Mars*, *The Long Utopia*, and *The Long Cosmos*, taking the series sixty years beyond 'step day', the momentous event that kicks off humanity's quantum migration. The two authors collaborated equally on the earlier drafts, though as Pratchett's condition progressed and he tried to complete as much work as he could, it was left to Baxter to do the tidying up, tweaking and redrafting needed to polish the work for publication. Pratchett had to crack on with other projects, and fast – it was becoming increasingly obvious to Terry, and those who knew him, that time was running out.

Chapter 19

Ever After

In November 2013, Doubleday published *Raising Steam*, the eighth Terry Pratchett novel since his PCA diagnosis six years earlier. It was, unbelievably, the fortieth book in the Discworld series. It would also be the last published during the author's lifetime. *Raising Steam*, thirty-nine novels and thirty years removed from *The Colour of Magic*, though not the final book in the series – there was still one more young adult novel to come – marks a clear point in the evolution of Discworld. Since *The Truth* in 2000, Pratchett had been pushing his creation into a cautious industrial revolution, which reaches a natural endpoint here as Ankh-Morpork enters the railway age. The invention of the steam engine effectively brings the Discworld into the modern era. Despite the magic, goblins, trolls and dwarves, it was now a landscape almost unrecognisable from the trad-fantasy world of its origins. It could only have been intentional. Pratchett had raised his greatest creation to adulthood.

Outside of his writing, it was becoming harder for him to ignore his illness. He would still claim in interviews that anyone meeting him without knowing his history would struggle to spot the difference between the PCA symptoms and the natural tics of any older man. That claim was becoming harder to accept. He was still lucid and interesting when talking to journalists but some were noticing that his answers, though usually stuffed with anecdotes, facts and oneliners, didn't always match the question he'd been asked. Terry was still good at giving journalists decent copy, but look a little closer and it does feel like those responses could be automated, the answers running along well-established grooves. As early as 2011 *The Times* journalist, Ginny Dougary noticed a decline in her subject in the three months since she'd last visited his home. 'Ideas segue into stories that are unconnected to the subject at hand,' she writes, 'and there is a certain rambling quality to his responses that wasn't there before. He also seems a bit disinhibited, kicking my calf repeatedly without noticing, adjusting his tackle and leaving the loo door open while he pees noisily.' While all of these could be attributed to the behaviour of any absent-minded older man, the difference in just a few months suggested that Terry's PCA was advancing more quickly than it had been. He was having other health issues, too. In 2012 he suffered complications following an attack of atrial fibrillation while on a promotional tour in New York. Rob Wilkins administered CPR in the back of a cab, and Terry was rushed to hospital. The attack had been caused by his blood pressure medication reacting with his hectic touring schedule. He was told to slow down and take life more easily, advice at which he characteristically grumbled.

By early 2014 anyone familiar with the energetic Pratchett of old couldn't fail to spot signs of his decline. There was a slight slurring to his speech, and an obvious reaching for words, creating long, awkward pauses. His hand-to-eye coordination issues were now so pronounced that he had given up using cutlery, finding it easier to eat with his hands. He would need sandwiches or drinks to be handed to him, as his eyes would struggle to find them on a table. Journalists would be warned not to take it personally if he didn't shake their hand – often he wouldn't be able to see their outstretched palm to grasp it. Still, these problems were largely restricted to the way he interfaced with the world. His imagination and sense of narrative were very much intact, and his memory, though occasionally spotty on labels and names, was working perfectly where it mattered. He was thinking and functioning, and was able to keep working.

The demand for new Pratchett products was a beast he was happy to keep feeding, and though his output had slowed to a single novel a year – in itself still pretty remarkable – Pratchett, Wilkins and Colin Smythe worked to publish a series of career-spanning anthologies to fill the gaps. First out of the traps was *A Blink of the Screen*, a collection of short stories dating back as far as 1962's *The Hades Business* and stretching up to 2010's *Sir Joshua Easement: A Biographical Note*. The latter was part of a series commissioned by the National Portrait Gallery called *Imagined Lives*, in which famous authors wrote fictionalised life stories of Elizabethan figures, whose real identities have been lost to time, but whose portraits remain.

In 2010, the *Bucks Free Press* had posted a series of Children's Circle stories online, some retyped, others scanned from the original pages. Unfortunately, no-one at the *Free Press* had done their due legal diligence, and Pratchett's lawyers were able to force the paper to take the stories down, the rights having remained with the author. Smythe went about assembling a more professional package for the old stories, releasing collections of Pratchett's children's writing in three volumes, *Dragons at Crumbling Castle*, *The Witch's Vacuum Cleaner* and *Father Christmas's Fake Beard*. All three were illustrated by Mark Beech, whose style echoed that of Pratchett's original artwork for *The Carpet People*. Pratchett couldn't resist making occasional tweaks to stories he'd written almost half a century ago, adding the odd sherbet lemon in the form of footnotes and cosmetic changes to the text. Fifty years after first having the idea, he found himself editing his original *Carpet People* story yet again.

That year – 2014 – also had the sad distinction of being the first since 1985 that didn't contain a new Discworld novel. Fans were placated with *The Long Mars*, the third volume in the Pratchett/Baxter *Long Earth* series, and *Dragons at Crumbling Castle*, which surprised both author and agent by selling extremely respectably. A second, adult-focused anthology, *A Slip of the Keyboard*, collecting Pratchett's articles, essays and speeches, was also published. His autobiography was still a work in progress, and Terry and Rob were both aware that the book, essentially being co-authored by this point, was likely to be his last. As a placeholder, *A Slip of the Keyboard* served rather well, containing many Pratchettian anecdotes tracking his life from childhood to well beyond his PCA diagnosis, the most recent entry being from 2011. The book contained a moving foreword by Neil Gaiman, discussing Pratchett's mixture of anger and compassion, an aspect of his friend's personality that Gaiman felt was often unnoticed. It's a lovely tribute, which was reproduced in *The Guardian* to promote the book. What didn't escape the notice of fans, however, was that it read a little too much like an obituary for comfort.

By the summer of 2014 Terry's disease had advanced to the point that he had lost ninety percent of his vision, which seriously limited his mobility and, even with the use of Talking Point, made writing more difficult than ever. He was, however, adamant that he would keep working. As well as his memoirs, he was determined to finish another

Discworld novel. It was a frustrating process as he struggled to settle on a plot from the numerous strands he always had dangling, and battled through the increasing fog of his worsening PCA. The book was to be the final Tiffany Aching adventure, and would involve the return of the evil Elves that had plagued the witches of Lancre in 1992's fan-favourite, *Lords and Ladies*. The story opens, more or less, with the death of Granny Weatherwax, one of the most beloved of all the characters in Discworld. Like the old baron at the beginning of *I Shall Wear Midnight*, Granny is given a good death, knowing it is coming due to her magical abilities (a precedent established in Discworld as early as *The Light Fantastic*), and greeting the figure of Death as that of an old friend. The symbolism couldn't be clearer.

That year's Discworld Convention was held in Manchester, and for the first time since the inception of the event, almost twenty years earlier, it was announced that Pratchett would not be able to attend in person. Instead he was ably represented by the usual suspects of 'Team Discworld' – Rob Wilkins, bringing with him one of Terry's black hats in place of his absent friend, Stephen Briggs, Bernard Pearson, and Colin Smythe, among others. Spirits were kept high, though there was a dawning realisation among fans that Terry's condition was declining, and perhaps the clock was now ticking a little faster. Convention guests were somewhat reassured by a filmed Q&A, in which Wilkins fed the author questions from fans. Terry seemed in good spirits, though keen to get through the interview as fast as he could so he could return to work. Wilkins announced that the next Discworld novel, the mere existence of which also gave fans some hope, was to be called *The Shepherd's Crown*. Attendees were given a limited-edition book, containing a short, new piece by Terry called 'Terry Pratchett's Guide To Life', a touching instruction to fans that they should live well, underlining the themes of treating people decently and challenging injustice, that dominated his books. The mood in the room was emotional, but chief of those emotions was happiness. Still, it escaped few people's notice that if Gaiman's piece had felt like an obituary, Terry himself seemed to have written a valediction.

If all of this feels remarkably serious, 2014 also contained much that was assuredly positive. In July, Stephen Baxter visited Terry in Broad

Chalke, and the two worked together on *The Long Cosmos*, the final book in the *Long Earth* series, adding a prominent section involving giant, skyscraper-sized trees that came from an idea of Terry's, and posing for photos outside Salisbury Cathedral. It would be left to Baxter to complete the final draft.

Back in 2012 Pratchett had formed a company, Narrativia, with Rob, Rhianna, and Rod Brown, producer of the recent Discworld TV adaptations, joining him on the executive team. The company would marshal and develop the multimedia rights and merchandising of all Pratchett-related future projects. First out of the gate was to be a full-cast TV series based on the Discworld City Watch novels, with Terry as executive producer and Rhianna on the writing team. By 2014, two more projects had been added. The first was a movie version of *The Wee Free Men* with a screenplay by Rhianna, a complete draft of which she presented to Terry as a Father's Day gift, printed out and tied with a red ribbon. Secondly, at long last, the ghost of *Good Omens* had stirred. BBC Studios had already acquired the rights to the book, officially co-producing with Narrativia and Neil Gaiman's Blank Corporation. The original plan would have seen Pratchett and Gaiman film a cameo, but otherwise leave the producers to get on with making the show they wanted to make. In 2014, that changed. Terry had always been protective of his 'old girl', even walking away from the first movie adaptation when he felt it had moved too far from the original work. With the ticking clock of his worsening PCA always on his mind, he was beginning to worry that he would never see justice done for his and Gaiman's cult classic. In autumn 2014, Terry emailed his co-author, formally asking if he would commit to writing the script for *Good Omens* himself. Gaiman, confronted with what was more or less his friend's dying wish, could hardly refuse. At the same time, and as serendipity would have it, a radio version was also being developed, adapted and directed by Dirk Maggs, the producer responsible for adapting Douglas Adams' later *Hitchhiker* books, and recent versions of Gaiman's *Neverwhere* and *Stardust*. The broadcast was slated to go out on Radio 4 over Christmas. Gaiman and Pratchett did indeed cameo in the first episode, as traffic cops observing as Crowley, voiced by Peter Serafinowicz, speeds away in his antique Bentley. The cameo was recorded in the back of Rob Wilkins' car on an autumn day, in the driveway of Terry's house in Broad Chalke. Terry was unable to read the script and simply repeated the lines read out to him. In the cameo he sounds frail and the performance feels a little forced, though it's still a welcome and charming addition to the show. The recording would be the last time Neil Gaiman would see his friend in person.

Terry and Rob continued to work on the autobiography, filming interviews that Rob could type up and edit later. Some of the footage would appear at the start of the docudrama *Terry Pratchett: Back In Black*, broadcast in 2017. The images are absolutely heartbreaking; a frail Terry, unable to complete a sentence as he grasps for the words hanging maddeningly just out of his reach, gesturing in frustration as if waving a magic wand. Rob admits in the documentary that they had probably left the project 'six months too late'. Still, they persevered. For Terry, it was a matter of getting as much work done as possible while there was still time to do it.

Despite his failing sight, mobility issues and other health concerns, he was productive and in good spirits as winter approached. The memoir was coming together, initial work was progressing on *The Watch* TV series and *The Shepherd's Crown* was a final polish and a handful of sherbet lemons away from being complete. He also had several works in progress in various states of completion, including a Discworld story provisionally called *Twilight Canyons*, about a troop of pensioners who foil the plans of a dark lord, plus a goblin murder mystery, following on from the events of *Snuff*. There were also sequels to his young adult novels *The Amazing Maurice and his Educated Rodents* and *Dodger* in the pipeline. Even at this stage, Terry was still thinking seriously about his next book.

Terry and Rob spent the morning of 5 December, a cold and foggy winter's day, working on the autobiography, and Rob had felt positive about the work they were doing. The two laughed a lot, as they often did. Rob Wilkins, after all, had become much more than a PA or business manager (the job title he had been given in Terry's final years). In truth he was more of a sidekick and a foil, the Stan Laurel to the older man's Oliver Hardy. The pair were best friends and co-conspirators. Later that day they made some business calls before Terry settled down to chat to his daughter on the phone. Talk turned to Terry's next novel. And then, at some point that evening, after working some more on the autobiography,

Terry turned to his assistant and friend and told him, quite simply, 'Terry Pratchett is dead now.' Rob tried to argue, but his boss would have none of it. 'No,' he repeated, 'Terry Pratchett is dead.' That was to be Terry's last day as a writer. A few days later, on 8 December, Terry's specialists agreed that his PCA had advanced to the point of being indistinguishable from full-blown Alzheimer's Disease. He spent much of the next few months slipping in and out of consciousness. As 2015 began, his vision, movement, memory and thinking were all severely impaired, and he needed help with the most basic of tasks.

On the morning of 12 March 2015, a bright, but chilly day in early spring, the time of the year when, as a younger man, he would always re-read *The Lord of the Rings*, Sir Terry Pratchett died. Not in Switzerland, not in a hospital, and not by his own choice, but from the complications of his disease, and in the home he loved, surrounded by his family. His cat, Pongo, was curled up on his bed. Later that day, Rob used Terry's Twitter account, @TerryAndRob ('Books written cheap') to share his friend's final short story. 'AT LAST, SIR TERRY, WE MUST WALK TOGETHER,' was the first tweet. The second: 'Terry took Death's arm and followed him through the doors and on to the black desert under the endless night.' The final Tweet read simply, 'THE END'.

Epilogue

Cigarettes

In Terry's 2004 novel, *Going Postal*, there is a tradition among the operators of 'the clacks', the big semaphore towers that work as the Discworld's cutting-edge communication system. When a clacks worker dies, their colleagues believe that their soul travels among the semaphore messages, and their name is 'sent' via the system to the tower closest to their home. If they have no home, or if their name should be remembered, then a code is added: 'GNU'. 'G' means that the message must be passed on, 'N' means it mustn't be recorded, and 'U' means the message should be turned around at the end of a line and sent back.[1] Thus the soul of the clacks worker stays travelling back and forth along the system, for a person isn't dead while their name is still being spoken. It's typically Pratchett – neat, melancholy, and satisfyingly nerdy. Shortly after his death a Discworld fan, posting on the discussion website Reddit, devised some HTML code called 'XClacksOverhead'. It could be copied into the basic source code of any website, and though it would be undetectable to anyone browsing the site, it would put the words 'GNU Terry Pratchett' into the fabric of the page. The idea quickly caught on. Soon thousands of coders and hobbyists across the world, including those running high-profile sites such as *The Guardian*, were sewing the name of Terry Pratchett into the web. His name, like his work, continues to run around the world.

The funeral of Professor Sir Terence David John Pratchett, OBE was held in Salisbury on 25 March 2015. The private ceremony was presided over by a Humanist celebrant (and Discworld fan), Kenneth Greenway. Terry was cremated in a wicker casket, near identical to the one in which Granny Weatherwax is buried in *The Shepherd's Crown*. Writing on the Humanist blog writerscafe.org, Greenway shared the feedback he had

---

1. In a typically Pratchettian touch, GNU is also the name of an open source operating system in the real world, which, very specifically, is not the same as UNIX.

been given by Rhianna Pratchett: 'Many thanks for all your hard work and support. It was hugely appreciated and you did a wonderful job of putting everything together. I think the service went really well and had it been for someone else and Dad was attending he'd have wanted one just like it!'

A public memorial was held on 14 April 2016 at London's Barbican. Rob Wilkins acted as host, Rhianna read aloud the obituary she had written in *The Observer* the previous year, Neil Gaiman read his foreword from *A Slip of the Keyboard*, and many more of Terry's friends and colleagues gave readings and speeches. Rob inducted several of those involved into the Order of the Honeybee, a select group charged with protecting their friend's professional legacy. At the end of the evening a pre-recorded video from Eric Idle led the crowd in a singalong of *Always Look on the Bright Side of Life*.

Terry's final novel, *The Shepherd's Crown*, was published in August 2015, and was celebrated with a midnight reading by Rob Wilkins in London. The book was, predictably, a huge success, though Rob admits in an afterword that the work wasn't as complete as its author would have liked. Neil Gaiman later confirmed that a subplot in which Granny Weatherwax's soul would occupy her cat, You, was never completed, though shadows of it remain in the story. Terry was unable to do his customary final polish, and his last book never got the sherbet lemons it deserved. To this day there are still fans who refuse to read *The Shepherd's Crown*, determined that there will always be one more Discworld novel left to enjoy. Both Rob and Rhianna have said that Terry would have hated this.

Remarkably, Terry kept his 'one new novel every year' streak intact until 2016, when *The Long Cosmos* was published, the final book in the *Long Earth* collaboration with Stephen Baxter. The following year, two collections of Terry's early children's stories emerged, *The Witch's Vacuum Cleaner*, and *Father Christmas's Fake Beard*.[2] He had managed an unbroken run of at least one new book every year, for thirty-one years.

---

2. At the time of writing, a final collection of Terry's earliest short stories, *The Time-Travelling Caveman*, is set to be published in September 2020. It is likely to be the last volume of Terry's previously unpublished fiction, though Wilkins' forthcoming Pratchett biography could well contain extracts from the memoir Terry was writing towards the end of his life.

In total he had written fifty-two full solo novels, forty-one of which were set on Discworld, and collaborated on a further six. There had been five short story collections, four volumes of *The Science of Discworld* (with Jack Cohen and Ian Stewart), *The Folklore of Discworld* (with folklore expert Jacqueline Simpson), the diaries, 'mapps' and *Discworld Companions*, *A Slip of the Keyboard*, documentaries, unpublished screenplays and other ephemera.

Despite his death, there has been no let-up in the demand for Terry's work. Gollancz continued to publish annual diaries and almanacs until the job was passed to Bernard and Isobel Pearson's Discworld Emporium, a mail-order service for Pratchett-based merchandise, with its own dedicated shop in Wincanton, Somerset. The town has been *officially* twinned with Ankh-Morpork. The emporium has published two 'atlases' (updating Stephen Briggs' mapps), its own range of stamps, special edition books and dozens of prints, bookmarks, jigsaws, models, cards and more. It remains a thriving business, as does Sandra Kidby's PJSMPrints.co.uk, now trading as discworld.com. Briggs, Pearson, Kidby, and other members of the Order of the Honeybee continue to make a career out of Discworld, something which Pratchett was keen they should do.

In 2019 the *Good Omens* TV series debuted internationally, a co-production between Narrativia, BBC Studios, Gaiman's Blank Corporation and Amazon. It had a star-studded cast including David Tennant, Michael Sheen and Miranda Richardson, was shepherded into life by Neil Gaiman, history's most hands-on showrunner, and met near universal acclaim. Near. A fundamentalist Christian group based in the US campaigned for Netflix to cancel the show, and the petition was signed by 20,000 people. Netflix were happy to agree to the terms of petition since A) There were no more episodes of *Good Omens* planned, and B) The show had been produced and broadcast by Amazon Prime, not Netflix. Amazon, for their part, have expressed interest in a follow-up series, though Gaiman is reluctant to go ahead without the blessing of his writing partner.

Narrativia's adaptation of the Discworld Vimes' stories, *The Watch*, began filming in 2019, though Rhianna is no longer involved and the concept has evolved away from Terry's original vision. It is one of several

Pratchett productions currently in development, including a hand-drawn animated movie version of *The Amazing Maurice and His Educated Rodents*, and an adaptation of *The Wee Free Men*, written by Rhianna Pratchett. Rhianna has said she wants Maisie Williams to play Tiffany Aching and Dame Maggie Smith to play Granny Weatherwax.

In 2017, as per his explicit instructions, a computer hard drive containing the only copies of Terry Pratchett's unfinished works was flattened with a steamroller by Rob Wilkins.

Mind how you go.
#GNUTerryPratchett.

Bibliography

Works by Sir Terry Pratchett

'Business Rivals', *Technical Cygnet*, Wycombe Technical High School Magazine, (December 1962)

'The Hades Business', *Science Fantasy*, Ed. Jon Carnell, vol. 20, no. 60, (August 1963)

'Letter', *Vector*, (21 September 1963)

'The Picture', *Technical Cygnet*, (c.1965)

'Solution', *Technical Cygnet*, (c.1965)

'The Searcher', *Technical Cygnet*, (c.1965)

'Look at the little – Dragon?' *Technical Cygnet*, (c.1965)

'Night Dweller' *New Worlds*, Ed. Michael Moorcock, vol. 49, no.156, (November 1965)

'Children's Circle' *Bucks Free Press*, High Wycombe, Bucks, (various issues 1965–1973)

'Marcus', *Midweek Free Press*, High Wycombe, Bucks, (various issues 1968–1973)

The Carpet People, Colin Smythe Ltd, Gerrards Cross, (1971)

'The King and I, or How the Bottom Dropped Out of the Wise Man Business', *Western Daily Press*, (24 December 1971)

'Warlock Hall', *Psychic Researcher*, Ed. Peter Bander, (various issues, 1974)

Bath and West Evening Chronicle, (various issues 1974–1976)

'Skepticism', *Undercurrents* – 'The magazine of radical science and alternative technology', (October 1975)

The Dark Side of the Sun, Colin Smythe Ltd, Gerrards Cross, (1976)

Strata, Colin Smythe Ltd, Gerrards Cross, (1981)

The Colour of Magic, Colin Smythe Ltd, Gerrards Cross, (1983)

The Light Fantastic, Colin Smythe Ltd, Gerrards Cross, (1986)

Equal Rites, Colin Smythe Ltd, Gerrards Cross/Victor Gollancz, London, (1987)

Mort, Colin Smythe Ltd, Gerrards Cross/Victor Gollancz, London, (1987)

Sourcery, Colin Smythe Ltd, Gerrards Cross/Victor Gollancz, London, (1988)

Wyrd Sisters, Victor Gollancz, London, (1988)

Pyramids, Victor Gollancz, London, (1989)

Truckers, Doubleday, London, (1989)

The Unadulterated Cat, Victor Gollancz, London, (1989)

Guards! Guards!, Victor Gollancz, London, (1989)

Diggers, Doubleday, London, (1990)

'History in the Faking', *London Evening Standard*, (2 February 1990)

Faust Eric, Victor Gollancz, London, (1990)

Wings, Doubleday, London, (1990)

Moving Pictures, Victor Gollancz, London, (1990)

Reaper Man, Victor Gollancz, London, (1991)

Witches Abroad, Victor Gollancz, London, (1991)

'Me and My Family', *The Daily Telegraph You and Your Family*, (4 December 1992)

Small Gods, Victor Gollancz, London, (1992)

The Carpet People, (revised edition) Doubleday, London, (1992)

Only You Can Save Mankind, Doubleday, London, (1992)

Lords and Ladies, Victor Gollancz, London, (1992)

'Slipped Discworld', *London Evening Standard*, (29 January 1993)

Johnny and the Dead, Doubleday, London, (1993)

Men At Arms, Victor Gollancz, London, (1993)

The Streets of Ankh Morpork (with Stephen Briggs, illustrated by Stephen Player), Corgi, London, (1993)

Dreams and Doorways: Turning Points In The Early Lives of Famous People, Ed. Monica Porter, Pan Macmillan Children's Books, London, (1993)

'Kevins', *The Author*, (1993)

Soul Music, Victor Gollancz, London, (1994)

Interesting Times, Victor Gollancz, London, (1994)

The Discworld Companion (with Stephen Briggs), Victor Gollancz, London, (1994)

The Discworld Mappe (with Stephen Briggs, illustrated by Stephen Player), Corgi, London, (1995)

Maskerade, Victor Gollancz, London, (1995)

'Roundhead Wood', *Playground Memories, Childhood Memories Chosen by the Famous in Support of Elangeni Middle School and Chestnut Lane Lower School*, Amersham, Ed. Nick Gammage, (1996)

Johnny and the Bomb, Doubleday, London, (1996)

Feet of Clay, Victor Gollancz, London, (1996)

Hogfather, Victor Gollancz, London, (1996)

Jingo, Victor Gollancz, London, (1997)

Unseen University Diary 1998, (with Stephen Briggs) Victor Gollancz, London, (1997)

The Last Continent, Doubleday, London, (1998)

A Tourist Guide To Lancre (with Stephen Briggs, illustrated by Paul Kidby), Corgi, London, (1998)

Carpe Jugulum, Doubleday, London, (1998)

'No Worries', *SFX*, June, (1998)

The Science Of Discworld, (with Jack Cohen and Ian Stewart), Ebury, London, (1999)

The Fifth Elephant, Doubleday, London, (1999)

Death's Domain (with Paul Kidby), Corgi, London, (1999)

'I Only Read The Brodie Notes', *Later*, (1999)

'Brewers Boy', Foreword to *Brewer's Dictionary of Phrase and Fable* Millennium Edition, (1999)

'2001: The Vision and the Reality', *The Sunday Times*, (24 December 2000)

The Truth, Doubleday, London, (2000)

Thief of Time, Doubleday, London, (2001)

The Last Hero, Victor Gollancz, London, (2001)

The Amazing Maurice and His Educated Rodents, Doubleday, London, (2001)

Night Watch, Doubleday, London, (2002)

The Wee Free Men, Doubleday, London, (2003)

Monstrous Regiment, Doubleday, London, (2003)

'On Granny Pratchett', *False teeth and a smoking mermaid: Famous people reveal the strange and beautiful truth about themselves and their grandparents*, Age Concern, (2004)

The Art of Discworld (with Paul Kidby), Victor Gollancz, London, (2004)

'Writer's Choice', *Waterstones' Books* Quarterly, 12, (2004)

A Hatful of Sky, Doubleday, London, (2004)

Going Postal, Doubleday, London, (2004)

Thud!, Doubleday, London, (2005)

Wintersmith, Doubleday, London, (2006)

'How To Be A Professional Boxer', Foreword to *Writers' & Artists' Yearbook*, (2006)

Making Money, Doubleday, London, (2007)

'An Embuggerance', PJSMPrints.co.uk, (December 2007)

Nation, Doubleday, London, (2008)

Unseen Academicals, Doubleday, London, (2009)

I Shall Wear Midnight, Doubleday, London, (2010)

Snuff, Doubleday, London, (2011)

The Long Earth (with Stephen Baxter), Doubleday, London, (2012)

Dodger, Doubleday, London, (2012)

A Blink of the Screen, Doubleday, London, (2012)

The Long War (with Stephen Baxter), Doubleday, London, (2013)

Raising Steam, Doubleday, London, (2013)

The Long Mars (with Stephen Baxter), Doubleday, London, (2014)

Dragons at Crumbling Castle and Other Stories, (including commentary by Suzanne Bridson), Doubleday, London, (2014)

A Slip of the Keyboard, Doubleday, London, (2014)

'A Little Advice for Life', *The MMXIV Green Folio*, Terry Pratchett and Rob Wilkins, (2014)

Shaking Hands With Death, Corgi, London, (2015)
The Shepherd's Crown, Corgi, London, (2015)
The Long Utopia (with Stephen Baxter), Doubleday, London, (2015)
The Long Cosmos (with Stephen Baxter), Doubleday, London, (2016)
The Terry Pratchett Diary (with misc), Victor Gollancz, (2016)
The Witch's Vacuum Cleaner and Other Stories, (including commentary by Suzanne Bridson) Doubleday, London, (2017)
Father Christmas's Fake Beard and Other Stories, Doubleday, London, (2017)
Mort (with an introduction by Neil Gaiman), Corgi, (2019)
Good Omens (with Neil Gaiman), illustrated edition, Victor Gollancz, London, (2019)

Books by other authors
Cabell, Craig. (2012) *Terry Pratchett: The Spirit of Fantasy*, John Blake Publishing.
Campbell, Hayley. (2017) *The Art of Neil Gaiman*, Ilex Press
Carpenter, Humphrey. (1977) *J. R. R. Tolkien: A Biography*, HarperCollins
Goldman, Joan. (1963) *Selected at Six*, Hodder and Stoughton
Hansen, Rob. (2019) *THEN: Science Fiction Fandom in the UK 1930–1980*, Ansible Editions
Hunt, *Peter.*, Lenz, Millicent. (2004) *Alternative Worlds in Fantasy Fiction*, Continuum
James, Ed et al. (2004) *Terry Pratchett: Guilty of Literature* (second edition), Old Earth Books
Kirby, Josh. (1991) *In The Garden of Unearthly Delights*, Paper Tiger
Kirby, Josh. (2001) *The Josh Kirby Discworld Portfolio*, Paper Tiger
Kirby, Josh. (1999) Langford, David. (1999) *A Cosmic Cornucopia*, Paper Tiger
Langford, David. (2001) *The Leaky Establishment*, Big Engine
Mcilwaine, Catherine. (2018) *Tolkien: Maker of Middle Earth*, The Bodleian Library
Robinson, Tony. (2016) *No Cunning Plan: My Story*, Sidgwick and Jackson
Sale, Charles. (1930) *The Specialist*, Putnam & Co
Tolkien, J. R. R. (1991) *The Lord of the Rings*, HarperCollins
Western, Peter. (2004) *With Stars in my Eyes: My Adventures In British Fandom*, NESFA Press
Whyman, Matt. (2019) *The Nice and Accurate Good Omens TV Companion*, Headline

Radio
On the Ropes, interview with John Humphrys, BBC Radio 4, (6 June 2014)
Hogfather, BBC World Service, (1996)
Live At The House Podcast, (13 April 2013)
'With fading memory, Terry Pratchett revisits *The Carpet People*', *All Things Considered*, NPR (USA), (11 March 2013)

Good Omens, (Dir. Dirk Maggs), BBC Radio 4, (December 2014)
Desert Island Discs, BBC Radio 4, (9 February 1997)

Television
Truckers, Cosgrove Hall Films, Thames Television, (1992)
Johnny and the Dead, LWT, ITV, (1995)
The Colour of Magic – screenplay, Rob Heyland, Catalyst Television, (1995)
Short Stories: Terry Pratchett's Jungle Quest, Channel 4, (1996)
Newsnight Late Review, BBC 2, (18 September 1997)
Terry Pratchett's Discworld TV-ROM, Channel 4, (1997)
Wyrd Sisters, Cosgrove Hall Films, Channel 4, (1997)
Soul Music, Cosgrove Hall Films, Channel 4, (1997)
Sir Terry Pratchett is interviewed at Minicon by Jim Young in Bloomington, Minnesota, USA, YouTube, (26 March 2005)
Blue Peter, BBC 1, (7 September 2005)
Terry Pratchett's Hogfather, The Mob Film Company, Sky, (2006)
Johnny and the Bomb, Childsplay, BBC 1, (2006)
Terry Pratchett's The Colour of Magic, The Mob Film Company, Sky, (2006)
Terry Pratchett: Living With Alzheimer's Part 1 & 2 (Dir. Charlie Russell), BBC 2, (2009)
Going Postal, The Mob, Sky, (2010)
The Richard Dimbleby Lecture, 'Terry Pratchett: Shaking Hands With Death', BBC 2, (2010)
Terry Pratchett: Choosing To Die (Dir. Charlie Russell), BBC 2, (2011)
Terry Pratchett: Facing Extinction (Dir. Charlie Russell), BBC 2, (2013)
Terry Pratchett: Back In Black (Dir. Charlie Russell), BBC 2, (2017)
Good Omens, Narrativia, BBC Studios, Amazon Studios, Blank Corporation, (2019)

Online resources
Alt.Fan.Pratchett newsgroup
Ansible.co.uk, edited by David Langford
Archive from The British Library sounds.bl.uk 'Terry Pratchett and Neil Gaiman, in conversation. Whose Fantasy?' (Recorded 14 June 1988)
Blog.patrickrothfuss.com/2011/07/meeting-terry-pratchett/
Delta4.co.uk
Colinsmythe.co.uk
College-of-arms.gov.uk
Discworld.com
Discworldemporium.com
Discworldmonthly.co.uk
Efanzines.com/PW/Stars/

Encyclopedia of Science Fiction, sf-encyclopedia.com 1979–2018 (Eds. John Clute, David Langford, Peter Nicholls [emeritus] and Graham Sleight)
Fancyclopedia.org/repetercon
Fialwol.org.uk/fanastuff, (Ed. Rob Hanson)
Lspace.org
Madison.com 'Terry Pratchett Interview', (2011)
Mandascott.co.uk/terry-pratchett-a-highly-abbreviated-memoir/
Oxford Dictionary of National Biography, oxforddnb.com
'Rood Words' 1996 Interview with Paul Rood re first DWCon geocitiesarchive. org/mxd/rainforest/3691//issues/7_roodwords.html#
Theguardian.com Terry Pratchett on religion: 'I'd rather be a rising ape than a fallen angel', Comment Is Free: video, (19 December 2009)
Ukwhoswho.com
Web.archive.org
Wiki.lspace.org

Articles, reviews and convention programmes

Yarcon Convention Programme, (April 8–11, 1966)
'Finding The Jokers', *The Oxford Times, (*May 1976)
'Widdershins World of a High Flyer', *Western Daily Press*, (21 May 1976)
'The Colour of Magic by Terry Pratchett', Colin Smythe, *Publisher's Weekly*, (26 August 1983)
'The Colour of Magic by Terry Pratchett', *Kirkus*, (15 August 1983)
'The Colour of Magic by Terry Pratchett', Louise James, *British Book News*, (March 1984)
'The Colour of Magic by Terry Pratchett', Jon Hutchinson, *The Times*, (1 March 1984)
'The Colour of Pratchett', Neil Gaiman, *Space Voyager*, p. 41, (June/July 1985)
'The Colour of Magic', *Computer and Video Games*, Issue 10, p. 60, (1986)
'The Colour of Magic', *Crash*, Issue 2, p. 52 (1987)
Andromeda Bookshop's Catalogue No. 116, (January/February 1987)
'Voyages Beyond', Wendy Graham, *Adventurer: The Superior Science Fiction and Fantasy Games Magazine*, (June/July 1987)
'Magical book of eccentric monsters', JB, *Somerset Standard*, (30 January 1987)
'Galactic Survival Kits', John Clute, *The Observer*, (26 April 1987)
'Terry Pratchett', Paul Kinkaid, *Interzone*, (September/October 1988)
'Adventuring in Discworld', Kevin Puttick, *GM: The Independent Fantasy Roleplaying Magazine*, Vol. 1, No. 11 pp. 52–68 (11 July 1989)
'A hit and myth venture for two Oxford writers', *Oxford Mail*, (4 July 1989)
'Teaching the Experts A Lesson', *Children's Book News*, (November 1989)
'Guards, Unicorns, Zool', John Clute, *Interzone*, Issue 33, (January/February 1990)

'Into the Nineties with Gollancz and Corgi', Marketing plan, Colin Smythe Collection, Senate House Library, University of London, (1990)

'Discovering Discworld', Nick Cairns, *The Magazine*, (February 1990)

'Oh, Good', John Clute, *Interzone*, (July 1990)

'Poltergeists versus pony tales', Christina Hardyment, *The Independent*, (17 November 1990)

'Death Goes On Holiday', Tom Wilkie, *The Independent*, (27 June 1991)

'Schlock Therapy', Jonathan Coe, *The Guardian*, (25 July 1991)

'Keyboard Addiction', Paul Golding, *The Sunday Times*, (17 November 1991)

'An Interview with Terry Pratchett and Neil Gaiman', Martin Tudor, *Gamesman*, pp. 20–22 (February 1992)

'Acclaimed author reports on the vivid world of fantasy', Steve Warren, *Bucks Free Press*, p. 6 (26 June 1992)

'Terry Who's Nome Brew', Tom Hibbert, *You Magazine (Mail On Sunday)*, pp. 34–6 (16 February 1992)

'The view from an elephant: Martin Wroe meets Terry Pratchett, a comic fantasist at home with elves and wizards', Martin Wroe, *The Independent*, (15 August 1992)

'Guardian Children's Fiction Award', various, (25 March 1993)

Martyn Taylor, *Vector*, Issue 174, (August/September 1993)

'Terry Pratchett Interview', *The School Magazine* (Australia). (c. 1994)

'Magical Mayhem', Rupert Goodwin, *The Times*, (5 March 1994)

'Dave Greenslade – Terry Pratchett's From The Discworld', Stuart Maconie, *Q Magazine*, (5 May 1994)

'The Dickens of Discworld', Stuart Jeffries, *The Guardian*, (18 November 1994)

'The Pratchett File', Robin Eggar, *Sunday Mirror Magazine*, (22 January 1995)

'Terry Pratchett', M. J. Simpson, *Book Collector*, No. 134, (May 1995)

'Spinner of Tales', Mark Edwards, *The Sunday Times*, (19 March 1995)

'One More Hit Disc for Terry', *Scotland On Sunday*, (28 May 1995)

'Bookers? Not for the loiks of oi', Giles Smith, *The Independent*, (12 June 1995)

'Jackie's at the helm for the 'flat earth disciples'', Matthew Edgar, *Lancashire Evening Post*, (16 November 1995)

'The SFX Interview. Head to Head with the Stars. Terry Pratchett', *SFX*, p.46 (December 1995)

'Thanks for the fantasy', Andy Beckett, *Independent On Sunday*, (2 June 1996)

'Putting Drivel Before Dickens', Susannah Herbert, *The Daily Telegraph*, (10 June 1995)

'All Men are Mort', *Starburst*, (July 1996)

'I'm Not Sure What the Word 'Nerd' Means: Terry Pratchett talks to Bill Gates', *GQ*, (July 1996)

'Weird But Wonderful', Mark Edwards, *The Sunday Times*, (7 July 1996)

'A life in the day of Terry Pratchett', Caroline Scott, *Sunday Times Magazine*, (4 August 1996)

'Tragedy on the Track', Sheena Walsh and James Mortlock, *Bury St Edmunds Mercury*, (September 1996)

'Designs on Success', *Chester Chronicle*, p. 10, (10 November 1996)

'Flights of Fancy worth millions', *Sunday Business*, p. 24, (8 December 1996)

Clarecraft Event Programme, (1997)

'What's The Big Deal ', William Lodge, *Nottingham Evening Post*, p. 28, (30 January 1997)

'Transworld lures Pratchett away from Victor Gollancz', *The Bookseller*, (25 April 1997)

'Special Edition Discworld Magazine', *SFX*, (May 1997)

'Misery Loves Company/Janus Stark', Jim Wirth, NME, (24 January 1998)

'Rich imagination of Discworld's doyen', Boris Johnson, *The Daily Telegraph*, p. 34, (11 May 1998)

'Jilted genres', Robert McCrum, *The Observer*, (15 November 1998)

'Money Matters: How The Other Half Spends', Natalie Graham, *Good Times*, p. 27, (February/March 1999).

'The Books Interview: Terry Pratchett', *The Observer*, (24 October 1999)

'Why the Discworld needs PCs', Hamish Mackintosh, *The Guardian*, (27 January 2000)

'A Conversation with Terry Pratchett – Part 1', Steven H. Silver, *SFSite*, (April 2000)

'A Conversation with Terry Pratchett – Part 2', Steven H. Silver, *SFSite*, (May 2000)

'Terry's magic words', James Delingpole, *The Daily Telegraph*, (7 November 2000)

City Life (What's On In Manchester), p. 55, (2 May 2001)

'A Conversation With Terry Pratchett', Claire E. White, *The Internet Writing Journal*, writerswrite.co.uk, (c. 2001)

'Terry Pratchett Interview', Gavin J. Grant, *Indiebound.org*, (c. 2001)

'In conversation: Terry Pratchett and Gerald Seymour', David Freeman, *The Guardian*, (8 November 2001)

'Neil Gaiman: Amazing master conjuror', *Boskone 39 Programme Book*, (February 2002)

'The Big Store', Programme for Bob Eaton's stage adaptation of *Truckers*, (March 2002)

'Pied Piper' brings belated literary reward', John Ezard, *The Guardian*, (13 July 2002)

'Terry Pratchett', Linda Richards, *January Magazine*, (c. 2002)

'Interview: Discworld Author Terry Pratchett', John Gardner, *New Zealand Herald*, (25 October 2002)

'My First Boss – Terry Pratchett, *The Guardian*, Karen Hainsworth, (23 November 2002)

'Night Watch by Terry Pratchett', Michael Dirda, *The Washington Post*, (24 November 2002)

'Life on Planet Pratchett', Sally Weale, *The Guardian*, (8 November 2002)

'Night Watch by Terry Pratchett', Therese Littleton, *The New York Times*, (15 December 2002)

'He's Got The World On A Disc', Trisha L. Sebastian, *SequentialTart.com*, (March 2003)

'Dispatches from Discworld', Joe Nazzaro, *Fantasy Worlds*, p. 74, (February 2004)

'Edinburgh festival: No really, it was wonderful', *The Sunday Times*, (15 August 2004)

'Tales of Wonder and Porn', *Noreascon 4: Worldcon Programme Book*, (September 2004)

'Terry Pratchett – Master of Speculative Satire', Drew Bittner, *SF Revu*, (24 September 2004)

'Strange Powers of the Discworld King', Stuart Wavell, *The Sunday Times*, (17 October 2004)

'Parenting: Only Need Not Mean Lonely', various, *The Sunday Times*, (7 August 2005)

'The Secrets of my Success – Terry Pratchett', Chris Hall, *The Daily Mail*, (7 August 2005)

'Terry Pratchett: Sod the Booker, this is popular', Giles Hattersley, *The Sunday Times*, (17 December 2006)

'Terry Pratchett Interview', *SFX*, (12 October 2006)

'James Jackson meets Terry Pratchett on the set of Hogfather', James Jackson, *The Times*, (9 December 2006)

'Terry Pratchett: "I had a stroke - and I didn't even notice"', Moira Petty, *The Daily Mail*, (5 November 2007)

'Terry Pratchett on the origins of Discworld, his Order of the British Empire and everything in between', Jim Young, *Scifi.com*, (January 2008)

'There's humour in the darkest places', Stuart Jeffries, *The Guardian*, (18 March 2008)

'Terry Pratchett, Lord of Discworld, fights to save his powers', Bryan Appleyard, *The Sunday Times*, (8 June 2008)

'Terry Pratchett hints he may have found God', Rob Davis, *The Telegraph*, (8 June 2008)

'Terry Pratchett', *TheGuardian.com*, (12 June 2008)

'The best science book ever written? Eminent figures pick their favourites', *The Times*, (12 June 2008)

'I create gods all the time - now I think one might exist, says fantasy author Terry Pratchett', *Mail Online*, (21 June 2008)

'INTERVIEW Terry Pratchett', *SFX*, (9 July 2008)

'I'm disgusted. I can get Viagra on NHS, but not a drug to help my Alzheimer's', *News of the World*, (17 August 2008)

'I'm slipping away a bit at a time . . . and all I can do is watch it happen', *The Mail On Sunday*, (7 October 2008)

'Terry Pratchett: "If I'd known what a progressive brain disease could do for your PR profile I may have had one earlier"', Deborah Orr, *The Independent*, (29 November 2008)

'Discworld author Terry Pratchett on Alzheimer's and his best work', Andrew Billen, *The Times*, (30 January 2009)

'One year on: Terry Pratchett the year I could never forget', Josie Ensor, *The Sunday Times*, (25 September 2009)

'Point Me to Heaven When the Final Chapter Comes', *The Mail On Sunday*, (2 August 2009)

'Sir Terry Pratchett interview for *Unseen Academicals*', John Preston, *The Telegraph*, (28 September 2009)

'Guardian book club: Unseen Academicals by Terry Pratchett', Sam Jordinson, *The Guardian*, (14 December 2009)

'Terry Pratchett – "I Will Always Be The Fellow That Writes Funny Books"', Anne Giles, *Bookwitch.wordpress.com*, (c. 2010)

'Sir Terry Pratchett wants to win control of how his own story ends', Damian Whitworth, *The Times*, (6 February 2010)

'The secrets of my success: Terry Pratchett', Chris Hall, *The Daily Mail*, (22 May 2010)

'Terry Pratchett: "I'm open to joy. But I'm also more cynical"', Aida Edemariam, *The Guardian*, (1 September 2010)

'Terry Pratchett on travel, writing and swearing at a PC', Dave Bradley, *SFX*, (14 September 2010)

'A Star Pupil', From *Celebrating 60 Years: Holtspur School 1951–2011*, (2011)

'I'm hunting a killer — but first I must clean up after the cat', *The Sunday Times*, (6 March 2011)

'Terry Pratchett writes in to Holtspur School for its 60th birthday', Lawrence Dunhill, *Bucks Free Press*, (4 May 2011)

'I pay more attention to the details of nature now', *The Times*, (21 May 2011)

'Death Knocked and We Let Him In', *The Sunday Times*, (12 June 2011)

'A Week in the Death of Terry Pratchett', *The Independent*, (18 June 2011)

'Meet The Superfans', Leo Benedictus, *The Guardian*, (24 June 2011)

'Discworld author Sir Terry Pratchett prepares real-life battle', Richard Eden, *The Telegraph*, (2 October 2011)

'Sir Terry Pratchett: Alzheimer's and me', Ginny Dougray, *The Times*, (8 October 2011)

'A Life In Writing: Terry Pratchett', Alison Flood, *The Guardian*, (14 October 2011)

'Terry Pratchett – Up to Snuff', Lisa Campbell, *Bookseller*, (9 November 2011)

'Terry Pratchett Interviewed', *Writers Online*, Writers-online.co.uk, (23 April 2012)

'Terry Pratchett And Stephen Baxter Interviewed', Ian Berriman, *SFX*, (24 July 2012)

'An Interview with Sir Terry Pratchett', Neil Gaiman, *Boing Boing*, (10 October 2012)

'World Book Night authors choose extracts to be given away with their work', Alison Flood, *The Guardian*, (17 February 2012)

'Terry Pratchett – I Thought My Alzheimer's Would Be Worse By Now', Elizabeth Grice, *The Telegraph*, (10 September 2012)

'Interview: Terry Pratchett, author', Peter Ross, *Scotland on Sunday*, (23 September 2012)

'The book that changed my life, by Rushdie, Pratchett and more', *The Times*, (29 September 2012)

'Terry Pratchett – What keeps me going is the fight', Arifa Akbar, *The Independent*, (11 October 2012)

'Dad copes with Alzheimer's in such a no nonsense way', Nick Duerden, *The Sunday Times*, (14 October 2012)

'Terry Pratchett on his medical diagnosis, his latest novel and more', Tasha Robinson *The AV Club*, (16 November 2012)

'Terry Pratchett – Fantasy is Uni-age', Stephen Moss, *The Guardian*, (22 April 2013)

'Sir Terry Pratchett in conversation: Virtual WCF 2013', *The Writer's Greenhouse*, (11 November 2013)

'On My First Job', *The Huffington Post*, (12 December 2013)

'Terry Pratchett: I started writing my new book when I was 17-years-old', *The Guardian*, (10 July 2014)

'Terry Pratchett: By The Book', *The New York Times*, (17 August 2014)

'Terry Pratchett Based Crowley on Neil Gaiman, and Other Tidbits from the Writing of Good Omens', Stubby The Rocket, *Tor.com*, (22 December 2014)

'Good Omens: How Terry Pratchett and Neil Gaiman wrote a book', *BBC Magazine*, (22 December 2014)

'Remembering The Wizardry of Sir Terry Pratchett', Gavin Haynes, *Vice*, (13 March 2015)

'Friends, Colleagues pay tribute to Sir Terry Pratchett', *bookbrunch.co.uk*, (13 March 2015)

'Terry Pratchett', Charles Stross, *antipope.org*, (13 March 2015)

'It Was Like Having a Full-Sized Hobbit for a Father', Maureen Patton, *The Telegraph*, (14 March 2015)

'Sir Terry Pratchett's schoolboy inspiration revealed', Patrick Sawyer, *The Telegraph*, (15 March 2015)

'Remembering Sir Terry Pratchett', Brian Gornall, The Society for Radiological Protection, sap-uk.org, (19 March, 2015)

'Neil Gaiman Reminisces about Sir Terry Pratchett', Maryann Yin, *GalleyCat*, (20 March 2015)

'"That's how I want to remember Terry": Neil Gaiman reminisces about Pratchett', Alison Flood, *The Guardian*, (23 March 2015)

'Letter: Terry Pratchett at the Discworld conventions', Elizabeth Alway, *The Guardian*, (5 April 2015)

'The teacher who inspired Terry Pratchett', Patrick Sawyer, *The Telegraph*, (8 June 2015)

'Terry Pratchett interview: a fantasy writer facing reality', Tom Chivers, *The Telegraph*, (27 August 2015)

'Neil Gaiman: the ending my friend Terry Pratchett never got to write', Alex O'Connell, *The Times*, (29 August 2015)

'Sir Terry Pratchett remembered by his daughter, Rhianna Pratchett', Rhianna Pratchett, *The Observer*, (17 December 2015)

Rhianna Pratchett, *Buckinghamshire County Council Website*, (2017)

'10 Things You Probably Didn't Know About Sir Terry Pratchett', Meghan Bell, *BarnesandNoble.com*, (28 April 2017)

'What I've Learnt: Neil Gaiman', Fiona Wilson, *The Times*, (2 September 2017)

Terry Pratchett: HisWorld: Official Exhibition Companion, The Estate of Terry Pratchett, Dunmanifestin, (2018)

'My family and other Moomins: Rhianna Pratchett on her father's love for Tove Jansson', Rhianna Pratchett, *The Guardian*, (12 March 2018)

'Before there was Discworld: Terry Pratchett's school notebooks give a fascinating insight into his teenage mind – including some very familiar-looking doodles', Keiligh Baker, *MailOnline*, (30 April 2018)

'The story behind the Oblivion mod Terry Pratchett worked on', Cian Maher, *Eurogamer*, (31 January 2019)

Video Games

The Colour of Magic, Delta4 Production, Piranha UK, (1986)

Discworld, A TWG/Perfect 10 Production, issued by Psygnosis Games, (1995)

Discworld II: Missing, presumed ...? A Perfect Production, issued by Psygnosis Games, (1996)

Discworld Noir, A Perfect/TWG Production, issued by GT Interactive Software (UK) Ltd, (1999)

Rise of the Tomb Raider, Rhianna Pratchett (writer), Crystal Dynamics, (2016)

Discworld Conventions

UK: 1996, 1998, 2002, 2004, 2006, 2008, 2010, 2012, 2014

US: 2009

AUS: 2012

Index